DRURY LANE TO DIMAPUR

Drury Lane to Dimapur

Wartime Adventures of an Actress

DOREEN HAWKINS

THE DOVECOTE PRESS

For my grandchildren, Natalie, Isabella and Julia,
who did not know their grandpa – a sadness for all of them,
and to my great-grandchildren, Eleanor, Alexander and Scarlett (so far)
. . . with love.

ACKNOWLEDGEMENTS

First, Caroline Knox – it was her enthusiasm that brought this
manuscript out of a cupboard, and got me working on it again.
Her constant encouragement kept me going.
Teresa Ransom, who was persuaded to read it and get the shears to it
– she reshaped what was an overlong rambling story, and actually
numbered the pages.
My son Andrew – for his practical help with all the modern
technology, and who also with his great knowledge of literature
corrected my appalling grammar and punctuation.
Thanks to all three, and David Burnett, for their patience
in putting up with me.

First published in 2009 by The Dovecote Press Ltd
Stanbridge, Wimborne Minster, Dorset BH21 4JD

ISBN 978-1-904-34966-2
© Doreen Hawkins 2009

The author has asserted her rights under the Copyright, Designs
and Patent Act 1988 to be identified as author of this work

Designed by The Dovecote Press
Printed and bound by MPG Biddles Ltd, Kings Lynn, Norfolk

All papers used by The Dovecote Press are natural,
recyclable products made from wood grown in sustainable,
well-managed forests

A CIP catalogue record for this book is available

Contents

INTRODUCTION

Ceylon, 1957

OH THE JOY of being on a plane that was airborne instead of the Britannia we had left behind like a dead bird on Istanbul runway. It had caused thirteen hours delay and an uncomfortable, freezing night on a lifeless, unheated aircraft.

Now I closed my eyes in the warm glow of anticipation of being reunited with my husband after too many long weeks. A glass of champagne at my elbow, I was enjoying the comforts of first class travel provided by the film company. I was becoming used to this pleasure – but never took it for granted – I could still remember the many uncomfortable journeys of wartime, which had to be endured along with other hazards.

I was returning to a country I never thought to revisit – Ceylon, now Sri Lanka. The circumstances of my leaving the city of Colombo in autumn 1945 were vastly different. At 4 a.m. I waited in line with other forces personnel for the prized airlift to Bombay. I was waved on board and made a swift move to the mailbags stacked at the front of the aircraft. I flung myself and kit-bag on the sacks, claiming my space. By now a seasoned traveller I was hoping to grab some much-needed sleep. It was a nine-hour flight and I had only recently had my amoebic-ridden appendix removed, in the hope the operation might rid me of the rotten disease that is endemic to the tropics. A recurring problem for the sufferer – back home to the temperate climate being the only real cure – the advice given, not to return to a tropical country for ten years. The timing was just right.

My husband Jack had been filming in the wilder parts of the island for some weeks now. *The Bridge on the River Kwai* was a movie first mentioned over a pleasant dinner in New York given by the producer Sam Spiegel for ourselves and the British director David Lean. The film was the chief topic of conversation – Jack confirming that the proposed Ceylon locations would be ideal. His knowledge of the region and the Far East was extensive as he had been commanding officer for troop entertainments there during the war. They wanted Jack for a major role in the film, but there were no definite dates, and as yet no completed script. Back in London our busy lives took over. Jack had more work than he could cope with so *The Bridge on the River Kwai* was put aside.

The call had come suddenly just before Christmas, asking Jack to join the unit in Ceylon. It caused great disappointment to our children, and frustrated fury for us, knowing Jack would possibly not start filming till after the festivities. Sam was covering himself. That was filming. It was not the first time and would certainly not be the last.

Now it was late February. The sky was darkening as we flew further east and began losing height to land in Karachi. As I walked down the steps of the plane the warm air embraced me as if in welcome. The stars so low in the sky I felt I could touch them. I inhaled the scent of the air around, a remembered part of me. I felt I had never left.

The previous time I had been in Karachi was on a three-day visit in 1944, the beginning of what became an extended tour of India and Burma with E.N.S.A. (Entertainment National Services Association), a wartime organisation providing entertainment for the Forces during the Second World War. Most of the theatrical profession joined to perform with ENSA during that time. I volunteered for overseas in 1943, joining a play company destined for the Middle East on to the Far East, eventually arriving in India nine months after our departure from Liverpool, by which time our company was depleted by exhaustion and sickness, with several members left behind in Cairo. India had been a new beginning; professional actors were loaned from the Forces, a new wardrobe, and a new director, Captain Jack Hawkins, who appeared as a shining hero to reorganise and redirect. He breathed new life into us, and a little magic into my life, as after the war we were married.

After a successful showing of *Private Lives* at the Excelsior Theatre in Bombay we were off to Karachi on the first leg of our tour. By day it was then a peaceful, colourful town to wander around. In the evening we performed to troops brought in by transport from various camps, giving them a much-needed laugh and outing to the theatre. We were billeted at the airport. Odd – but there was nowhere else suitable for us to stay. In 1957 I found the airport larger, and extended of course, but I was shown into a 'basha' hut: that flimsy construction of bamboo and palm leaves was still in use – not so flimsy after all. This one had been modernised for 1st Class passengers for a few hours relaxation on a stopover.

My only wish was to get out of those crumpled clothes, have a bath and a few hours sleep before flying on to Colombo. When I was wakened with a cup of real Indian 'char' – one sip and I knew I was back.

Freshened with the change into a cool, chic outfit, which I knew would please Jack, I was on yet another plane – the last lap of a long journey. I was mystified by the numerous forms I had to fill in before landing; then I realised the massive change that had taken place in Ceylon, with the exit of the British and the end of the Raj.

There he was – the wide grin, arms out-stretched to hug me. I couldn't wait to run into them. But the days of casual airports were over. Forms had to be examined, rubber-stamped. There was a new air of officialdom. However, seeing Jack impatiently waiting they let me through. The filming on the island was well known for having brought work to many and a prosperity that could not be ignored. We headed for the Galleface Hotel where Jack had a room reserved for the length of his stay – I could see that beautiful shimmering Indian Ocean in the distance. It made me long to swim in it again.

Fortunately Jack was not recalled to the location until late the following day, and I went with him. We were driven up there in what was a reasonable car for these parts, no air-conditioning as yet, but bearable with the windows wide open (to hell with the dust), air was more important. We soon left Colombo behind and were climbing into increasingly wild parts of the island. Gazing out of the window it was just as I remembered it: monkeys stared down at us, leaping from tree to tree, chattering loudly at the interruption. Jack was in deep conversation with the wife of Bill Graf, the American representative of Columbia Films. Betty Graf could talk of nothing but 'The Bridge', and the worries of the production team about the planned explosion.

On we drove through increasingly dense foliage. With darkness falling we entered a narrower track, suddenly coming upon a collection of lighted buildings, where a blazing banner erected by the crew across the gates announced 'Sam's Place'. After five bone-shaking hours we had arrived, thankful to be out of the car and able to stretch ourselves. We made for our quarters – yet again the good old basha hut. Sam Spiegel had bought the bungalow off a tea planter, who like many of the British Raj was forced to sell up with the new regime. Sam had built all the huts and showers in a compound around the main bungalow, which was made into a kind of mess for all to use. There was a large dining room, two well-stocked bars, one with beer and soft drinks, the other with spirits, almost impossible to get locally, also some recreation rooms with billiards and games. Around the bungalow stretched a large veranda. Good mosquito screening everywhere.

I noticed some fishing equipment in the corner of our basha. Jack told me Alec Guinness had left it for his use with a note that it might help save his sanity. It had just preserved his! Ominous, I thought. Alec had already left, having finished his role of Colonel Nicholson he was on the next plane home. A pity, Alec was really good company.

We wandered into the mess. Jack wanting to introduce me to Bill Holden with whom he had struck up a warm friendship. William Holden was an actor I admired, particularly for his performance in the film *Sunset Boulevard*. At the bar he greeted us warmly and we began to talk easily. Presently Ardis his wife joined us, proceeding to mix dry martinis. Bill said she was the expert and that this was their evening ritual. Jack and I tended to avoid that lethal pre-dinner aperitif. We were saved by the arrival of Sam Spiegel.

'Baby (he called everyone Baby) - how lovely to see you' - kisses - 'When did you arrive?' Before waiting for an answer he called out 'Bettee', and up came a stunning girl in very Beverley Hills pants with the long slender legs to fill them. Sam put his arms around us both, insisting 'come babies, we will have dinner together.'

Guiding us into to the dining room - Jack trailing behind - he continued, 'We have some delicious salmon tonight flown in from Scotland, and I have an excellent wine to accompany it.' Say what you like about Sam Spiegel, and there were many that did, you could not fault his wonderful taste – always shown in food and wine.

The dining room was almost empty and quiet: the crew, always hungry after a day's work, would have eaten early. As we sat down I saw David Lean sitting at his table with three very young Thai girls who were working in the film. Smiling, he waved to me in greeting, but didn't come over. Jack told me that the tension between Sam and David was such that they rarely spoke to each other. Right from the early days Kwai had been a film of stress, now especially so with the preparations for the explosion, Sam was here for final meetings with the engineers about the laying of charges. Once the explosives had been placed in water they would only be active for twenty-four hours, after which they would be useless. Everything had to be accomplished in the shortest time and with the greatest precision.

Jack and I finally escaped to our basha hut. The first thing I realised was that Sam and Betty were next door and the walls were only made of straw. We could hear Sam's voice pleading and Betty's firm rejection. 'No, Sam.' 'Oh, Baby.' 'Absolutely *not*, Sam!' – and so on. I looked at Jack: he was smothering his laughter. We were talking in whispers. So I hissed, 'Do not even think of it!' I let down my mosquito net, tucking it firmly into place.

Jack left very early the next morning for filming. When I went to the dining room for breakfast, it was empty.

I knew the unspoken rules of being a location wife: not to visit the location or set unless invited, and not to hang around too often watching the work. This was easy for me. In my own career as an actress I had done my share of hanging about studio sets. It is tiring and boring. I always had a stack of books waiting to be read and little time for reading, along with the many film scripts that Jack received, of which I would usually be the reader. So in shorts and the essential hat, I found a relaxing chair, the chosen book I was itching to read, and settled down with the intention of ridding myself of my English pallor.

I looked at the surrounding garden, filled with English plants which someone had lovingly persevered with. All tea plantations were high in the hills and had majestic views of the colourful scenery, the bushes of tea sloping in lines downwards. During my time in Ceylon we were only billeted once on a plantation. I remember the air being fresh and clear, and welcoming the change of altitude and lack of bugs. I looked at this bungalow now housing a film company. It had probably belonged to a family of several generations, now uprooted in the wake of independence. Several depressed wives had been returning to Colombo on the same plane as myself, unsuccessful in their search for somewhere to live and start afresh. The lack of money and materials in post-war Britain provided an inadequate supply of housing to help the refugees who were entering Britain in ever-increasing numbers. For those whose lives had been here in Ceylon the future was one of uncertainty and unease. Those bungalows on the south coast of England beckoned, 'Shangrila', 'Mon Repos' – but could hardly replace the magical views or a house full of servants.

When the film unit returned in the evening I was fresh and rested. Jack and Bill made for the showers, Ardis and I sat chatting, getting to know one another. She had fine bone structure, dark eyes and hair cropped short at the time. In her mid-forties, I supposed. She had been a well-known film actress until she met and married Bill, putting an end to her career.

Ardis and I spent most of our rather empty days together wandering down to the small village nearby – a gathering of huts and one tiny shop. But we enjoyed each other's company, lunching back at Sam's Place. She told me about her life in Hollywood, I told her a little of my time spent in Ceylon with ENSA during the war when we travelled all over the island performing to the RAF, with their incredibly disguised airfields to keep them safe from enemy air attack. She remarked that my exploits with ENSA sounded amusing and interesting enough to be written down. I replied that I might do that, for my family's amusement.

Most nights we would be a foursome enjoying dinner together. When there was any free time we drove down to Colombo and the air-conditioned hotel rooms considerately provided by Sam Spiegel. He and Betty kept a suite at the Galleface. It was very humid in those bashas at Sam's Place. There was one more sequence to be filmed before the blowing of the bridge.

Back in Colombo Jack and Bill Holden were shooting a scene at the familiar Mount Lavinia Hotel. It had been dressed up to resemble a convalescent home with bandaged, wounded extras wandering around in the background. Sitting on the terrace I thought of the blissfully happy two days Jack and I had spent there in 1944. Smartened considerably – no peeling paint or flapping shutters now – I was watching Bill and my husband in their scene together playing with the ease of experienced actors. I was floating into the past and my then unhappy insecurities about our future together. How could I know then it would all fall into place in such an un-dreamt of way.

Jack finished for the day and came to collect me for a rare lunch together, to be relished.

Ardis and I decided to visit the new location, going with our husbands in the morning. (We were invited!) Sitting high on a hill overlooking miles of thickly foliaged jungle, hazy and purple in its intensity, we were eating cold chicken. The packed lunch for a location. For once, Jack and Bill were cleaned up and in pukka uniforms, shooting an office scene where Jack, as Major Warden presses Shears (Bill Holden) to lead a small group of commandos to retrace the terrible jungle trek he had made following his escape from the Japanese prisoner of war camp. The object, to blow up this infamous bridge that the oddball Colonel Nicholson (played by

Alec Guinness) had been lending his expertise as an engineer, and the men under his command, to construct. 'Co-operating with the enemy' – a dreadful wartime offence. The unfortunate Shears has to agree to this mad operation as a few unsavoury items from his past have been conveniently dug up to persuade him. This crazy bargain points to the idiocy, the misery, the cruel waste of life, and sheer horror of war, that the film so clearly portrays: the story of *The Bridge on the River Kwai*.

The momentous day finally arrived. Bill had left early along with everyone else because he had to dirty up to get in the water at the right moment. The whole of Sam's Place was empty apart from Ardis, myself and Jack, as he was not involved in this particular sequence. Knowing the delays of filming, we had decided to make our way to the site later in the morning, for we knew the train containing the dummy Japanese soldiers was due to cross the bridge at around midday. The explosion was to take place when the train was halfway over, the bridge then collapsing into the water below and the train going with it. It was very costly and could only be filmed once. Tension was high. Sam had gone down to the site early, partly because he couldn't bear to stay away, but also to greet his guests. He had invited the Prime Minister, his wife, and many other dignitaries, including anyone who had helped to facilitate the exceedingly difficult creation of a bridge in the middle of a jungle. There were military posted for miles around to keep any locals away from the area, and out of danger.

Dressed in slacks and the necessary hats, we wound our way on a narrow track through the dense green, taking with us a large thermos flask full of lethal iced Bloody Marys mixed by Ardis, a drink that was the rage in California in 1957. Jack carried the thermos, Ardis some plastic cups and I trailed behind with the sandwiches. We had to go in single file, brushing back the tangled branches as we went down towards the river. Finally we emerged from the thickness into a vast open space, it was my first sight of the bridge, which was tremendously impressive and much larger than I had visualised. Its immense timber frame straddled the partially dried up river, which flowed gently past large, flat, exposed stones. I confess I thought it rather a sin to blow up such a fine structure.

The group of grandees were sitting at tables under umbrellas, sipping iced drinks as though they were at a garden party. It was an astounding sight. Because they didn't understand the vagaries of filming they had assembled early, so were already hot and restive as the midday sun was beating down. I was glad I had a hat. We found a collection of flat stones to sit on but they were burning hot on the behind so we tried to cool them with water then sit on them quickly.

Bill was way over the other side of the bridge. The camera crew were hidden in separate foxholes, their cameras covering different angles. When the train approached and blew its whistle, that was the signal for each camera operator to press a button to show that he was safely in his foxhole. This gave the all-important green light to the director, David Lean, and the chief cameraman, Jack Hilyard. Only the director could give the signal to set off all the charges so carefully placed and concealed for the explosion.

Nothing seemed to be happening, we opened the thermos. Sam was waiting among his guests. The heat was unbearable. I took off my hat, fanning myself and Jack. I knew it was ridiculous to be sitting in this sun. 'Do you think it will really happen today?'

'It must,' replied Jack.

'It has to be today, or unimaginable disaster,' said Ardis, topping up my plastic cup. I looked over to Sam, who, by the way he was flicking around his fly switch in a state of agitation was obviously nervous. It was so unlike him. I opened the sandwiches. Then the train whistle blew. We held our breath, sandwiches half-bitten.

Everyone was all attention as the little train appeared out of the jungle. We didn't move a muscle – the heat was forgotten. It was chugging across the bridge, dummy soldiers lolling against the glassless windows. It reached the centre of the bridge, but it was carrying on – Jack, Ardis and I leapt to our feet. 'Blow you bastard, blow,' Jack hissed between clenched teeth. But no – on it went. Now Sam was at the edge of the water, at the edge of everything it seemed.

'Oh, no – *no*' he moaned in utter despair. Then the noise of a collision as the train reached the other side, surely becoming derailed. But no, disaster had been prevented by a generator placed across the tracks at the far side of the bridge – where the train should never have arrived. Complete derailment was averted, though some minor damage was done to the train and the dummy soldiers from being thrown about.

There was a deathly silence.

Sam had disappeared, to find David. No doubt they would be speaking now. The guests were melting away. There was a state of shock all round. What went wrong? That was the big question. What would happen now?

Jack poured out the last of the drink. Suddenly a splashing noise, a figure all blacked up was doing a rapid swim towards us. Jack waded into the water. 'Go back, Bill Holden, go back, we have drunk it all.'

Bill staggered out of the water and sat on one of the flagstones, grabbing a sandwich out of his wife's hand. He chewed on the sandwich for a moment. 'What about that?' he said. 'If it isn't blown within twenty-four hours all the charges have to be renewed.'

'Does anyone know what went wrong?' Jack asked.

'There is talk that one of the cameramen didn't push his button – without that safeguard – no explosion.'

It was a very subdued trek back to the mess. It was like being in the presence of death. Sam's Place resembled a morgue. Men slowly filtered back, then disappeared. There was no one at the bar and silence had settled over all. During the afternoon Jack put together the story of the disaster. The first mishap was the driver of the train who was to jump clear as soon as the locomotive reached the bridge. He jumped all right, but was in such a hurry he neglected to adjust the throttle to the arranged speed. He suffered a minor injury to his ankle. The train sped over the bridge and rammed into the generator, which was now hanging over the ravine. Whatever manpower could be summoned was using every means to stop it crashing into the river, and to get the train back on its tracks. A crane was needed, but to get a suitable one here in the middle of the jungle was no easy feat. At the time the bridge was constructed there were teams of elephants to haul the heavy equipment, but the engineers and workers had all dispersed. The explosive experts brought in by Sam from ICI would not stay for more than three days – and the explosives would anyway not last. It was time that now counted, every minute costing a fortune.

I could well understand the look of despair on Sam's face when he climbed the steps to the veranda with David following. Darkness had fallen – Jack and I just sat there in the semi-dark watching the unhappy pair as they took their seats side by side at the other end of the veranda. Normally at this time of the evening there was the loud buzz of conversation and the laughter of men. But it was so quiet I could hear the great bullfrogs croaking, the chorus of crickets and all the distant jungle noises I hadn't noticed before.

I do not believe I have ever known a film in which there was not a disaster or some major hitch, but this had the makings of one of the most costly and spectacular.

Nodding towards Sam and David, Jack muttered they must be trying to reach a decision. They certainly looked as though the weight of the world was upon their shoulders. Hunched forward, elbows on knees, David's face was cupped in his hands. Sam looked faintly ridiculous in his khaki shorts, hat still on his head, fly whisk dangling in his hands, he, too was leaning forward, deep in thought. He turned to David every few moments when they would talk in low tones. I felt desperately sorry for Sam; so much depended on what he decided. It was all down to him to find the extra money, which, one guessed, was not there. I was confident he would use all his wits and wiles and considerable knowledge of producing to save the film and his own future credibility. David appeared calmer. His face was controlled and still handsome in spite of the dirt and fatigue lining it. His extraordinary eyes glittered with determination to save his film. If anyone could achieve the impossible he would.

17

Thank heaven Bill and Ardis appeared and we moved to join them, mutually agreeing to go straight into the quiet and almost empty dining room. As we finished and were about to leave the table, David Lean entered bringing with him the cameraman who had failed to take cover in time. The man who forgot to press his button! Not one of his colleagues was speaking to him, or worse, they were laughing at him. David had decided to sympathise, much to Sam's disgust.

In the small hours, the news came through that the train had been levered back onto the track. It was decided to make every possible effort for a blast-off around midday. The next day when Jack and I breakfasted alone we were told everyone was at the site except for Ardis, who eventually made a late morning appearance. Bill was down at the bridge in hope of the prayed for explosion.

We decided to make the trek down again taking drinks and sandwiches, just in case something happened. Once more we stumbled along the little path, but then halfway down we suddenly heard the train's whistle. We broke into a fast trot, ignoring brambles and overhanging branches, and panting hard, reached the dried stones of the riverbank.

Just in time. At that moment the train had reached the centre of the bridge. There was an enormous explosion, followed by another – then, the incredible sight of the bridge blowing apart. The train fell as if in slow motion into the water below, realistically spilling out some of the dummies. As the smoke and debris cleared shouts and cheers came from the other side of the bridge, taken up by those on the near side. We flung our hats in the air and we were dancing about and waving and cheering. Oh, it was great!

No – more than that – it was a stupendous event in the history of the movies.

The Bridge on the River Kwai went on to win seven Oscars, and remains a cinema classic.

PART I

ENGLAND

ONE

England, 1924

The spotlight shone on the centre of the stage. Its beam picked out the tiny doll-like child, blond hair cut into a fringed bob, dressed in blue organdie with a pink sash and a bow at the waist. The walk from the wings had been unhurried, the limbs moving jerkily up and down as if a mechanical doll. When I reached centre stage, I turned towards the audience. Applause rang out, though I couldn't imagine why. Instinct told me that something more could be done to please the smiling faces half-hidden in the shadows. I did a mechanical bow, loudly squawking 'Mama' as my own doll did when bent forward. This brought even more applause. Satisfied, I turned and continued my jerky walk to the wings where I could see my father waiting. He scooped me up in his arms.

'Clever girl, whatever inspired you to say "Mama!"'

I shook my head, I was only four years old.

'You are a born actress,' Pop exclaimed, giving me a kiss.

A rosy dream that neither of my parents had the remotest idea of achieving. I was delighted that I had pleased the most important person in my life.

The local paper, reporting on the Missies Bird's Dancing Academy's annual matinee at the Grand Theatre, Southampton, gave me a piece all to myself. Great excitement in our house, I was the only one actually named, and given a whole sentence saying I was the success of the afternoon. It was possibly the best notice I ever had, and is certainly the only one to survive, now faded and yellowing in an ancient scrapbook.

When I was older I was sent to a rather posh, girls only, day school in Southampton. An excellent school, which I only saw as a waste of time. As well as endless dancing lessons, I was also doing odd performances at the Grand Theatre, playing various children's parts. At school in the morning, if I had performed the evening before, I would wearily sit at the back not taking anything in. When I was about fourteen I spotted an advert in *The Stage* – the weekly publication for theatricals, which my father had regularly delivered. He was a keen amateur actor, in fact had spent a short time as a professional when young, before joining up to fight in the First World War. Up-to-date news on London productions dropped regularly on to our doormat. I thrived on this literature. Seeing an advertisement for 'young ballet-trained dancers to join Madame Katrina's Girls for pantomime at a top theatre. Solo dance for suitable girl', I showed it to my mother because I thought it was something I could do during the Christmas holidays. Mother was glad to agree. I think she was keen to be rid of me. In due course she took me up to a shabby old house in Peckham to audition, where I danced for Madame Katrina whose exotic foreign-sounding name was made less convincing by a broad Cockney accent. When I finished, she praised my technique and engaged me to join her girls in a pantomime that Christmas.

*   *   *   *   *

It was pitch dark. I stood leaning against the door and held my breath. I had just eased my mother out of the door knowing that if she stayed I would have to put up with tears – always near with her. She might even have insisted on taking me home again. Instead I was alone with my suitcase in the hall of this strange house in Peckham.

My eyes became accustomed to the dark. Then I heard girlish giggles. I felt my way up the stairs, hanging on to the banisters, until I came to a chink of light. I opened a door into the room I had auditioned in, with its upright piano and barre against the wall.

Over by the fire sat three girls, their feet propped up on a fireguard. Their hair was platinum blonde like Jean Harlow, the film star of the time. They suddenly saw me.

'Come on over and join us. Have a ciggie – they are Gerald du Maurier,' said one of the girls importantly. I took one. No one had ever offered me a cigarette before. I began to feel grown up, puffing away without coughing. The girls began to ask questions about myself which I managed to avoid. Finally, 'How old are you?'

'Fifteen,' I lied.

'That's young,' said the girl with the northern accent, putting another piece of coal on the fire. 'She's a mean old bugger with the coal.'

What did that mean? It was new to my ears, but then so was almost everything.

My mother had stamped some cards for me to send to her. I told her that all was fine and I was happy with my new friends. So the semi-deception went on. The sheer hours of work were exhausting. The head girl, Peggy, who had joined our group and was tutoring us, was patience in the extreme, particularly with me. The excitement was breathtaking. I was able to get a bus with another girl to the Lyons Corner house in the West End for supper after rehearsals, clutching money given to me by my father. The buzz from this first taste of freedom and from learning the new dance steps was exhilarating.

Lying in bed at night – my mother had insisted that I have my own – I listened to the talk of the older girls, which was revealing. I continued to send the stamped cards home. I suppose my parents imagined I was rehearsing 'Swan Lake' or similar – best let them continue to think that. I was in a fairyland of my own making. Discomforts went unnoticed. I was involved in the musical theatre and loving every moment of it.

It was the platinum blonde hair that finished me, putting an end to freedom. Walking towards my parents on the station platform, I can still see the horrified look on their faces. One wet Sunday during the pantomime we were bored in the digs so the girls decided that as I was a natural blonde it would bleach easily. Some dreadful mixture was applied (which stung) then washed out about an hour later. Miraculously my hair survived, emerging blonder than any of them.

My grandmother entered the fray. All this had passed her by until now. She was dismayed. She was also angry at what had happened to her granddaughter. My father was her much-loved eldest son, but she wasn't blind to his faults. He had neglected the business built up my grandfather, instead spending his days on amateur theatricals writing plays and composing musicals at the piano. Although his head was in the clouds, my grandmother felt my mother was more to blame for my behaviour. Granny had always been a little unsure of this orphan her son had married. My mother was one of five, the result of a disastrous romance and runaway marriage. This ill-fated pair produced five children before they were thirty and were dead by the age of forty – he of drink, she a few years later (worn out I imagine), leaving the five children to go into an orphanage or rely on the generosity of her mother. My great grandmother could not face the children going into an orphanage, so aged sixty and after bringing up her own large family, she took them in. My mother, the third of this sad family, was always considered some sort of hysteric. I think she was and she had a reason.

I loved my grandparents' house. The huge sloping garden, the orchard, the nut wood, the tennis court, the stream that ran through at the bottom of the garden with the bridge across it. Remarkably, it all existed close to the centre of Southampton. All the children's playthings were still there, albeit covered in green moss. There was a rocking horse, swing and a miniature roundabout. All emblems of a happy past. In my imagination I could see my father and his siblings playing together before the Great War brought its terrible losses and tragedies, jolting the unhappy world into the twentieth century.

My earliest memories are of grandpa getting me out of bed, helping me to dress then leading me by the hand out into the dew-laden gardens before going to work, which he did at 8 o'clock. After inspecting the soft fruit (popping white raspberries in my mouth) and vegetable gardens, we toured the flowerbeds and tall leafy trees that gave the garden its shade.

My grandfather was a self-made man who had started work as a boy in Southampton. He became a respected businessman and landowner, having built up a fortune outfitting ships' crews – notably of the White Star Line, including the ill-fated *Titanic*. He frequently travelled with granny to visit his relations who had emigrated to America and Canada. I was always taken on board to say goodbye, and the tearful farewells left me with an insatiable desire for travel.

My occasional weekend with them was a treat. From my grandmother I learned (I hope) a certain elegance that has stayed with me. I used to watch the table being laid and meals prepared in the kitchen – with the occasional taste. In the evening, grandpa would sit me on his knee and twiddle the knobs of that magic box – the Crystal Set – putting earmuffs on my ears so I could hear Children's Hour. It must have been about 1924.

He died of a stroke one Sunday. Arriving for lunch we were met by a white-faced parlour maid. My father rushed straight past her. We were bundled back into the car and home again. He was only sixty. I was eight years old. It was my first heartbreak.

And now my platinum blonde hair had upset my grandmother. I was miserable, and cross with myself that she had become involved. It was all my fault that I was going around looking like a student-tart. Impossible now to return to school; those boats well and truly burnt. With their strict rules on dress and behaviour I doubt they would let me in the doors. Anyway the derision would be unbearable. Most of my decent clothes had been swapped for what can only be described as 'tat': some stupid too high-heeled shoes and an idiotic hat amongst the collection. But what to do with myself? I was clearly driving everyone mad. I went to daily ballet workout and took singing lessons from an old-fashioned teacher. I inspected my hair roots daily and wished they would grow faster. I had a few local friends and began to realise that I was held with some respect and an aura of glamour. To have had such a daring adventure made me different. But I had left any school friends behind, moving on precociously into a future I was unsure how best to carve out.

The next move came as a complete surprise: indeed, the unexpected was to be the pattern of my future.

*   *   *   *   *

The Grand Theatre, Southampton, re-entered my life. Running the repertory company was leading man a Mr Alfred Kennedy (everyone was Mr or Miss in those days). For the coming season he planned to to take his company north and put on contemporary plays, one of which was a comedy about some teenagers left alone in a house whilst their parents were away. Kennedy was finding it difficult to cast the lead role of a flirtatious teenage girl who as a guest in the house, caused general mayhem. Strangely enough I leapt into his mind! He and my father were friends. He had heard of my problems, so he suggested I join the company.

Life brightened considerably. I was thrilled to be asked but slightly scared. My mood varied between sheer fright and exhilaration. I shut myself up in my bedroom learning the lines until I was word-perfect, saying them out loud to practise my voice. I had not travelled further than London before, and, to my relief, discovered that I was to be accompanied north by an actress called Newsome McCormack who was also joining the Kennedy Company. She seemed old to me, but I suppose was about thirty. I called her Miss McCormack.

On the Sunday we set out I put on a bright face to ward off mother's tears. One seemingly endless train journey followed another. When we began to cross the Pennines Miss McCormack announced that we were nearly there. Finally we arrived in a strange town. It was cold and closed, a provincial Sunday evening in Huddersfield. Everyone spoke in a funny accent. Once delivered to my lodgings, I was left alone with a forbidding looking landlady who was obviously fed up because I had ruined her evening. I found it difficult to understand her broad Yorkshire accent. The room was cold with a put-u-up bed. Thankfully the fire gave a weak but warming glow.

What to do? I thought of the first rehearsal awaiting me in the morning. Some unappetising cold supper was put on the table. For a moment I thought I might cry out of sheer loneliness and fear. But I had taught myself years ago not to indulge in that useless emotion. Instead I thought about school. I could be returning there. I ate my supper, unpacked my suitcase, found the bathroom, let down the put-u-up and went to bed.

Looking back I know that my performance as the teenage tearaway was a success. I was thrilled when I spied Mr Kennedy standing in the prompt-corner watching and laughing along with the audience. I know he did not regret taking a chance on me. I had the advantages of being the right age, of having my own gym slip and school uniform, even my own hockey stick with which to make my first entrance and create a laugh, and I had a natural ability with timing. My limited talents were boosted with theatre know-how acquired from my recent experience with the pantomime. Having the movement of a dancer helped me to walk about a stage with confidence and ease, something that takes a long time to learn. But most of all was my own conviction that I could do it, and do it well.

This was the beginning of years of hard work, a ceaseless pursuit of self-education. Not for me the tennis parties and dances for girls of my age, but a stimulating and rewarding life. Buoyed by success, my days took on a sense of purpose. I was willing to do anything bidden and was asked to stay on as a member of the Huddersfield company. I was only just fifteen and very naïve. I should really have been at school, but instead I was living alone in digs and acting in a repertory company, for which I earned the grand sum of £2.10s a week, topped up by my father with an extra ten shillings.

A romance in Huddersfield when I was only sixteen with the leading juvenile, ten years my senior, brought my mother up with all speed to the theatre where I was playing. It was true, it had started during the very first rehearsal, playing Vane, when I was required to slap his face. Not knowing the theatre techniques I gave him a hard slap. It was not that I hurt him, it was that I broke his spectacles that miffed him. I was blushing with embarrassment and remorse. The director managed to calm the situation, explaining to me the art of the 'stage-slap', and promising the actor that the repair of his spectacles would be reimbursed. But a frisson remained between us, a flirtation developed, increasing over time. The leading juvenile had written to my father saying he was in love with me and Pops was absolutely incandescent and threatened to call the police. My mother carted me off to Southampton. I was gated.

In those days to be engaged was a sign of being grown up. The men I met were of course mainly actors from whichever company I was in, and in due course my poor parents suffered several so-called engagements to various young men. But for now I was housebound in Southampton in disgrace, and was soon was bored stiff. One day an actor named Bill Waddy, who played character roles with the Kennedy Company, rang to say he was now at the Grand Theatre with Peter Coleman and his company. They needed a young actress to fill a small role and he had thought of me. As it was local, my parents relented, and I was at rehearsal the following day.

Once in, I did some more work for them. Peter Coleman, who was to become a great friend, told me they were planning to produce their own pantomime. There would be stars from London to play the leads, and speciality acts, would I care to be involved as I could dance. Would I? To work over Christmas in a pantomime was my best way of spending it. That was when I first met Peter Cushing.

* * * * *

27

My first sight of Peter Cushing was so memorable that I can see the whole episode in detail some sixty years later. It was the autumn of 1936 and I was in the audience of the Grand Theatre with my parents for the first night of a new play. It was about a composer, Lizt I think, with Peter Coleman in the leading role. Peter was perfectly cast, romantic to look at with the voice and acting ability to keep the audience riveted. Half way through there was a scene set in a German beer garden. In the background were a few tables with extras and whoever could be spared from backstage, dressed as drinkers. Peter Coleman was downstage in the foreground in full flow. Suddenly the audience began to titter and then laugh out loud. Peter was completely thrown, wondering wildly what was wrong. Were his flies undone (always the actors nightmare)? We in the audience were aware that one of the bit players was doing the unforgivable, drawing attention towards himself. Peter Cushing, for it was he, was acting a drunk and playing with a sausage on a fork. The laughter increased his antics.

Peter Coleman was furious when he came off stage, demanding the head of the culprit who had ruined his scene. He was only mollified when the success of the play at the final curtain was obvious from the applause; followed by the tears of shame and protestations of innocence by the 'sausage swinger'. Peter Coleman was a kind man and Cushing, well he was different. He had certainly learnt a big lesson, and never ruined another actor's scene again.

Come the pantomime Peter was still in his job as ASM (assistant stage manager). Coleman gave him a second chance, this time as an actor in his dream role, King Rat, in which he could not only overact but also devise a make-up so intricate he had to be in the theatre early in the morning to be ready for the matinee. Dressed complete with tail in the bottom half of the rat costume, and in his terrifying make-up with whiskers and all, he rushed around the theatre frightening everybody, banging on dressing room doors at the overture and beginners call, and doing the million jobs given to the ASM. Shades of future ghouls.

In pantomime, it is a wonderful thing before the curtain rises to hear the excitement of the children on the other side – the noise of their voices, the seats banging up and down, the anticipation. First Peter had his big moment, dramatically appearing through the curtains with thunder, lightning, flashing lights and smoke to declaim the scary prologue with the children screaming, booing and hissing. Then the curtains parted to show the usual village scene with singing and dancing. Peter was rushed off his feet, seeing to all the props and scene changes, occasionally leaping on stage as a fierce rat. He was good looking with a splendid profile and dark wavy hair. His warm humour was always there throughout all the backstage panics. He just loved being part of the theatre, as I did, so we became practically inseparable. His visits to my home won my parents approval. They grew fond of him – everyone did. Was it love? I thought so, but I was only seventeen. He was sure it was, at twenty-four, but so unworldly and unsophisticated that I often felt the elder. Our relationship became close and loving. We kissed and hugged and held hands with always a great affection between us, but never more.

Of course we did crazy things at times, I was led on by him. When a film came to the next door cinema we wanted to see and the only free time was between the shows, Peter persuaded the manager of the cinema to let us creep in. We covered our costumes with coats, found two convenient seats and sidled into them, hidden by the darkness. Worried about the time towards the end of the film, I checked Peter's watch. It was with some consternation I saw this rat face protruding from his overcoat collar. I could hardly wait to make our exit before the lights came up, though he protested strongly when I dragged him away while the credits were rolling.

After the pantomime Peter and I went up to London. He had enormous confidence and ambition and was determined to find a London agent. So we went up and down Charing Cross Road and St. Martin's Lane where all the theatrical agents used to have offices, he carrying a portfolio of photos. He then took me to meet his family who lived on the outskirts of London. It was a charming warm home called Clearview; which describes it well. His were the dream mother and father. She was nicknamed Tiny, again descriptive, and obviously adored this odd son who was determined to be an actor. David the other son was at college learning to be a farmer. We were served a delicious dinner (we were starving) and I was pressed to stay the night in the comfortable spare room. A perfect end to an exhausting day.

We found a job together in a repertory company in Lowestoft, not at the end of the pier but in a proper theatre that was well attended. Out of season it was easy to find digs with two bedrooms and a sitting room in a boarding house on the promenade. We spent all our free time walking on the beach, fooling around like two kids and watching the herring fleet arrive at the little port. The women moved down the coast for the herring season and, fascinated, we watched them gutting the herrings, their hands red with cold, knives flashing, before flinging the fish into salted barrels with great accuracy.

We bought an ancient drop-head Ford for seventeen pounds, which was cheap even then. It was a real jalopy, and there is no way it would be allowed on the roads today, but it moved. Peter drove it and began to teach me. On one of our Sunday jaunts I stalled the engine. We were holding up the traffic and causing a cacophony of hooting when a policeman approached and took in the car with a mixture of amazement and amusement. He asked for my licence and I showed him my provisional one. He then looked at Peter.

'Are you instructing this young lady Sir?'

'Oh yes officer,' said Peter grinning broadly.

'Can I see your licence?'

I was sure he had it but in which pocket? When he got out of the car I thought the policeman's eyes were going to pop out of his head. Over his shirt and flannels, Peter was wearing his dressing gown, a shortish very flamboyant and colourful one adorned with dragons. Large feet in battered carpet slippers protruded from his trousers.

'Excuse me sir, but do you always drive around dressed in this manner?'

Peter gave him a disarming smile and produced his licence. 'Not really officer, but it is Sunday.'

The horns were still blowing, but not as loudly. Most of the waiting drivers were so fascinated by the scene they were hanging out of their windows. Peter was now at the front of the car struggling with the starting handle. When the engine fired, the racket it made was appalling. The policeman told him to drive so I moved over, but it took a good push from two of the watching drivers plus the policeman to get us moving. Off we went with Peter waving and thanking everybody. I was so used to his eccentricities that I did not find this encounter particularly odd, or his mode of dress. He did have a jacket and shoes in the back of the car

We worked together for a while near Manchester, where we spent our free time seeing performances by all the London companies. Peter would present his card at the box office and nearly always got two free seats for the matinee. Sitting comfortably in the stalls, we read in the programme we were to see a 'prior to London' opening of a play called *Autumn*. The leading actors were Flora Robson and Jack Hawkins, both of whom I had seen in films. Jack's name was also familiar because he had been in the original cast of many contemporary plays, and so it appeared in the editions handed out at rehearsals. When he made his first entrance as a young barrister I was riveted. I could not take my eyes away from this actor who really knew his craft. Just the way he walked slowly towards Flora Robson, exchanging trivial conversation with her. They meet centre stage and he grasps her in his arms in a passionate embrace. A surprise gasp from the audience – it is obvious they are embroiled in a clandestine affair – guilt is everywhere. I was enjoying an afternoon of complete magic, transported from Manchester to a drawing room in Belgravia. I was rather naïve and immature at eighteen. I did not have the luck to see many West End productions. The plays were less sophisticated and violent in 1938. As Peter and I hurried back to our own theatre for the evening performance

I felt depressed. The standards of production were simply not comparable – what could be hoped for with one week of rushed rehearsals, cramming the lines, endeavouring to get some sort of wardrobe together. Theirs was another world – but how to get into it?

In 1938 the company moved to Scarborough, again on the sea and also out of season. It was a lovely theatre to play in, and always full. By this time Peter had advanced to playing leading juveniles, frequently opposite me. He was quick to learn and listened to advice and direction. He had learned to cope with his overlarge hands and feet, for in his early days he didn't know what to do with them – yet he was the most exquisite watercolour painter, and painted many pictures for me. We were content together.

On one of our spring jaunts into the country with a picnic, disaster struck the car and our affection for the old motor turned to hate. On our way back it conked out, nothing would start the wretched engine. It was a weekday and we had to be at the theatre for the play – in fact we opened it. We nearly went crazy. It was too far to walk. The road was deserted and there was no telephone box in sight. Miraculously a lone bus appeared and Peter leapt into the middle of the road, waving his arms frantically until it stopped. The bus then crawled along stopping frequently. We were both sick with worry and finally arrived at the stage door to be met by a furious director, the manager, everyone. They had held the curtain for five minutes. We were flung onto the stage just as we were, luckily it was a modern dress play. Nothing like that has ever happened to me before or since. It is every actor's nightmare.

Peter was so anxious to get on and prove himself he never ceased writing to managements and agents. He didn't have much luck except for Harry Hanson, newly in management with the young George Black, whose father was a successful London impresario. Peter was told there would be a place for him in their Leeds company. It would mean more money and a step up, so I told him to grab the opportunity.

I had had my eighteenth birthday and we became engaged, but because Peter fretted that he didn't have the money to buy me an engagement ring I wore his signet ring instead. He was worried about the forthcoming parting, but I sensed we needed some time apart. We were so close in all ways but one. Peter was an honourable man. I knew he desired me and could sense there was a frustration building up within him, but my early strong feeling for him had now become a loving friendship.

Peter's frustration finally exploded after the theatre one night at Mrs Morgan's digs. We were having spaghetti supper in the sitting room. Peter was in a strange mood. I think he was a bit miffed that I was not showing more regret at the parting. When I told him I was sure he had made the right decision he took it the wrong way and a heated argument began, in which he accused me of seeing someone else. It was ridiculous, we were never apart. The next thing I knew there was a plate of spaghetti in my face. There was a moment of stunned silence, I, wiping spaghetti off my face, had to laugh. It was so idiotic – the old custard pie routine. Peter burst into tears and ran out of the house. Now I was worried, and followed. I could hear his running footsteps in the empty street. I guessed he was making for the nearby flat of our manager and his wife. When I arrived, Peter was being comforted over a cup of tea. They looked at my face and hair with strands of spaghetti still clinging to it and tried not to laugh. I said Peter and I should leave them in peace. 'Look after him,' was their farewell. I began to realise that was really what my future might be. Although there was about eight years difference between us, he frequently called me mummy.

In letters exchanged while he was working in Leeds he was full of the new company, how he loved all the actors he was working with, plus news of a cricket team they had. I in turn wrote how much the company missed him, but I could not in all honesty say that I was desperately missing him. At this time late nights were no problem for me so I was enjoying myself. There were picnics, dances, excursions to the beach. Everyone appeared to getting as much pleasure as they could out of life as the awful spectre of war drew closer.

In the last letter I had written to Peter I had told him I was leaving for home at the end of the season in May, before Scarborough became full of summer visitors. I was hoping for a job in one of Hanson's companies and said I thought we should both pursue our careers and not think about marriage for the time being. I agreed with my parents that I was too young to marry. I really didn't know my own mind.

When I was on the train crawling into Euston on my way to Southampton, I saw Peter on the platform anxiously scanning the carriages. I knew he was going to meet me and I knew it would be an emotive encounter, but when I saw his mother and father as well I realised this was going to mean a confrontation. I was right. Peter was upset and his parents were there to persuade me to continue the engagement. We drove to Waterloo Station and over tea and cakes had a heartbreaking farewell. I loved them all but I had to do what was best for both of us; even then I could be strong when faced with a critical decision. I remember it all so vividly. His dear mother asking me to think again; Peter's father talking to him in the background, with his arm round his shoulders to comfort him; Peter crying. Finally, as the train pulled out, the tears began running down my cheeks. But I knew I was right.

It was a crucial moment in Peter's life. His father, hoping to console him, gave him money enough to go to Hollywood and to keep him until he found a job, which he did in no time at all. English actors were in demand and it was before the days of the dreaded Green Card, so he could work easily. He wrote me warm and loving letters, but more important was his growing success in films. Peter Cushing had found his vocation. Without either of us realising it at the time, I had given him the chance he needed.

TWO

Sheffield, 1939

At the beginning of September 1939 we began rehearsing Terence Rattigan's hugely successful comedy *French Without Tears* in a room above the bar in a pub opposite the Lyceum Theatre in Sheffield. The play had recently concluded it's London run with the all-star cast of Rex Harrison, Trevor Howard, Roland Culver, and with Kay Hammond playing the entrancing female lead, Diana. I had been given that part, so this was my big moment. It was a dream part. I could show Hanson and Black that they had made no mistake in employing me. At my interview in London they said they thought I was too young (and I had already added a year to my age). I tried to convince them, quite truthfully, that I already had considerable theatrical experience. Then they thought I might be rather tall, another wretched drawback. Between the ages of fifteen and eighteen I had shot up and was now nearly 5ft 7inches; this was often a problem because most male actors were on the short side. But what finally decided them in my favour was my blond hair and long legs. Diana, the lead, has to be young and slim as she wears a bathing suit throughout most of the play. So, to my elation, I was given the part.

When we gathered for our first rehearsal, unbelievably all the men were tall. Playing opposite me was a splendid young actor, Myles Eason. Rehearsing in the pub in Sheffield, Myles and I had come to the crucial scene where he finally loses his temper with the flirting, teasing Diana and swings her around to kiss her. At that moment the door to the rehearsal room burst open and the theatre manager made a dramatic entry and announced 'War has been declared!' There was a deathly hush then everyone spoke at once. The manager raised his voice above the din to tell us he didn't know what we were to do but that he would speak to London on the phone. We fell silent. The inevitable had at last happened.

Eventually the director spoke. 'Well, I suppose we should continue from where we were in the script.' Myles and I repeated the dialogue up to the kiss and then he swung me around and kissed me so fiercely that he bit me! We just stared at each other – my lip bleeding – he horrified. He stammered out an apology and gave me his handkerchief. We both laughed, somewhat hysterically and everyone joined in. Our director sensibly called for a break and we filed downstairs to the bar, which was buzzing. A glass of beer was some comfort and though the talk was loud, underneath it all everyone was nervous and scared. The dreadful certainty was that we were almost totally unprepared for war.

The theatre was abruptly closed by the management. We were given money for fares and told to return to our homes until further notice. No one knew what was happening. Invasion was expected and places such as theatres where lots of people gathered were not considered safe. There had already been one air raid warning, very fightening, but a false alarm.

*　　*　　*　　*　　*

The first time I got to know Patrick was on the railway station on my way home. On reflection, stations and trains provided the main background for our romance.

Sheffield Station was bedlam, filled with a mass of worried travellers trying to get onto trains. Most of our company had families in the north and had wisely decided to stay where they were, while two or three others, London bound, had gone by road whilst there was still petrol. So I was alone with my suitcase when Patrick, who was our stage manager, came pushing towards me through the crowd.

He was broad and well over six feet tall, and looked as though he would be a helpful ally. We were both making for London, then on to the South Coast, so we needed to board a London-bound train. When an engine steamed in there was a mad rush. Patrick took my case, told me to hang on to him and managed to clear a path through the crowds. A carriage door was open, so he flung in our cases and jumped in, hauling me after him. A miracle; there were two vacant seats which we immediately occupied.

It was a so-called London Express, but the train halted at every station and sometimes in the middle of nowhere, so the journey was long and tedious. Gradually our carriage became less crowded. Out of sheer boredom we began to exchange backgrounds. His parents lived near Hastings. Mine had evacuated from Southampton and bought a house in Christchurch near the River Avon. He told me he had volunteered for the Palestine Police when he was nineteen and had just returned to England after three years there. I knew nothing about it and he did not expand, except to remark on the high mortality rate; most of his pals had been killed and he was lucky to return. Aware that his hopes for peace were likely to be short-lived he had taken this temporary job with Harry Hanson. He had known Harry in his earlier days when he was running a repertory company at the end of the pier at Hastings. Patrick had joined as an ASM when he left school.

I was curious about Harry and longed to hear more of our bald, humorous but strict boss. Apparently he had begun his career as an Adagio dancer, partnering his sister. When she left to get married he started a repertory company in Hastings. George Black, then a top impresario in the London musical theatre, including the London Hippodrome, was searching for some means of giving his son, George Junior, experience in theatre management. Because of Harry's success in his tiny Hastings theatre George was teamed up with him. In no time at all Hanson & Black had companies in most of the large cities in England. Their reputation was as high as their standards. Almost all the actors I knew during the war had worked in one of their companies.

Harry himself was a memorable personality, sporting a

reddish toupee, which would be switched to grey if he wanted to sack someone, cut salaries, or deliver a lecture. He was strict; compliments were not frequent, but he was well liked though the butt of many jokes. A flashy but tasteful dresser, he was always the first to criticise our wardrobe which we had to provide ourselves. It was no use pointing out that we were underpaid! He was gay but always discreet about his partner. Homosexuality was neither admitted nor legal in 1939.

At last we arrived in London. Chaos once more. How was I to get myself to Waterloo Station? All the entrances to the underground were blocked by a mass of humanity struggling to go down the stairs, or up, all with luggage. Patrick managed by magic to find a taxi and helped me in, pushing my case in after me. I thought he was joining me, but he slammed the door, waving goodbye. He faded into the crowds and out of my mind.

I was only at home for a week. The little house my parents had hastily fled to in Christchurch was bursting. My brother was home from school. My aunt and her daughter had come from London, and other members of the family from Southampton. It was a major upheaval of everyone's world. All I could think about was missing my opportunity to play Diana in *French without Tears*, so I was overjoyed when the call came to return to Sheffield. My mother made me a money belt that I wore strapped around my stomach with fifty pounds in it, a small fortune then. If the Germans invaded it was to be used to find my way home.

Once the train from Christchurch arrived in Southampton, the passengers for London piled in. The corridors were full of men standing. I fortunately had a seat but squeezed myself into a corner to make more space. By the time we reached Waterloo the fellow squashed next to me was becoming too friendly. He had a flask of whisky from which he took constant nips and kept offering it to me. My polite refusal did not stop his whisky fuelled chatter. He said that he had just arrived back from Palestine. I remarked that I knew someone who had served in the Palestine Police. He looked at me with renewed interest. 'A close friend?'

'Oh no,' I replied wishing that I had never spoken.

'Well he's lucky to be alive. Those boys have a rough time.' Arriving at Waterloo, my companion, by then a little high on his Scotch, asked me my next destination, so I told him Euston and then Sheffield. He was also bound for Euston.

People were milling around trying to find a train or crowding into the underground. The crowds were immense and desperate. Taxis were scarce and quickly snapped up – however, this was a travelling man. He parked me in front of the baggage, then disappeared. I was beginning to wonder if I would ever see him again when suddenly he was by my side urging me to hurry. We grabbed our bags and ran towards a taxi already containing two people who were also Euston bound. I didn't worry how he had achieved this miracle – cash probably – there were bribes being offered for taxis. I was just thankful.

At Euston more chaos. Hundreds of men in uniform laden with kit bags, a new sight that was to become familiar. The man, I never asked his name, found a way through to one of the refreshment bars, and guided me inside. The noise was deafening and we were enveloped by clouds of cigarette smoke. There was not a table or chair free. Then a sergeant put his head in the door yelling some orders. Within minutes the room emptied of all in uniform. The man seated me at an empty table and made for the bar, returning with two large whiskies. I was beginning to wonder how to extricate myself from what was becoming an increasingly awkward situation, when across at the bar I saw a tall broad figure and recognised Patrick.

'Excuse me,' I said, ' I see a friend over there who may know about trains.' I quickly made my way across to Patrick and asked him to rescue me from my companion, who had just returned from Palestine. Patrick went over to the man and spoke to him in fluent Arabic. I have absolutely no idea what he said, but quite suddenly the man picked up his bag and walked away so abruptly he left his drink behind.

'Whatever did you say?' I asked.

'Never mind,' said Patrick as he finished the man's whisky.

The platforms at Euston resembled a minor riot. Patrick returned to where he had left me guarding the luggage, with news of a train departing for the north. If we could find and board it, we might eventually reach Sheffield. Once on the platform we jostled with the waiting crowds. Finally the engine crawled into the station, puffing steam. The carriage doors were flung open, disgorging troops with full kit, all young in ill-fitting brand new uniforms, followed by civilians struggling with their luggage. The result was chaotic with waiting passengers trying to force a way on whilst the others were still trying to get out. I only recall hanging on to Pat's belt, pushing our way through the mass of humanity and kit bags. Panting and triumphant we made it in the end and Pat put the luggage down in a small space in the already jammed corridors. We sat on it for a moment to get a breather and to stake a claim for the spot. It had been dark for hours. All the bulbs on the train were painted blue and hardly any lights were allowed on the station. The blackout, new to us, was already in force. That lengthy journey north in a blacked out train was going to be a test of endurance.

'By the way,' said Patrick 'wouldn't you be more comfortable without that ridiculous hat on your head?' There was no point in explaining that in 1939 without a hat you were not properly dressed. The war would soon change us. Scarves were to become the popular headgear of the war.

We must have been waiting to start for almost an hour, so it was a relief to feel the train moving and to know we were finally on our way. I just prayed we were going in the right direction. There was no doubt it was going to be a long night. Patrick fitted the cases together and placed his coat over them leaving space for people to squeeze by in the corridor. I tried to relax on the 'bed' he had made for me. It was so good to lie down, the last time had been at home early that morning, so I lay back on the suitcases and lost all sense of time. Patrick took off his jacket to put under my head as a pillow and leant back against the wall. I fell asleep. I have no idea how long I was dozing, it was impossible to sleep for long with all the activity. I had the sensation of lips on mine. Not sure what to do I kept my eyes closed, it was not unpleasant. 'Were you kissing me Patrick?'

Silence, then 'You looked so irresistible lying there.'

I said sleepily 'I rather enjoyed it.'

We arrived in Sheffield just before dawn, where Pat eventually found a cab, and piled me and my case into it. I should think he was glad to be rid of me

The theatres remained open and cinemas re-opened. The phoney war took everyone by surprise. We were expecting bombs, gas, germ warfare, invasion, all of which had been threatened, but instead there was nothing. But this extraordinary breather we were having gave us the God-given time needed to gather our forces together and, very important, time to re-arm. Living in Sheffield, the home of steel, we were only too aware of the mills and factories working all hours trying to make up for precious lost time.

Life just went along as usual, with only call-ups affecting us. Before the end of the season we lost two of our male actors, and then after we closed at Sheffield, Myles Eason. Petrol and food were both rationed and it was becoming increasingly difficult to buy many basics. Black-out, torches and gas masks became a way of life.

I was asked by the Hanson-Black management to play Eliza Doolittle in *Pygmalion* for one of their companies. I was overjoyed and flattered to be offered such a prestigious role in the famous Shaw play. I was also fortunate to have a talented director who helped me master the all-important Cockney accent, which must be authentic and is not as easy as it sounds. I made a big success of Eliza, due to our hard work. Both bosses came to see me and I actually received compliments, very rare, in case you became big headed and asked for a raise! Immediately after *Pygmalion* I was asked to join another of their companies for a play called *The Housemaster*. The cast were all young and we had a lot of fun. But even as we partied, we could sense that the war was beginning to hot up – and this time in earnest.

41

In a moment of great patriotism, fairly early in the war, I had presented myself to the local recruiting office in Sheffield. I told them I was willing to volunteer for any service, the WRENS being high on my list. The lady behind the desk regarded me for a moment; then came the questions. When did I matriculate? How many languages – if any? What age? Could I drive a car? As this went on it became perfectly clear that I was of no possible use because I had left school far too early with no real qualifications, certificates in ballet were of course not worth mentioning. I spoke school French, my driving licence was still provisional because tests were discontinued with the shortage of petrol. There was obviously not much point in continuing the interview. I *could* if desperate, join the WAAF or ATS as a driver but at the moment only girls with more experience were required.

The woman looked at me kindly and leant across the desk.

'Miss Lawrence, I am a regular member of the audience at the Lyceum Theatre and you are a versatile young actress. You are helping so much more by staying in your own profession. Something you do well is making people happy. We all need the escapism of entertainment, a good evening at the theatre. I think that you are genuinely contributing to the war effort in a way that others cannot. But if you wish to do more I suggest you consider the ENSA organisation. Then, when you are twenty-one, you can join them and volunteer for service overseas. They will need people like yourself.'

It was one of the best pieces of advice I have ever received

THREE

Sheffield, 1940

Fate has frequently stepped into my life, as in Sheffield in 1940. Because of the city's importance to the war effort, bombs increasingly targeted it as the spring wore on. At first, when the air raid sirens sent out their eerie warning, the theatre management would make an announcement from the stage, giving the audience the choice of leaving or staying in their seats, but the play continued. At the final curtain, if the 'All Clear' had not sounded and bombs were still thudding we would remain on stage and do our best to entertain the usually packed theatre. I don't remember anyone leaving during a performance. It was safer inside than facing the flying glass and debris in the streets. Mainly I think they stayed for the warmth of companionship, people were happier in groups. Short of a direct hit it was the safest choice.

We tried sing-songs, the band in the orchestra pit striking up one well-known tune after another as a way of keeping the audience from thinking about what was happening outside. It was a great relief when we heard the 'All Clear' finally sound because we, the actors, were absolutely worn out. We had lines to learn and a rehearsal the following day for the next week's play. After a while we had to call a halt and everyone had to take a chance.

Personally all I cared about was the lack of trams. They did not run during an air raid and it was a long way to the digs at Brocco Bank, but safer than central Sheffield – Valerie Skardon, a fellow actress joined me there. If a bombing raid occurred during the show it was often a prelude to another attack, but one could risk a dash for home during the break between raids.

One night there was a direct hit on the house next door to Patrick's digs while he was in the theatre. On returning he found the air raid wardens evacuating his house as unsafe, so he spent that night in the theatre. The following day he moved to Brocco Bank with us. Valerie had spoken to our landlady, Mrs Jennings, and the dear woman was so soft-hearted that she found a small room upstairs for him.

Patrick, sensing my unease, said it would only be for a short while. He had already volunteered and was waiting for further orders. I occupied the 'best front room' with a coal fire. Sometimes Val would join me for a late night supper which Mrs Jennings would leave to warm in the kitchen range oven, and we would sit eating by my fire. It was usually shepherd's pie, tripe and onions, stew, anything she could manage on our ration books. It seemed churlish to exclude Patrick. Valerie was engaged, which in straight language meant she was having an affair with another Patrick who in peacetime was in theatre management. He was now an officer in uniform and stationed in the north. He frequently arrived unexpectedly for weekend leave to share Val's double bed.

For this reason, Pat and I often found ourselves alone together. Events galloped along at speed. I tried to struggle against any romantic entanglement, my instincts told me it was a mistake, but inevitably through the many pressures of the war and the heightened emotions, we became lovers. He was an expert in love-making and I became a willing pupil.

The theatre was forced to open earlier, by 5.00pm. The aim was to get people off the streets and into their homes before the now nightly raids. All public transport ceased early and it became hardly worth the journey back to the digs between rehearsal and the evening performance. It was often easier to go to a local café and eat what was on offer.

Telephones were rare. I had to find a call box if I wanted to phone my parents. There was no phone at my digs and the one at the stage door was only for essential calls. One relied upon letters for news, and letter writing was during snatched times at the theatre, in the dressing room during waits. So much time was spent in the theatre that everything went on there. Washing smalls in the dressing room basin; desperately altering clothes to meet H.H's high standards. Fellow actresses and I formed a lending circle out of necessity. Cards from actress friends in Leeds or Nottingham or wherever brought their requests. 'I can send you my best grey if you can loan me your lace negligee', or similar exchanges. A trip to the post office was all that was required.

When Patrick's call-up papers came he had a week to make ready to join the Irish Guards. It was a frantic time. He told me he was in love with me, I said I thought I was with him. Then he was gone: to where? I had no idea and he was unable to tell me.

I hadn't realised how that brief, but all too ardent relationship with Pat would affect me. I suffered a longing that I had not felt before. I needed to be near him – touch him – laugh with him – have him hold me close. I thought it was love. With hindsight I'm afraid it was lust.

Valerie married her Pat and we all trooped to an early morning ceremony at a registry office. Marriages were taking place with little thought of anything beyond the precious moments to be spent together. Valerie's marriage was one of the few to last. She produced two daughters before the end of the war and remained with Pat until his death.

* * * * *

At last I heard from Patrick. He was stationed in the south, somewhere near Caterham and longed to see me while it was still possible. Could I take a night train down on a Saturday so we could spend Sunday together? Officially I was not supposed to leave the area in case I became trapped or could not return, when the company would be short of an actress. We were about to put on a play in which I had only a minor role. I decided to go the weekend immediately prior to the opening. I could travel all Saturday night and return over Sunday night to be in time for

Monday's dress rehearsal.

Terrible things were happening in the war. Our army in France was being pushed towards the coast and although the news was sparse, it was all too plain that it was in retreat and being driven back. Many prisoners were taken, whole platoons just surrounded. Retreat was staring us in the face, but no one would speak, or even think of, the word defeat. If we had to face invasion, even though we knew that we were not sufficiently equipped, there was to be no capitulation. We did not talk about it much, it was too frightening, though we made jokes about what we might do to defend ourselves.

Night trains were no longer crammed with civilians, so there were only troops in the gloomy blacked out carriages. Blinds had to be drawn and bulbs dimmed, making it impossible to read or even sleep because of the crush of kit bags and rifles. I had nothing with me but a handbag and the obligatory gas mask. As no one inspected those ridiculous cardboard boxes we wore slung round our necks, I had taken out my mask and replaced it with a toothbrush and a few toilet oddments. I'm sure the masks would have been useless anyway.

The atmosphere in the carriage was stifling, tense, and full of smoke. The conversation was all about the retreat in France. These boys had thought they were to be sent across the Channel, but there was no point now. From what I could gather there was chaos. All the lads struggling to return to England were being bombed and strafed to hell on the French beaches. We had heard nothing of this in Sheffield, but in the dark of the carriage, where I was squashed unseen in a corner, my companions swopped rumours and scraps of news in tense whispers.

I had caught the midnight train, having confided in Val so that Mrs Jennings would not be worried by my absence. The train would crawl then suddenly gather speed. When we approached London there was an air raid in progress. The train halted , then moved on once more. The journey seemed never-ending. We made it into Euston as dawn was breaking and the 'All Clear' sounded.

The bombers had gone for the night.

I had to find my way to Waterloo. Where there are troops there is always a N.A.A.F.I, or some other kind soul who had a kiosk open with tea, so after swallowing a cup I followed the masses. I managed to squeeze onto a tube to Charing Cross, I could walk from there to Waterloo if needs be. When I emerged at Charing Cross the station was completely empty. In those days it boasted a Ladies Waiting Room with clean lavatories and wash basins, even a woman in charge who despite her surprise at seeing me at such an hour handed me a clean towel.

Feeling refreshed, I wandered out of the Embankment entrance into the most beautiful morning. It was so early there was not another soul about, not even a sound – it was eerily quiet. I crossed over to the parapet and leant on it, looking at the glorious view of the river sparkling in the sunlight. To my right were Westminster Bridge and the familiar silhouette of Big Ben. There was no traffic and I felt I was utterly alone in this great city of ours. I looked down at the flowing Thames, unwittingly at night the guide for German planes into the heart of London. Oh God, I prayed, please do not let our country be taken from us. Do not allow this city we love be filled with our enemies, please help us to keep our land free. I stayed there lost in my thoughts. Big Ben struck. I had plenty of time before the first train, if indeed there was one, so I started walking to Waterloo Station.

I did not know that the great evacuation of Dunkirk was taking place – how could I know? We were not given any news on the radio or in the papers until after the exhausted and wounded men had been ferried home to England by any craft that floated and could make it to France and back. A miracle of courage and endurance was taking place – the queues of men on the beaches patiently waiting to be hauled aboard anything which could carry them. Bombed and shot at, they must have wondered why our aircraft were not there to protect them. The sad reason was a lack of planes and trained pilots, though our pilots were preparing with all speed for the Battle of Britain that lay ahead.

At last the train crawled into a small Surrey station and the porter called out the name, necessary because all name boards had been obliterated, as had all signposts. It was part of a safety precaution to confuse the enemy in case of an invasion, it certainly confused everyone else. The station was virtually empty and I was the only person to alight. Patrick's tall figure stood alone on the platform. I was so delighted to see him that I jumped into his arms, my weariness quite forgotten.

He was clutching a tiny posy of violets because he knew I was fond of them. Linking arms, we wandered away from the station eagerly exchanging news. Where could we go? It was Sunday in England in the country, and not a single café was open. Pat said he had reserved a table at a hotel for lunch, but it was too early so we wandered up into the woods nearby. I sat on his jacket on the grass, just talking. He told me how much he loved me, the parting had made him realise how deeply. I spoke about my loneliness after he had left and how much I had missed him. He said he was against a wartime marriage because it would be unfair to me, but I protested that as it was impossible to see anything ahead, it seemed we should grasp at any happiness no matter how brief. The future was unknown. Patrick knew he was to be transferred to the Intelligence Corps, but had no idea when or where. I dreaded that he would be sent overseas. We knew little of what was happening to our Forces in France.

We lay back on the grass and we both stared at the extraordinarily blue sky above us.

Finally he asked 'Will you marry me? I could get leave for marriage soon, if I were to apply.'

I paused, my parents would be unhappy, possibly difficult, after all they had never met him. I knew that I had not even mentioned Pat in my letters home and it would be an unpleasant shock for them, but there was some inborn puritanical rule lurking within me. You did not sleep with a man unless you had marriage in mind. I tried to ignore this thought, it was old fashioned, a rule to be broken in such desperate times. I also felt that marriage might give me a sense of much needed security. Anyway, at that moment I thought we would be lucky if we lived to next Christmas. So I turned to him and said 'Yes.'

He laughed and hugged me. 'We can get a special licence.' He pulled me to my feet. 'Come on it's opening time – twelve o'clock – let's celebrate.'

*   *   *   *   *

Events moved swiftly. I was working hard with long roles to be learnt and rehearsed, trying to find the time and the courage to write to my parents. There seemed little point in explaining our brief relationship. I thought it might be better just to come straight out with our plans for a marriage. This was wartime. Bombs were now a nightly occurrence. There was so little time to waste. Patrick obtained his leave; I'm sure his commanding officer was inundated with similar requests.

Our intention was to have a quiet ceremony, but it did not work out as easily as we had thought. My mother was furious, and would not be pacified, but my father wisely did nothing to stop me. Even my friends in the theatre were hardly overwhelmed with joy when I spread the news. Their objections were the haste and my youth – I was still only 20. Even Harry Hanson rang to demand if I had taken leave of my senses. However, he sent a small cheque and everyone was supportive when the moment came.

I knew my father would come up to Sheffield to give me away and he arrived with mother, still in a black mood. To my surprise he was bearing presents from his staff, old retainers who had known me all my life. I was very touched.

More surprises. My cousin Jean arrived from London. She was about to join the WAAF and with her was an old school friend of mine waiting for her call-up to the WRENS. Mrs Jennings, wonderful and accommodating as always, found room for the two girls, one of whom shared my bed.

Patrick and I were to spend our wedding night at the Grand

Hotel, the best Sheffield could produce. We were to be married on Saturday morning, and of course I had to work on Saturday night, which meant Patrick and I only had Sunday together, for on Monday I had the dress rehearsal of the new play which opened that night. Always one play a week.

Patrick arrived with his kit bag on Friday night as I was making a quick change in the dressing room. We hardly had time to embrace when I had to rush back on stage. Patrick dumped his kit bag and watched me from the wings, which I found somewhat distracting. Later he told me he was in a state because his parents had turned up unexpectedly. I hadn't met them and knew little about his family background, but I did know his mother was unwell, she had recently had a major operation for a brain tumour so I could understand his concern.

Far from the quiet, swift, happy wedding we had planned it was becoming one of fraught agitation.

I had spent all my coupons and money on a chic new outfit and had splashed out on having a hat made. White weddings were almost unheard of at this time.

Because we were so crowded in the digs we all had a restless night and worst of all I awoke to find I had started my period! I'm afraid I had entirely forgotten about the dates.

Mother was still in a black mood but I did my best to ignore it, as I did my stomach ache. Pop and I sat alone in my bed-sit on the Saturday morning. He was concerned that I had eaten nothing that day but I couldn't face food. I was suddenly nervous, but it was too late to admit to qualms. The car was at the door, and with my father holding my hand we were off. The moment of no return.

I saw Patrick and Mike Aldridge, the best man. As Mike and the groom had never met, he hardly qualified for the job, but I had talked him into it as we were waiting at the side of the stage the night before. He could hardly refuse, there was no one else! I gave them a big smile as I joined them, which faded when I was nearly knocked unconscious by the brandy fumes. The bridegroom and best man had obviously been getting acquainted.

The company had arranged a small get together on the stage during the afternoon with a cake and a photographer from the local press. Then there was the rush to make up ready for the evening show.

Much later we made our way to the Grand Hotel for supper. It was the first real food I had eaten all day. Eventually we fell into bed; I was absolutely exhausted with the emotional strain, hard work and not feeling very well. We heard the air raid siren, but had every intention of ignoring it. It was not to be. Staff at the hotel were banging on all the doors, telling guests to go down at once to the ballroom taking only their most important possessions. Flinging on dressing gowns we joined the throng. Bombs were dropping unpleasantly close and the whole building was shuddering. As the other guests gathered around the ballroom tables we found ourselves with the well-known tenor, Richard Tauber, who was playing at Sheffield's other principal theatre, the Empire. We struck up a friendly conversation, and ended up spending our wedding night sharing a bottle of Scotch with Richard Tauber.

It was dawn by the time the 'All Clear' sounded and we all trailed off for what was left of the night. With the combination of whisky and the events of the day and night, I fell sound asleep.

At nine o'clock the telephone by the bed rang. Who on earth would ring and disturb us on our one day together? It was Patrick's father. From the strained tone of his voice I realised something was wrong and I sat up in bed.

Pat was saying, 'I can't, this is supposed to be my honeymoon and we've been up all night.' Silence, while his father pleaded with him. 'Alright. I will come if you are sure it will help.'

He hung up and I looked at him. 'What is it? Your mother?'

He nodded and made for the bathroom. 'My mother won't leave without seeing me, she is being difficult, my father can't deal with her.' I just looked astonished. He left saying he would return shortly.

I had breakfast in bed, then a leisurely bath. Finally I decided to go over to the pub where Patrick's parents were staying to find out what had happened to my new husband. I looked at my finger – yes – I was certainly wearing a gold ring. Once there, and not knowing what to do I sat downstairs at a small table and ordered a baby Guinness.

After about half an hour a distraught Patrick appeared. Apparently his mother was having one of her attacks; she wouldn't get out of bed to get dressed and ready for the journey home. They had already missed their train. Both he and his father had tried every kind of persuasion. I said I would go up and talk to her, after all she was my mother-in-law. Patrick was hesitant but longing to get away, so thought it worth trying. I had not expected the scene that greeted me. The lady in the old fashioned double bed was either indulging in a dramatic bid for the attention that she knew would keep her husband and son by her side, or she was genuinely crackers. She ignored me, clinging on to Patrick, begging him not to leave her. Her wretched husband explained over and over again that her son was not only married, but that his duties to King and Country meant he had to leave all of us. I realised my presence only exacerbated the situation, so I bade them farewell. Patrick then stated firmly that he was leaving with me. This was all that remained of his honeymoon and he did not care if she took root in the bed. The echo of her cries followed our exit.

We returned to the Grand without a word. What was there to say? Emerging through the swing doors into the hotel, who should be at the nearest table but my parents, and my mother was actually smiling. After an amazingly convivial lunch, we were saying goodbye on the hotel steps when a large car rolled up, one of the few with a gallon of petrol left in its tank, and out spilled some local friends who had come to sweep us off to a celebratory party.

It was a late return to Brocco Bank that night. I became guilt ridden about the dress rehearsal awaiting me tomorrow. Although I was not playing a leading role there was an important scene that needed work. Married or not, it was the job that came first. So there we were, sitting up in bed, script in hand, Patrick cueing me, until we both fell asleep.

Between the dress rehearsal and the opening, there was only enough time for tea and the usual sausages at the local café. As always on a first night I was consumed with nerves and could only think of the performance ahead. During the show Patrick had to leave to catch the train to make the long journey south to report in again for duty. It was almost three months before we saw each other again.

*   *   *   *   *

We next met when I went to join him in Winchester for two weeks. For me it was ideal. I was close to my family in Southampton and rather proud of my new married status. Pat had leave at weekends, otherwise he was going 'over the wall' as he described it, returning to me unofficially.

There was 48 hours when he was on duty and unable to get out. I took a train to Southampton to see my much-loved Pop, intending to go on by bus to stay with a friend who owned a cottage in the New Forest. Once in the city, I made my way down to the docks where our ship's outfitting business was situated. Pop was surprised and delighted to see me, but begged me to get out of the city as quickly as possible.

'Why the hurry?' I asked.

'As dusk falls there will be panic – everyone trying to leave.'

When we reached the city centre I could see what he meant. Every vehicle was crammed with people. Tramcars were overflowing, with desperate human beings hanging on to them in the effort to get away from the nightly raids – many opting for just a blanket in the New Forest. My father was determined to take me to the bus station. They were all packed, but he helped me squeeze on one. Waving goodbye, I was scared that he might miss his train home to Christchurch.

That night Southampton was blitzed. Burned to the ground. The cottage I was staying in shook. The windows rattled so much we

53

thought we would be safer outside. From the garden, we watched in horror as bombs exploded and flames devoured our hometown. The area near the docks were the main target. Ships lit up in the blaze were at the mercy of the bombers.

I have bitter memories of the losses: Grandpa's business, the properties, possessions, all gone. Luckily no loss of family lives. The young were all away in the Forces. The older members of the family had wisely moved out. Telephone lines were all down, so I returned to the relative peace of Winchester without news. It was several days before I knew that my father was safe.

On Patrick's 'prior to embarkation' leave we went to visit his parents. As we neared Hastings the skies were alive with aircraft, with the constant roaring noise of planes flying low before climbing high over the Channel. Airfields had been hastily constructed, particularly in Kent, and all were a hive of activity. This was where the war was being fought now. These courageous young pilots were doing their utmost to keep Hitler and his armies away from our shores. The feared invasion had not taken place so far.

I was not looking forward to this visit after my last encounter with Patrick's parents, who lived in a small house perched on the cliffs outside Hastings. However, we were given a warm welcome. His mother was obviously keeping herself under control, but I couldn't help regarding her somewhat warily; her permanent state of nerves made us all uneasy. His father was a delightful man, but I noticed that he treated his wife as a semi-invalid. Patrick was always taking me out for walks which finished at the nearest pub. There was also the strain of the inevitable parting. He had to return to Winchester and we had only one more night together.

I left for more work in Peterborough, where Harry wanted me to join his company. Would I see my husband again? He hoped to be given a final leave to say goodbye, but we couldn't be certain, so it was one more awful parting.

I had hoped for peace after the bombs in Sheffield, but I had chosen the wrong place. Peterborough was surrounded by airfields which were attacked most nights. I managed at last to find digs,

but not near the theatre and with no public transport. Everyone
cycled or walked. One of the cast found an old bicycle for me for
seven and six pence, cheap even then, on which I wobbled home
every night with the skies bursting with tracer bullets and shells
lighting up the whole area. It was like a firework display, without
the fun.

One night in early 1941 I was in my dressing room at the
theatre when I heard the sound of stomping boots in the corridor
outside. I stopped still – so did my heart. A bang on the door and
in walked Patrick. He had had no time or means of informing me.
Overwhelmed with delight and surprise I didn't think of the reason
for his unexpected appearance until later. He had been given a four
day embarkation leave. We set about making the most of it.

There was a party in the Green Room. The touring company
from the other theatre usually joined us, their stage door was
directly opposite ours. That week it was Emlyn Williams in one of
his own plays, who brought over a much prized bottle of Scotch.

During the show the following night a telegram from Patrick's
father brought the shocking news that his mother had died. What
to do? We had only two days left. Of course he must go, but he
was upset and kept repeating 'Why did she have to do this to me
– why now?' I thought it a strange reaction, but it was a sudden
death for a woman in early middle-age. Naturally I was distressed
too, it was an awful thing to happen. I realised that I was being
selfish, hating to sacrifice an all too brief leave.

Our director came to see me and said that I was to go to Hastings
with Patrick on the following day and he would ask the understudy
to take over. At least we could be together and maybe I could give
Patrick some support.

So back to Hastings. Patrick remained unusually silent. It was
an unhappy return. The little house was cold and creepy. Patrick
found the key under the mat. Fortunately we were soon joined by
his father. I let them have a quiet conversation together and then
we left the gloom for some food in a restaurant.

The next day we were surprised by the arrival of his mother's sister. She was a terrific light relief, a total opposite to her sister, and swept us all out to drinks at the hotel where she was staying. The gist of the family conversation was that it was always going to happen, 'poor soul, her son going overseas was too much.' I was left to draw my own conclusions. I had promised to return to Peterborough on the Sunday night for the dress rehearsal the following day. So that was our goodbye.

* * * * *

Sheffield was to open for another season and Harry did his best to persuade me to return there after Peterborough. I didn't want to go. I needed the work but I was sick of the treadmill of weekly repertory. I really wanted to work in London, and perhaps join one of the many touring companies of West End players and actors. The bombing in London was at its height. Several theatres had been hit so the provincial theatres were benefiting from visits from many top companies. It was a boom time for the profession. Theatres and cinemas were filled to capacity; people would not allow the bombs to keep them away. Harry Hanson raised my salary (a miracle), enticing me with a list of plays, including several by Bernard Shaw with good roles for me. It was tempting.

The decision was made for me by unexpected news from Patrick. Through a code we had devised, as all Forces letters were censored, I gathered he was still in England in the north awaiting departure. If I returned to Sheffield we might be able to meet again. So I did, back to Brocco Bank and Ma Jennings with her tiny husband and fat dog. Sure enough Patrick arrived.

For weeks, his regiment had been holed up in Liverpool awaiting embarkation. They were billeted in appalling discomfort in cold, damp warehouses with no facilities. The docks were a prime target, under heavy nightly bombing. The convoy was late in arriving, either not available, or more likely unable to enter the docks during raids to embark the troops. I think the commanding officers were glad to send those away who could take short leave nearby. So we had four more days.

The morning when I was to begin rehearsals was our last. We were at the bleak railway station at 9.30 am. It was a gut-wrenching departure, we knew this time it was the final one. Patrick leant out of the window of the train, hanging on to my hands until he had to let go. I watched through the steam and my tears until he was out of sight then turned and left the empty grey platform to walk down the slope from the station towards the theatre. The weather was as cold and dismal as I felt.

Then, through the stage door a warm greeting from the old keeper – Charlie, Joe, whatever his name – I was glad to see him again. Then back up onto the familiar stage. Oh great, Alexander Marsh was going to be the director. He had helped me so much with Eliza in *Pygmalion*. The actors were all greeting each other; it was great to see old friends and meet the rest of the cast. I was further cheered when 'Marshie' confided to me that my old friend Peter Coleman would be joining us. I began to feel warmth again in my body and in my soul. I was at home on any stage. Working light, curtain up, the vast auditorium beyond, dark, empty and hushed. I inhaled that familiar musty odour of any theatre backstage. I was back in my own environment. Scripts were handed out by the stage manager, pencils at the ready we made a start. The play was *Quiet Wedding* and I was playing the bride.

FOUR

London, 1942

Soon after Patrick went, sometime in the spring of that year, I had reached the dead end of being able to churn out a new play every week. I always seemed to have the most lines to learn, and my brain had reached saturation point. So when a fat script was dumped on my lap with a part I knew I was totally unsuited for, a wee Highland lass from the Scottish Isles (I couldn't even master the accent in the time allotted), I struck. Not usually a person to take a stand, I made for the stage door and only telephone and rang Harry Hanson in London, telling him I had reached the end, and could he find someone to take my place?

H.H. was quite suddenly a different person, soothing and kind to the hysterical young actress, suggesting a rest with my parents. I was so relieved and amazed for not being berated for leaving him in the lurch, that I failed to realise that this left the door open. He was never going to let me go. As for replacing me – if only temporarily – with so many out-of-work actresses there was always one eager to step into your shoes.

My final final curtain call at the Lyceum Theatre, Sheffield, marked the start of a fraught night. Peter Coleman was also leaving, so we planned to catch the last train to London. Our optimism faded as the train grew later and later. The manager of the Station Hotel, a regular patron of the theatre, seeing us pacing the platform in frustration, took us into his private apartment and gave us a welcome drink. As a leaving gift he gave me a box of *marrons glacé*, not seen in England since the war began. I smiled my thanks but it was yet another box to fit into my overflowing carrier bags. When the train arrived we pushed our way on board into an already crowded compartment. We made frequent stops, sometimes for lengthy periods. Sitting there in the blacked out carriages I at times wondered if we would ever get started again. It was obvious there was trouble ahead: London had raids most nights but this must be a heavy one.

Finally we came to a shuddering halt and we were off-loaded as quickly as possible and told to find shelter, the train was going no further, presumably it wasn't safe. Perhaps Euston and Kings Cross had been blitzed – stations were always targets. Clutching our belongings, Peter and I looked for somewhere to shelter. We could see a hut nearby, which was already full of people huddled together. They made a space for us. No one was talking. In the distance we could hear the odd crump and thump of the bombs. As my eyes grew accustomed to the darkness I could see it was a hut for railway workers. Finally Peter, his clear actor's voice breaking the silence, asked where we were. Harrow-on-the-Hill we were told. Silence was resumed until Peter said he was starving, I agreed, we were talking in whispers for some odd reason. Apart from a drinks only farewell party after the final performance we had eaten nothing since lunch on the previous day. Our stomachs were rattling, but all I could produce was a bottle of sherry and the sticky French bons bons. However we were desperate and attacked the *marrons*, washing them down with the sherry.

Dawn broke. The sky lightened, and the bombers departed. We emerged wearily from our emergency shelter. Eventually an electric commuter train pulled in and took us to an underground station on the outskirts of London. As we sped into the city, each stop revealed the white, drawn faces of people lying on every kind of bedding, closely packed together, trying to get away from the bombs. Peter's Notting Hill station approached. He didn't want to leave me on my own, but was desperate to see if his wife and their home were alright. 'I'll be fine,' I replied to his query, with a confidence I did not feel. When he left, making his way through the bodies lying on the platform, I felt so alone.

I had been told no trains would go beyond Charing Cross, so I had no choice but to walk to Waterloo struggling with my suitcase and carrier bags. When I finally reached the ramp leading up to the station the sight that greeted me was unbelievable – the early morning light revealed the chaos and damage of the night's bombing. It seemed I was the only occupant of this vast silent building, which along with most of London had been blasted all night in one of the worst raids of the war. There would certainly be no trains today. I was afraid for the first time in that long night and in despair flopped, exhausted, onto the only chair remaining upright in what was left of the buffet. The eerie silence was broken by the odd piece of glass or masonry dropping from the roof.

What to do? Oh God, what to do?

I couldn't walk another step if my life depended on it.

A lone station attendant appeared, sweeping the broken glass with an inadequate broom. Startled at the sight of this pathetic girl collapsed in a chair, clutching a bunch of dead flowers, wearing a hat and surrounded by bags and a suitcase, it must have given the poor man a nasty shock. In an astonished voice he urged me to get out.

'Miss, you can't stay here, it's not safe.'

It was true, bits of the building were falling around us. He was wearing a tin hat.

I simply said 'Not another step, just let me sit here.'

He took charge, gathering my possessions. 'Follow me.'

My legs did as they were told, automatically propelling me to keep up with him down that slope again. At the bottom was a bus taking on passengers. He somehow squeezed in me and my luggage. We were to be taken to Clapham Junction and from there hoped to get trains to our various destinations. I shouted my thanks as we lurched off, standing so tightly packed it was impossible to fall. How could I find words to thank a man who had helped me when I truly thought I had reached rock bottom? He will always remain tucked in my memories with gratitude.

After three weeks at home I began to get bored. I missed work and the camaraderie of the theatre. But I had arrived home exhausted and at first it had been wonderful to just sleep and sleep in my own room in my own bed. Mother and I would sometimes take a picnic onto the nearby sand dunes, often watching the acrobatic dogfights in the sky over the Channel, the planes zooming and whirling. Until we heard the sudden burst of guns firing it was difficult to realise that young lives were at stake above us in that vivid blue sky. The tiny cemetery nearby was already the burial place for young German airmen

As I began to look and feel normal again, the urge to work grew stronger. Madness! Harry Hanson was a wily bird, he timed his telephone call perfectly. After three weeks he rang inquiring about my health, saying how much I had been missed, flattering me and suggesting I might feel well enough to come back to work. Apparently they had a crisis at the Empire Theatre in Penge, a south London suburb in Bromley. They needed an Eliza Doolittle for *Pygmalion*. Could I reprise the role I had played so successfully before?

It was tempting. On leaving Sheffield I had determined not to go north again. It was nothing to do with the city, because I had made lots of friends and spent many a Sunday exploring Derbyshire's dramatic countryside. But I needed to be in or near London to carry out my plan of going overseas. I desperately needed to see Patrick again, we were married for such a brief time before he was drafted, but to where? As he was an officer in the Intelligence Corps and spoke fluent Arabic it was not difficult to guess. The war in the Western Desert was raging fiercely – Rommel and Montgomery facing each other like two mad dogs across the endless sand. Both were determined to fight to the last man. The cost in lives was enormous.

Of course I went back to work, H.H. making all sorts of promises. He even gave me a smidgen of a raise. I knew most of the actors at the Penge Empire and as they just managed to catch the last train to London after the night's performance I did the same. By day I gathered information on what was going on in the theatre world, and more importantly, news of ENSA – about which I knew absolutely nothing. I either stayed with Irene, my mother's younger sister, who was very dear to me and had a flat in St John's Wood, or a friend from the Sheffield days who had a spare room in her studio flat high up in Chalk Farm. I was lucky. So much of London had been destroyed in the Bliz that accommodation was virtually impossible to find.

*   *   *   *   *

In a small café near the Odeon Cinema in Leicester Square, we actors hunched up over our coffee cups eager for any gossip or theatre news, anything that might lead to finding a job; or in my case a better one. By late morning that cold autumn there was usually a group of actors sitting about, tired and foot-sore from from the daily round of seeing agents, rehearsals, or yet another audition.

I was particularly attentive, eager for information of work overseas.

'I tell you darling, all I know is that Drury Lane is casting for a drama group to go overseas.'

'Is it going to the Middle East?'

'Where else?'

'How do I find out more about this company? Do you think I'm in time?'

'You ring Drury Lane and ask to speak to Henry Oscar. He seems to be organising it.'

I said goodbye and left my share of the money, saying I had to run to make the evening performance. Because of nightly air raids the theatres had taken to opening around five o'clock which left little time. The exciting news I had just heard would have to wait until tomorrow.

At Victoria Station I leapt onto the train as it was moving. I had become quite adept at this and always caught it. The Empire in Penge was a large barn of a theatre, a poor relation of the London

Palladium, and used for variety and musicals. In 1942 it housed Harry Hanson's repertory company and was packed out every night. Every evening all theatres, cinemas, pubs and restaurants were jammed with humanity, but going into central London was difficult and risky. People were desperate for entertainment. A chance to briefly forget the war and the need to be with others was uppermost. Better to be bombed in company than alone at home and, if possible, having a good time.

When I finished my rehearsal the next morning I made for the telephone box next to the stage door. I didn't want my conversation to be overheard. I was nervous. Drury Lane Theatre was closed for the duration of the war. Now it housed ENSA – Entertainments National Service Association. I had only learnt all this over coffee yesterday, everything was so secret then.

I dialled the number of Drury Lane and asked for Henry Oscar, waiting with beating heart and dry throat. He came on the line and I launched into my rehearsed request about the overseas tour, giving my name, what I had done in theatre, what I was currently doing. When I paused he asked me to come to Drury Lane for an interview when was I free. They were casting for the Overseas Repertory Company – to be renamed the India Repertory Company – right now. Could I manage tomorrow?

I presented myself to Henry Oscar, who was sitting looking important in a dressing room in the lovely old theatre. He was an actor of some note, mostly cast as a villain – he had that kind of persona. I took off my coat and sat down. Yes, there was to be a tour, the first of its kind, to see how the troops responded, because previously ENSA had only sent singers, dancers and musical acts overseas. The India Repertory Company was a response to repeated requests from the Far East for entertainment. They felt they had been ignored with all the attention on the Middle East.

I nodded, though I knew little of the war in the Far East.

The company was to perform a repertoire of six plays, the first to be Noel Coward's *Hay Fever*. My faced was wreathed in smiles, I had played the daughter, Sorel, and thought the comedy was a good choice for the Services. He said I would be cast as Sorel, the rest of the plays to be rehearsed en route. I told him I could leave Hanson by the end of the next week when the play I was in finished.

'Fine. You'll start the rehearsal for *Hay Fever* the week after you are free. You will get telephone calls about all of this. Now go and apply for a passport.'

The excitement and awareness of what was happening slowly dawned on me. It seemed unbelievable that it was really coming true.

Suddenly fixing me with his strange eyes Harry Oscar leant across the desk. 'I see you are married.' My heart fell a few storeys, this was where it could all go wrong.

I replied clearly that I was, though I was now nervous and off balance.

'Is your object of joining this tour to see your husband? Can you tell me where he is?'

I said as far as I knew he was in the Middle East but he could be moved at any time.

'I must ask you this,' he pressed on, 'if you should by chance catch up with him would you try and remain with him?'

'Oh, no,' I answered truthfully. 'Of course if we were in the same vicinity and he was able to get leave I'd want to see him. But as always the job would come first. Staying would be out of the question. I'd never break a contract.'

'Do I have your assurance on this?'

'Of course,' I said firmly.

'Good. Please be ready to meet the rest of the company and rehearse *Hay Fever*. Now go and get your passport. This is urgent.'

The interview was over.

I left the room euphoric. I couldn't believe it had been so easy. Outside someone waited to take me to the Passport Office where I spent what was left of the afternoon answering absurd questions about my lack of Japanese or German ancestry. With my thoughts

Me as a fairy, aged 2½. How to grab an audience, wave a wand.

After the early death of their parents in about 1900, my mother and her siblings were placed in an orphanage. Mother and Aunt Irene are in the front row, second and third from the left.

My mother and Aunt Irene rescued from the orphanage by my great-grandmother, and enjoying themselves.

My mother and father as
Anastasia and Uriah Heap, with
theatrical aspirations.

Posed for the hornpipe on point
aged thirteen in one of Pops
shows, and saluting life ahead.

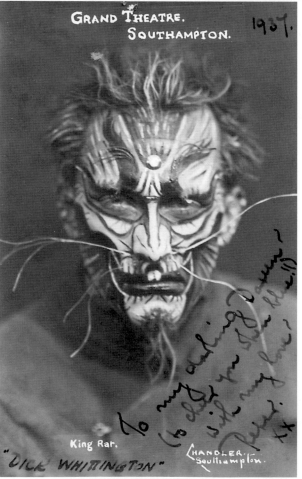

A rare moment with the family: Pops, Mum and my brother Alan on the Isle of Wight, summer 1938.

Peter Cushing in excessively intricate make-up in 1937 as King Rat at the Grand Theatre, Southampton.

Peter on one of our Yorkshire picnics.

Me and Peter. A couple of young actors with burning ambitions.

Jack Hawkins was already a big star when I first saw him in *Autumn* with Flora Robson, at the Manchester matinee. I was riveted to my seat watching him act.

Sheffield blitzed in 1940, but at the Lyceum we continued to perform (*courtesy of Sheffield Newspapers Ltd*).

A Sheffield tram, my usual form of transport, having taken a direct hit (*courtesy of Sheffield Libraries*).

The overworked cast taking a break on the sagging sofa – my final rehearsal in Sheffield 1942.

The India Repertory Company in a dress rehearsal of *Hay Fever* at the Theatre Royal, Drury Lane before our departure. Ros Merrivale and Pamela Roberts can be seen as the escaping guests.

Reunion with Patrick in Cairo, autumn 1943, after 2½ years apart. He was a complete stranger to me. A photograph posed for the families back home.

Celebrating Christmas 1943 on board a troopship bound for Bombay – myself, Joanna Duncan and Pamela Roberts.

far away, I made it out to Penge in time to make up and be ready for the next performance, but with every sense tingling at the prospect of this new adventure ahead.

I wrote to Harry Hanson trying to explain my hasty departure. For one final time I ran up the hill in Penge after the evening performance with the other actors. We were all panting, tearing at the train door, flinging ourselves into the blacked-out carriage. I was never going to do this kind of soul destroying work again, no matter what the future held. This time it was final.

I was escaping into the unknown.

*　*　*　*　*

The first rehearsal and gathering of the cast of the India Repertory Company took place in the Circle Bar of Drury Lane. I can't remember who the director was, but the middle-aged actress named Jean (her surname escapes me), who played Judith the actress, could and would give an adequate performance. With her experience and timing she would get the laughs, which was most important. Charles, another middle-aged experienced actor, was playing the diplomat. He looked the part and knew what he was doing. Coward's great wit comes through in the writing – it plays itself.

A tall willowy actor called Maurice Braddell was cast for Judith's author husband. Maurice had understudied Noel Coward in *Private Lives*, in which he was to play Elyot when we got around to rehearsing it. Why he was exempt from military service no-one ever asked, one didn't ask those kind of questions. All able-bodied men between the ages of nineteen and thirty-eight were liable for service, so there was a terrible dearth of actors. Godfrey, the actor playing Simon, my brother, looked about fifteen though I discovered later that he was older than that. Quite definitely an oddball – not enough to put him away – but he was alright for ENSA.

There was another service reject named Roy who was partially deaf, and a pretty girl called Pamela Roberts, who was younger than me and had very little experience. Oddly, Pamela's lack of training was an asset in playing the daffy girl in the blissfully comic scene with the diplomat – though we were to discover that this was about the extent of her acting ability. More crucially, she had staying power and guts, both essential for the future. Next came Betty Potter, who was cast in the gem of a part, the dresser, now housekeeper, to this strangely dysfuntional theatrical family and who I watched with interest. She was certainly verging on dippy, but had plenty of humour and wit.

A tall dark actress was playing Myra, and I instantly found in her a kindred spirit. She was the daughter of Philip Merivale, a well-known actor who after the death of his wife had married Gladys Cooper, a famous beauty and a name from my childhood. From that rehearsal onwards Rosamund Merivale and I embarked on a life-long friendship. After the first rehearsal finished Roz suggested we have tea together and guided me to a little patisserie she knew in nearby Soho where we indulged ourselves in tea and cakes and exchanged a few confidences. At twenty-eight, she was several years older than me, more travelled and sophisticated and knew more interesting people. She had played a season at Stratford-upon-Avon. The age difference was unimportant, for years I had been with older people but at last I was no longer the baby of the cast, Pamela Roberts had that honour and she was welcome. We mutually agreed, having met the cast with whom we were to share this journey into the unknown, that we would need to stick together.

The uncomfortable first vaccination was soon over, leaving a sore arm which when knocked accidentally caused real pain. No warning arm-band was allowed: it might give away (to whom?) the possible journey ahead. We were bound by secrecy. 'Careless talk costs lives'. Not a word of any destination was to be given. As we knew so little ourselves it was easy to obey orders. More jabs were given against the many hidden diseases lurking in the tropics.

My greatest excitement was shopping for clothes! I had been too long with Harry Hanson and didn't realise that 'all wardrobe provided' meant *new* clothes. Drury Lane provided the necessary clothing coupons and one of the girls from the wardrobe department took me shopping. I was free to buy what I wanted, including an evening dress. Everything had to be suitable for the tropics, cottons were high on the list, silk being unwearable and prone to rot. Then we were measured for leather mosquito boots and fitted with a Bombay Bowler, an outdated pith helmet.

The excitement increased when we were given leave to say our farewells – not easy with the Official Secrecy Act, of which we were given constant reminders. Christmas 1942 was close. Would we be here or not? Aunt Irene had saved her coupons for months intending to blow the lot on a tin of turkey. She hoped to get a day's leave from the BBC in Portland Square, where she toiled away throughout the war and she hoped I would be there on Boxing Day to share the tin. All my heavy baggage had gone to Drury Lane to travel separately. To where? The call would come by telephone.

The day after Christmas I had the order to be at Drury Lane at ten in the morning. A group of us hung around the foyer clutching our hand luggage. The mood was one of anticipation. Finally we were put on a bus and driven to Kings Cross, where an official from Drury Lane announced we were to embark on a train to Pickering in North Yorkshire. There was an audible gasp from the India Repertory Company, then silence. Someone had the temerity to ask 'Why Pickering?' 'No idea. Obeying instructions.'

Rosamund and I sat facing each other in the train going north wondering what in heavens was going on. Deep snow and temperatures below zero were not what we were expecting – or dressed for. On arrival we were split up for billeting, though Roz and I remained together. Both here, and eventually abroad, we were classed as officers, an unexpected promotion, but one that proved to be a very necessary perk.

This particular day, as it was growing dark and snowing, we were thrust into the unwelcoming house of a lady who was as surprised and unhappy as we were. She pushed open a door, shoving us and our belongings into a freezing bedroom with no heating of any kind, and with a double bed. Rosamund opened her mouth to protest – the rule was you always had a bed to yourself – but decided to remain silent. The room temperature was well below freezing, perhaps body warmth was our only hope of making it through the night. The lavatory was along the corridor and there was no bath, but we were brought a can of hot water every morning for a strip wash, not endured since schooldays. In all the strange happenings of the future, I only had to remind myself of the unpleasant shock of Pickering, our initiation into the odd quirks of ENSA.

Why we were here became quickly obvious. Almost immediately we were entertaining the troops under canvas in Pickering awaiting orders. The nightly shows were our contribution to the war effort and the reason for us joining ENSA. Nigel Patrick, a peacetime actor who Rosamund knew, was the head of entertainments trying to keep the troops occupied during the evenings. Not easy. *Hay Fever* helped him for a week, and the audiences hugely enjoyed the comedy, which was gratifying for us. The all male audience was noisy and verbal, letting off steam with wolf whistles and catcalls. It was slightly reminiscent of pantomime and a theatre full of children. We didn't mind, it was to become part of our way of life and proved our efforts were appreciated. It was to be a long time before I played before a civilian audience again and then it seemed oddly quiet and disconcerting.

These Army and Air Force camps were all over England. Much training was necessary as the professional army had been badly thinned out at Dunkirk, a terrible loss, with many remaining Prisoners of War for the length of the war. But as Hitler had invaded Russia and the threat of invasion had receded, we began to breathe a little easier. Factories were working flat out making the vital weapons and equipment we had lacked at the declaration of war. No-one knew what was really around the corner. All these huge encampments of men ready to fight, but where? We were to perform at quite a few in the next three months. We ceased to ask what was happening and just got on with the job.

After Pickering we went to Kings Lynn and the many East Anglian airfields. A manager arrived from Drury Lane who had been invalided out of the Air Force and was furious about it; he had been a pilot flying Hurricanes. With him was a fellow called Ron, with a false leg, who was only twenty and became very dear to us. No-one asked how he had lost his leg. We were so frightened about idle chat that curiosity about each other was virtually non-existent. Ron became our stage manager and proved to be a great asset, happily striking scenery and moving furniture, despite his artificial leg.

Our next move was to Canterbury and the airfields of Kent, the front-line through the Battle of Britain. Many Australians were now based there, and *Hay Fever* cheered them and us. It was good to provide a few hours of relaxation and laughter to men so far from home. After that it was to Wiltshire, where suddenly it was spring and warmer. We were billeted in a hostel that had been a splendid country house commandeered for the war, but was now rather neglected. We slept in camps beds, six to a room, setting off in a bus every evening to perform at whichever camp was on the list. Coming back we all sang, it was the only way to pass the time on what were often long journeys. One night, just after we set off, the bus came to a screeching halt near the gates of the house; the reason appeared to be a young girl with pretty golden hair and a lovely face dressed from head to toe in bright green including bag and shoes. Rosamund nudged me. 'She didn't buy that outfit in England.'

She climbed aboard and our manager announced in a full voice. 'This is Joanna Duncan who has just arrived from America. She is to join us on the tour and will be the general understudy.' The poor girl sat in silence while we all sized her up. Finally someone said something and we all joined in with words of welcome.

Just as we began to enjoy the warm sunshine and the untended garden, we had a call from Drury Lane. We were to go on leave for three days. There was a buzz of excitement – were we preparing for the off? Would it really happen this time?

A blacked out bus took us from Drury Lane at one o'clock in the morning. All very secret. We were deposited with our hand baggage onto a darkened station. We were not told which London station or where we were bound, but looking around most of us noticed it was that great monument to Victoriana, Saint Pancras, so we must be going north to Liverpool. We were high on excitement, after several false starts the great adventure was beginning.

We piled on to the train and were given seats with a group of young officers, sharing sandwiches and drinks with them. Hardly bothering to sleep we sang for most of the journey. It was the usual stop – start – wait – wartime train. At dawn we were shunted into a siding and eventually unloaded to climb the gangway onto a large liner painted in wartime camouflage grey. At the top of the gangway stood a young naval officer who clasped me to him, giving me a smacking kiss. Surprised, I took a closer look.

'Doreen,' he said, 'It's your father's assistant to his magic tricks.'

I laughed, recognizing him. 'John! You've grown since then.' As a schoolboy, John had been my father's assistant when he performed as a magician at children's parties. Pop was a man of many talents, alas making money was not one of them.

Pamela Roberts and I were pushed into a tiny cabin with two bunks. I made for the top as she preferred the lower. We had brought only light luggage. Unpacking, I opened a drawer in the only chest and small creatures ran out. I let out a startled yell. A steward appeared saying he would be looking after us and not to let a few cockroaches alarm us – they were all over the ship, its permanent residents. He became an asset in our new surroundings, providing information that we would not have got from anyone else, the name of our ship *Athlone Castle* for a start.

We spent several days off the port of Liverpool, waiting, we supposed, for the rest of the convoy. With Liverpool's recent history of bombing everyone was nervously scanning the skies. Now the Secrecy Act made some sort of sense. The time was filled by lengthy lectures from senior officers on the tropics and their nasty bugs and the many rules that would apply throughout the voyage. These were mostly delivered in the main dining room, but there was also a convivial little bar, which provided one of the few other places on board for meeting and making friends, and to enjoy a laugh. Almost all the public rooms of the ship had been converted into sleeping accommodation for the hundreds of serviceman who had boarded – the same with all troop ships I was to discover. Officers (which included us) were also allotted a portion of the deck, about half the size of a tennis court, for walking.

After four days of waiting and wondering I awoke in the night to the tremor of the ship's engines, which became a rhythm to accompany us for several weeks. My delight at knowing at last I was on my way – nothing to stop me now – was immense. I fell back into a peaceful sleep to the gentle rocking of the ship.

I awoke to a beautiful April day. We were gaining speed to keep up with the convoy. The decks were crowded as we were passing the last sight of our homeland, the Western Isles of Scotland, an emotive sight for all. The sound of male voices was first heard from the lower decks, singing 'The Skye Boat Song', soon to be taken up by other decks, and then the entire ship was singing lustily as we sped on into the unknown.

PART II

AFRICA

FIVE

The India Repertory Company, April 1943

Over the next weeks, as we zigzagged across the North Atlantic as far as Greenland (we later learned) before turning down to the Azores, we dutifully assembled for the daily ritual of Lifeboat Drill. Our convoy was sent out in April 1943, only a month after U boats sank 120 Merchant Navy ships in the North Sea. We were instructed never to be without our life-belts, 'Mae Wests' as they were nicknamed, in tribute to the busty blonde comedienne with her risque one-liners. To be caught without your life-belt could mean being 'put on a charge', so as a constant companion over five voyages with ENSA, I became attached to my Mae West and its many uses: pillow, cushion for the back and to sit upon – thank heaven, I never had to put its real use to the test. There were U-Boat alarms yet I don't remember ever being afraid. Being on deck, watching the giant whales diving alongside then rising and blowing jets of sea water, was a wonderful sight. It would be a mistake to think about what might be following us lurking below.

The rest of the days we kept ourselves occupied by, among other things, walking on our allotted deck-space – and that meant serious walking, in lines, with some wag totting up our mileage.

Once we were under way, our manager Maurice Braddell approached the CO. about performances. To sort out our costumes, we had to go down to the lower decks of the *Athlone Castle*. Seeing what the men had to endure was a sight I cannot ever erase. They were massed together like cattle, bunk upon bunk, some in swinging hammocks, and sitting wherever there was a space. An officer went in front of us to make sure there were no naked bodies and to warn the men ladies were approaching. There were just silent stares, no wolf whistles here, but only unspoken misery. Finally on the lowest deck of all we had to make our way across massed bodies to our trunks of costumes. We were below the waterline. The heat was tremendous and there was no air. Many men had been sick and the stench was appalling. Once a day they were assembled on deck for P.T. and drill, which must have come as a relief, but there were so many of them it had to be one section at a time. I suppose this was the same with eating. I felt so impotent amidst such suffering. The officer escorting us agreed that the conditions were 'not ideal', but what could be done about it. The officers' quarters were also cramped, with six to a tiny cabin. Many years later, a close friend who had been a young volunteer airman going out to Africa on board a troopship, told me that there were so many servicemen on board that they had to take it in turns to sleep.

Having recovered our costumes, we gave many performances over the following weeks of *Hay Fever*, and began rehearsals for our repertoire of other plays. We were there to entertain and that's what we did.

When our troopship finally sighted land, we lined up on the decks watching this strange, steaming continent emerge on the horizon. As we drew nearer hills appeared, covered in thick foliage. That morning I had a word with our steward, always a mine of information – 'Athlone Castle,' he told me, 'she always does the African run – even in peace time.' We had only been able to guess where we were but now we knew it had to be Africa. I asked our friendly steward which port we were slowly making our way towards.

'Freetown, Sierra Leone, a bastard of a place – never go ashore' was the answer. The next piece of information came from the CO. over the tannoy, who told us to pack our bags ready for disembarkation. Of course we had no choice – presumably we were to be off-loaded, but why? As far as we knew this convoy was bound for the Far East and India.

The ships remained off shore and dropped anchor. Canoes came alongside, paddled by natives pleading for us to throw pennies overboard which they then dived for and retrieved in the most incredible feat of underwater swimming. Our divers were limited to a few words of English taught them by British troops – it was very fruity indeed. For once we did not lack amusement or entertainment, it was the best fun we had had since the Liverpool boat train.

A steel staircase was assembled and hung over the side of the ship. When, from the top, you viewed the small boat waiting below it looked a very long way down – rather similar to the view from a block of high flats. Sailors carried our hand luggage down, which was just as well. After we'd all managed the climb and jumped into the boat, the crew took us ashore and left us, rather ominously wishing us luck.

A perspiring, red-faced officer came to meet us, who looked fed up and not at all welcoming. 'What are you doing here?' he demanded brusquely.

We didn't know and were not at all happy with our reception.

Maurice, our manager, asked 'Where is the Entertainments Officer? What is happening to all our things, theatre props, clothes and scenery?' There was no answer.

It was humid and unbelievably hot. Coming from a frozen England our blood had not yet had a chance to thin down, although it soon would. We were wearing our pith helmets, and soon learnt they had not been worn since World War I except, I suspected, in films. Whatever their purpose it was not to keep you cool, we were all dripping with sweat. Also, either from my theatre tuition or from watching films, I had assumed a white linen suit would be the very outfit for the tropics. Big mistake.

The officer realised he had to do something with us, if only to dump us on someone else. We were taken to what was laughingly known as the officer's mess, a bamboo and straw constructed bungalow with a veranda, where we were thankfully seated in the shade and given a cold drink. Finally we were left in the care of the few officers, who kindly provided us with a truly forgettable lunch. This was very much an outpost of the Empire.

Finally the officer reappeared looking a little more cheerful. He had arranged various billets for us for one night and tomorrow we would be transported to Takoradi. Where was that? No one had any idea.

Rosamund and I were driven away in the staff car and told we were to spend the night with the British consul and his wife.

The consul's large, white house was built on stilts and covered with bougainvillaea. We climbed the steps up to the entrance, where we were welcomed by the butler and shown into the living room. I have never forgotten it. The house was on a hillside and from the wide open windows we overlooked trees and bush falling away to the dazzling sea and surf we had just left. We could see our ship and the convoy still at anchor. There was a heavenly breeze blowing gently through the room and we felt blissfully cool for the first time. We were taken to our bedroom by the consul's wife, who apologised for us having to share a room – little did she know. When alone we hugged each other with delight, a day that had begun so disastrously was going to finish in a totally unexpected and exciting way. I couldn't wait to drag off that linen suit and fling myself on the bed. Then the bath – I felt positively beatific as I lay in it soaking up the warm water. On the ship there were only salt-water baths and we had to take our turn over those.

Rosamund and I took our time about dressing for dinner, both wishing we had more than the one silk dress we had with us. Uncertain where to present ourselves we decided to make for the veranda, it was so delightfully cool and with that incredible view. The lush colours of the tropical trees descended towards the huge surf and sparkling sea. After factory chimneys, blackouts and total gloom, this was a fairy-tale coming true. A servant arrived as soon as we were seated carrying ice and drinks. What would we like? I looked at Rosamund, hoping for a lead. She was socially more adept and more sophisticated and worldly than I was. Most of my teenage and adult life had been spent in the theatre with actors as my constant companions, but now I was beginning to realise that there was a whole other world out there full of people who knew nothing of acting and the stage.

Rosamund asked for Scotch with water and ice. I did the same. It was delicious. Like everything else alcohol was scarce in England. On a tray there were nuts and other goodies, and though we tried not to eat too many we were famished, having eaten nothing all day. Time passed. The servant reappeared and refilled our glasses. There was silence in the house, we were obviously far too early and began to feel uncomfortable. Then up the stairs bounded two young naval officers who were also given drinks. We introduced ourselves, then the consul and his wife appeared. After chatter and more drinks, dinner was served, and not a moment too soon. It was the first decent meal I had had in years, the highlight of which was fresh fruit, not readily available in Britain after 1939. It was a delightful evening, there would not be many like it for a long while.

Finally we were told about the mosquito boots issued in London as part of our tropical equipment. Knee length and of soft leather, we were advised to wear them every night as malarial mosquitoes were a great danger in West Africa, and were especially active after sundown. We eventually said goodnight. We were exhausted and more than happy to tuck ourselves up under the mosquito nets. Over the following years I became so used to their protection that I was uneasy without one.

We were awakened by a soft-footed servant with early morning tea – the English carried their habits to many far-flung places. Sunlight filled the room. We jumped out of bed to look at the sea and noticed the convoy had slipped away quietly in the night. I dug out my shorts and cotton shirt bought from the ship-board shop that sold khaki cotton men's clothes. I'd bought the smallest sized shirt and trousers they stocked. Joanna Duncan and Rosamund did the same, and we cut the trousers short, creating cool but practical outfits.

That morning, when we climbed into the back of a lorry bound for Takoradi, we found only hard benches without any padding. Little did I know how many times in the future I would have to climb in and out of lorries. It was just as well we didn't realise what was ahead of us. Takoradi was a day's drive away along a rugged and primitive road. The heat and humidity were frightful. As we bounced along we were flung from side to side, so it was easier to sit on the floor surrounded by props and scenery and tin trunks filled with our costumes. We used rugs or anything we could find to protect our poor bottoms. The NAAFI had provided sandwiches and bottled drinks, which we sipped sparingly. Then I spied a wonderful sight. We were driving parallel to the sea and there were these beautiful coconut trees dipping onto the white sand with the sea and surf beyond. We hammered on the partition for the driver to stop. The ghastly jolting ceased. Climbing out, followed by the others, I ran headlong into the sea, wading in and letting the surf crash all over me.

Finally, much later and too dishevelled and exhausted to care, we were driven into a RAF station. We had a warm, if surprised, greeting. It seemed we were to be billeted with them in Takoradi. We women were given a bungalow consisting of a bedroom with six cots and mosquito nets, and a bathroom with a primitive lavatory, which was to become a normal part of our lives in the future. None of us had every encountered a thunder-box before. It consisted of a wooden seat with an appropriate hole in the centre and a bucket underneath. At the side was another bucket with a shovel and sand to pitch down the hole, hoping for a straight aim. There was no loo paper, only odd bits of old African newspapers, and so one of our main purchases whenever we were in civilisation was paper, which we carried around in our knapsacks everywhere.

The officer in charge apologised for the rather hurried arrangements, but he had no idea we were arriving etc. etc. However we were welcomed and the RAF were smiling happily to see us. They gave us drinks and food and we smiled in return in spite of our sore bottoms and aching backs.

*   *   *   *   *

It was the time spent in Takoradi which at last made us feel needed.

A makeshift theatre was rigged up with a stage and somewhere to dress and make-up, half for the men, the other half for the women. The audience sat in the open which, apart from the mosquitoes, was better and cooler.

As I recall 'Tak', as we all came to call it, was a small African port. As we were with airmen we could only assume they were involved in transport and there must be an airstrip somewhere. There was a large contingent from the South African Air Force.

Our first production, Noel Coward's *Hay Fever,* was enormously well received and revived our appetite for work. There had been no entertainment on the station apart from the odd film, so we did repeat performances until everyone had seen the show. In the meantime we brushed up another play from our repertoire. When we asked the commanding officer how long we would be staying he just laughed and said he had no idea, indeed had not expected us in the first place. There was no point in trying to find out where our next journey would take us, or even why we were there at all. As we were called the India Repertory Company, why were we in Africa? We had obviously been destined for India, possibly via the Middle East, which was what they had told us at Drury Lane, but as we had long ago discovered, their information was always inaccurate. One piece of news was so good no one kept it secret. The Americans had made a successful landing in North Africa and along with the Allied Forces were forging ahead through the desert. For the first time it seemed Rommel was on the defensive.

Africa was definitely getting to me. After the extreme cold and discomforts of England, the minor misfortunes here were nothing. I love heat. I would rather be dripping than shivering and I loved the people of West Africa, they were so beautiful and graceful. I adored it as night fell suddenly and the fires were lit. I know they were made of cow dung and heaven knows what else, but I loved the scent of smoke in the air and the smells of the African cookpot. I loved the sounds of the night chorus, every insect and animal joining in, with the croak of the enormous bullfrogs drowning all. Everything, everybody was larger there. Above us the myriad of stars made a great deep blue canopy over all.

I was stimulated and deeply content at the same time.

I'm not sure how long we were in 'Tak', but I do remember that the night before *Private Lives* was due to open Rosamund was taken seriously ill during the dress rehearsal and carried off to the camp hospital. There was no way she could work and I was understudying her part of Amanda, the leading role and one of the longest written by Coward.

Maurice, our manager, asked me how quickly I could learn and rehearse it. What a question! I had of course watched the performances, so was familiar with most of the moves. Everyone offered to help, but I knew from my repertory days it had to be pure slog on my own. My memory has always been good through learning so many lines over the years – almost photographic. So I set to work, sat up, lay on my bed, walked about and didn't sleep all night. Godfrey, the male juvenile, nobly brought me coffee and offered to hear my lines, but I waited until morning before calling for help. We worked for several hours. I slept briefly, then learnt the final act, which was the easiest. We had a rehearsal, mainly of the fight scene, which would be impossible to do without making the moves co-ordinate with the words.

I played that night, and to my amazement sailed through without a mistake. The reception was tumultuous, both from the audience and from my fellow actors. I should have been near collapse but was on such a high that I thoroughly enjoyed the party they laid on for me afterwards. When I finally reached my bed I slept for about fifteen hours.

On the fifth night of *Private Lives* we were told to pack up and be ready for embarkation the following day. It was a tremendous rush. Luckily Roz was better – anyway, she had no intention of being left behind no matter how ill she might feel.

SIX

Accra, Lagos & South Africa, 1943

The little boat slowly made its way towards the grey convoy of ships in the shimmering sea, though we were not sure which one we were boarding. As usual the names were obliterated. Finally we drew alongside a great brooding-looking monster. The decks were lined with men curiously watching the arrival of this strange group of civilians. The lower deck predictably welcomed us with a surprised and rather weary sounding wolf whistle, but the upper decks gazed down in silence. It was a long climb up the wood and rope ladder. After being welcomed aboard we were shown our cabins – one for the men and one for the women. It was hotter than Hades and the portholes were about to be closed and clamped for the night: the blackout. There were six in our cabin, and Jean, our leading lady in *Hay Fever*, was as usual snoring! Oh well. We each grabbed a bunk and stowed our possessions and life belts. I was at the top where I like to be.

Rosamund, Joanna and I decided to make for the bar. It was packed with men and filled with cigarette smoke. Cigarettes were either duty free or supplied by the NAAFI, so cost next to nothing, and at that time everyone smoked. Drinks were also cheap, although it wasn't long before American influence forced all troopships to become dry.

There was a sudden hush when we walked in, but before we had time for embarrassment there was a rush towards us. What would we like to drink, where had we come from, why were we on board and where were we going? A dozen questions. Then it was our turn. Where was the convoy heading? Drinks in hand we all exchanged news and information. The men had been issued with Bush hats, they were definitely Far East bound. Perhaps we were to go with them, after all, we *were* the India Repertory Company – if so it was certainly a long journey ahead.

The dining room was small and with the portholes clamped shut the heat was unbearable. Sweat dripped down on to our plates, but as the food was inedible we made for cool of the deck as quickly as possible. That night as we lay sweating in our bunks we felt the familiar tremor of the ship's engines. The gentle rocking and swaying, the blessed breath of air through the open door meant we were on the move again. I went to sleep through sheer exhaustion.

Our manager, Maurice, approached the C.O. about entertainment. Would he like us put on some performances during the voyage, as we had on the previous ship? It was decided that although it would be a welcome diversion it was not worth our while to go down into the hold to unpack our costumes and scenery until we knew how long we were going to be on board. We would know this when we reached the next port, although no mention was made as to where, or which port. I have to admit we were all relieved: doing a show below decks in such heat wouldn't have been enjoyable for either players or audience.

I have forgotten how long we were at sea – ten days maybe, perhaps longer. We had constant U-Boat alarms. Supposedly we were steaming south with – so it was rumoured – a U-Boat following us. One of the officers with whom I had become friendly, Owen Feldman, was a champion swimmer with the cups to prove it and said that if we were torpedoed I was to stick with him. He gestured to the life rafts tethered to the deck. 'Those rafts will be the safest to make for, it will be impossible to launch the lifeboats in time.'

Finally the ship's engines slowed down and we saw land and a port of some size. The ship was waiting its turn to dock and everyone was on deck speculating as to where we were. No jolly fellows diving for pennies here, just gentle rocking, silent waiting.

Rumours abounded but as usual my best information came from our steward. 'Accra,' he said, 'main port of the Gold Coast.'

The port had a safety barrier around it to prevent U-boats entering. The barrier was only opened when it was safe to allow the convoy in, and then quickly closed to make certain a U-boat didn't slip in as well. During the night the throbbing started as the engines gathered speed and we hurried into the sanctuary of the port.

As usual the company were the first to disembark and I said goodbye to Owen Feldman – the next time I was to see him was in hospital in Secunderabad.

We were met by two officers. This time the Army had provided cars for us instead of the usual three-ton lorries. We were billeted on the American compound, which had more suitable accommodation, and were allocated a bungalow on stilts, to keep out scorpions, lizards and the possible snake. It had two bedrooms and a living room with a good sized fan which helped to keep the many flying insects at bay. We were able to persuade Jean (the snorer) that she was entitled to her privacy in one of the bedrooms, while Roz, Betty, Jo and I crammed into the other bedroom and Pamela opted for a lone cot in the living room. We had oil lamps, a shower and the usual thunder box.

Accra was quite a town with a bustling port and was undoubtedly the closest we had come to civilization since arriving in West Africa: now of course it is the capital of Ghana.

We were to perform in its town hall, which had a large stage, two good sized dressing rooms and most importantly, electricity, which meant lights in the dressing rooms, footlights on stage and lights in the auditorium.

It was to the town hall's grounds that we were invited to the mayor's party on our first evening. We wore the long cotton dresses run up for us in Takoradi, whilst the African women were resplendent in their colourful national dress topped by sensational headgear. When we arrived the band was playing all sorts of jolly tunes, mostly from old musicals. They looked magnificent in their scarlet jackets with gold trimmings and a fez hat – the dress uniform of a West African Regiment, obviously worn with pride. Suddenly they struck up *High Life* and all the Africans rushed onto the wooden dance floor. It was their dance, the beat so exciting it set the pulses racing. We were urged to join in, the men in their white tuxedos not listening to our protests of our inability to follow their rhythmic gyrations. Our English inhibitions were soon forgotten. I happened to glance at Pamela, normally so prissy and now dancing with the most abandon.

After that night we joined the *High Life* whenever it was danced. It must have been the origin of the funky music played today in clubs and parties, anywhere where the young gather to dance and let themselves go. I am thankful that I have not missed out, and was able to enjoy that throbbing beat when I was young in West Africa.

* * * * *

We remained in Accra for about three months and began rehearsals of another play. We were now doing a repertoire of three, putting on one or the other almost every night and performing to packed and enthusiastic audiences of troops from nearby camps. There were many Americans stationed in Accra, also a contingent of civilian Americans involved in the oil industry – important for the war effort.

Time passed quickly. We found ourselves coming to the rainy season at the end of July with the humidity increasing uncomfortably. For once we were told in advance where our next posting was to be, Lagos in Nigeria.

We had real luck with our transport to Lagos. The American Air Force had an airstrip at Accra and a transport plane available. What a joy! Not the hot crowded stuffy cabins and the crammed decks, but just a few hours flight down the African coast. It was my first flight and I was thrilled as we flew low, clinging to the coast, it was a wondrous sight.

85

We landed bumpily on a makeshift airstrip, more like a field, where we found lorries waiting, plus a British officer who told us we were to stay at the Grand Hotel, which I'm afraid did not live up to its name. We women were housed on the top floor with four in one room, and Jean and Betty in the other. We had a bathroom with a spasmodic water supply and a twin-seated thunder box for the whole top floor. When I removed the lid from one of the seats, I stared down five floors to the ground below. An awfully long drop. We unpacked and tried to find sufficient space in the meagre cupboards, which didn't look particularly clean and smelt musty. I decided to go downstairs to investigate. I found a desk, an ancient telephone on the wall and a room that could be the dining room. I wondered how long we would be here.

I fished into my handbag for a telephone number given to me in Accra by one of our American Oil friends. On impulse I dialled the number, amazed the instrument worked. It was answered almost immediately. Within fifteen minutes I was collected by car sent by George, one of the Accra fellows who had been transferred to Lagos. Soon I was lying luxuriously in a hot bath, followed by drinks with the other occupants of their comfortable mess. Theirs was a reserved occupation which gave them a better life-style to that of the armed forces, but they had their own problems to cope with. Extreme boredom – loneliness without their wives – always in some far away place. But their generosity to us in Lagos cannot be forgotten. They made it bearable with their bathrooms and four flushing lavatories!

At first sight Lagos seemed larger than Accra, the people not so tall. We had been on the Gold Coast since late May and we were now well into July. Here in Nigeria the rainy season had started, so the humidity was high and the bugs multiplied. My legs were covered with bites, mostly mosquito. No one felt particularly well and some of the actors were so ill they couldn't work. The plays were performed nightly and we changed them frequently, but suddenly so many of us were sick we couldn't muster a full cast for any of our three plays.

We were supposed to go inland into the bush but we had to cancel. The tropics were getting to us and we couldn't carry on without some changes. We were contemplating what to do next when we were told to pack and be ready to leave in two days. We knew it would be our last time in West Africa – our next destination was to be South Africa.

The day we left it poured with rain, real tropical rain, which cleared away some of the unbearable humidity. Once on board ship we were shown to our cabins on what would have been the promenade deck in peacetime, and which thankfully had portholes that opened. Somehow we seemed to have mislaid Betty Potter! Had she requested to be returned to England or advised to go? She was not seen by any of us for over a week and, when we asked, we were told she was in hospital.

The ship seemed empty, but then there was a great noise of tramping feet and gear being brought on board. According to Jo, who went on deck and was soon moved out of the way, there were white Army officers leading companies of African troops on to the ship. The last to come on board was a medical team with a young man on a stretcher. It was a distressing sight. I had never seen anyone look so dreadfully ill, his tropical tan was grey-green and he was skeletal under the thin blanket. I heard from his fellow officers that he had Black Water fever. The very worst. It is malaria in extremis, from which few recover. He was taken straight to the sickbay, but we never heard of his eventual fate.

I suppose we must have found the dining room, although I had little appetite. I just recall exhaustion, lying on the bunk and being unable to sleep. We were all very wan and apathetic and although the weather was squally and rough, it was good for me and I think the others improved in health too. The change from the dreadful humidity plus the lack of bugs made up for the cramped conditions. Jo and I loved being on deck when it was rough, going forward as far as we were allowed to watch the spray breaking over the bows. The ship was full of African troops. During the day they were brought up on deck for drill, mainly I think to give them fresh air.

Most had come from bush tribes and had never been further than their villages. Being squashed below deck in rough seas must have been awful for them.

One morning we went on deck to a calm sea and a sky of heavenly blue. The air was clear and fresh and there was no rain. It was the most brilliant and beautiful morning. Suddenly I was amazed to see a large ice floe drift by with, astonishingly, penguins standing on it – then more penguins. Someone remarked that although a great distance away, the South Pole was opposite South Africa. It was all so new and exciting. Then suddenly through the mist and sunlight land was in sight and we glimpsed Table Mountain. We were slowly gliding into Cape Town. It was magic – it couldn't be happening to me.

I can't remember whether we went into the harbour or laid off for supplies. I know we were not allowed ashore but had to set sail again, making for Durban. As we waited for orders in Durban harbour, we saw twinkling lights, making the whole place looked like a fairyland. It was the first time we had seen lights since before the war. There was no blackout here, no U-boats, no bombs. No war! Shore leave was uppermost in our minds.

The film of *Casablanca* was showing. We all applied for leave to see it. Unbelievably it was granted. To be on land again – even though every now and then the ground beneath us seemed to sway – to eat in a proper restaurant, then see such a terrific movie was more than a treat. It was an Event.

We were delighted to be told that we were to stay in Durban and on leave for a while. Our manager had received the instructions from the Army or our headquarters: probably the Army, as in all honesty I don't think the ENSA office in Drury Lane had any idea where we were. It was lovely to be on dry land, and in South Africa. We four girls were in one room in a pleasant small hotel in walking distance of anywhere we wanted to be.

There was only one problem – no money. Here we were surrounded by shops brimming with all the things we had been missing for years. Shoes, nylon and silk stockings, dresses and cosmetics, including lipstick and nail polish. Our accommodation was paid for, but nothing else. We were taken out to dinners and night clubs so we lacked for nothing in our social life, but our savings were small and certainly not enough to go on a shopping spree. We all had money in bank accounts at home. Mine was Barclays and I had a lengthy, pleading conversation with the manager of the Durban branch. It was to little avail, the bank had no contact with England and all foreign exchange had ceased. However, I came away with five pounds, and I think that was given out of kindness. It certainly never appeared on any later statements. Five pounds was worth a great deal more in 1943.

Winter was coming to Durban and the temperate climate was doing wonders for our health. We lost our weariness and regained our energy. The South African's generosity was incredible, I have seldom met such hospitality. Although the country was stunningly beautiful, I was not alone in being upset by apartheid and the unpleasant realities of segregation. Separate buses, lifts, beaches for white and black. We hadn't come across anything like it in West Africa. I began to speak of it to one of our new South African friends and was abruptly told that I didn't live there so should not talk about situations I knew nothing of – in other words 'shut up'.

The thing, however, that was really spoiling my enjoyment was toothache. My final wisdom tooth was trying to come through which was becoming increasingly agonising and I was beginning to resemble a bad case of mumps on one side. After having dinner one night with some friends of Pamela Roberts who watched me in such obvious pain, they insisted I visit their dentist the next day and kindly made an appointment for me. The tooth was very badly impacted and the dentist said I would have to have an operation under anaesthetic. No wonder it was such agony. Realising that I was on constant stand-by for departure he arranged to perform the surgery the next day and Pam came with me. I was put on the operating table and bliss came with unconsciousness. The news, when I came round, was that it had been a really difficult extraction and he had been forced to cut and stitch the gum. He was concerned that it could become infected (this was before antibiotics), so I must take care to rinse with the special prescription he provided and follow-up care would be needed. The next day I could not open my mouth to eat, or even drink until someone found me a straw. I consoled myself that at least the operation was behind me. As it happened, we were instructed to pack and be ready to board ship the following day so there was no time for even visiting the dentist again and further treatment had to be abandoned. As I could hardly speak, I could only write a note of thanks. I hope our manager did something about the account for the operation though I doubt it. So in this uncomfortable condition I left South Africa. We were not informed where we were going to next.

Our accommodation this time was even more cramped, with all five women sharing one cabin. Shortly before sailing another woman appeared, in civvies, and was billeted with us. She didn't look at all happy about this – anymore than we were. It is difficult befriending a complete stranger when you are a group of actors used to being with one another and enduring shared discomforts. We felt sorry for her as an outsider and did our best to welcome her. I cannot remember, and am sure she didn't tell us, what her particular mission was. A high-ranking officer's wife, or Queen Bee of one of the women's forces in mufti? Anyway she regarded us with some disdain. ENSA – odd sort of strange folk, jugglers, dancers, actors – certainly not part of her world.

We went all went up on deck to bid farewell to South Africa. We were slowly slipping out of Durban Harbour when a woman in white, holding a megaphone so all could hear and standing at the end of the harbour wall, began singing her heart out as we glided by, ship after ship. The soldiers were leaning over the side cheering her and waving goodbye. The ships must have listed to port with all the men determined to see her – the final goodbye from their homeland. The South African officer squashed next to me told me she was known as 'the lady in white' and sang for every convoy that passed through Durban. Later I learned that she did so throughout the entire war until VJ day in August 1945. No one who was on one of those convoys will ever forget her. There were tears on our faces as her singing grew slowly feinter. We gathered speed into the Indian Ocean.

The ship and her officers were Dutch, who had made a run for it when the Nazi's invaded their country and were using their freedom to ferry troops to where they were needed. Almost the entire ship was filled with South African officers and men returning to active service after leave in their homeland, a reward for the way they had fought in the battle of El Alamein; that heroic victory in the Western Desert and one of the turning points of the war. They were returning to Egypt for what? Invasion of Italy seemed most likely, and seasoned troops were needed, so it was back to Cairo for them and re-posting. For us – the forgotten, depleted, worn out India Repertory Company – heaven knows!

South African beer and Bols gin seemed to be the only tipple on board. I have never liked gin and Bols seemed to be an acquired taste, but with fruit juice it helped with the more or less constant ache from the tooth extraction. The medical officer confirmed what I most feared. Infection had set in. It was made even more difficult because I could not open my mouth properly for inspection, and there was no dental officer on board. With no antibiotics the only help was for one of his orderlies to syringe my mouth with carbolic. I would agree to anything for relief.

Everyone left the cabin, unable to watch. A bucket full of carbolic was attached to a rubber tube and nozzle which was forced into my mouth so it could reach the back of my jaw. That was purgatory. Then the poor lad had to pump the liquid through into the infected spot – a towel I draped round me was soaking when he had finished. He would pack up his props and depart as quickly as he could, not daring to even glance at the writhing suffering body he left behind. This was repeated daily until I could stand it no more. It did, however, have the desired effect on the infection. I could eat a little and the swelling slowly reduced. After those sessions I learnt to appreciate Bols gin, but anything would have been welcome.

We rarely caught a glimpse of our fellow occupant. She spoke to us only when necessary and otherwise disappeared, mostly to join the senior officers whose table she sat at in the dining room. One morning we were confronted with what was virtually an accusation. Her pearls were missing, had we seen them? No one had. I don't think we had ever even noticed her wearing them. We had no jewellery, we had no occasion to wear any except for costume jewellery on stage. We suggested she had a good search and then forgot all about it.

The next day we were all in the cabin dressing when there was a knock on the door. An embarrassed officer presented himself. He gulped, then informed us he had been ordered to search our belongings. We didn't know whether to be angry or to laugh. We were most certainly shocked. The officer and the two accompanying NCOs were ill at ease, bright red in the face, at the awful task they had to perform. The Javanese stewards had already been interrogated. Jean was starting to protest angrily, she was obviously going to make a fuss, but that wouldn't help a really difficult situation for everyone. Pam told them to go ahead, I just laughed and the others joined in. Roz said the whole affair was preposterous. The officer asked shamefacedly would we mind opening our luggage. Fortunately we never had much with us as there was such limited space, so this highly tricky situation could only be brief. Of course nothing was found. The officer departed with many apologies and thanks.

The woman who had mislaid her precious pearls was nowhere to be seen. We had an outburst of anger and outrage. 'What kind of people does she think we are? Rogues and vagabonds?' After we had vented our fury and had a good laugh we packed our bags again.

You can imagine our elation when we heard that night that the famous pearl necklace had been discovered. Better still, the whole ship knew. The pearls had been found nestling between the CO's bunk and the wall of his cabin!

SEVEN

Cairo, 1943

The first smell of approaching land was appalling, like burning rubber. It turned out to be oil from Port Tewfick in Egypt. We were bound for Cairo but the Suez Canal was closed and we were loaded into a small boat to be taken ashore, then by lorry to a waiting train.

The long journey through the empty desert seemed never ending. Our thirst was terrible, and any bottles of liquid we had brought with us, soon drunk. We were unused to the dry atmosphere, totally opposite to the humidity to which we had become acclimatised. I really felt my tongue was beginning to swell in the hot, very hot, dry heat. At last we saw the lights of a city. Since Monty's victory at El Alamein the war was over here. Slowly we drew into Cairo Station. It was now night and thank heavens much cooler. We must have looked a bedraggled, dusty group and not difficult to find on the platform. The Entertainments Officer approached us immediately. He took off his cap and scratched his head. 'I don't know what you are doing here, we thought you were in East Africa.' A familiar greeting.

Thankfully he managed to find Rosamund and I and a few others accommodation at the Victoria Hotel. The rest must have gone somewhere else.

We found our work in Cairo very demanding. We were out in the desert many nights, entertaining units of the Eighth Army left behind to clear the debris and destruction of the tremendous battles in the Western Desert. There were arduous journeys in Army lorries or rickety ancient buses to wherever there were pockets of troops in the desert. There was rarely a proper stage, but somehow they managed to create one for us. The men we performed to felt isolated and abandoned, either waiting for leave in Cairo or just returning from it, bored and lonely. I suppose they were there as an occupying force, which must have seemed an anticlimax after the tremendous action and struggle for survival. The Western Desert was an unwelcoming place, full of potholes and shell craters. We passed the odd overturned tank and all the aftermath of warfare. I thought of the terrible loss of lives and shuddered. Not only was the desert back-breaking to be driven over, but I found it deeply depressing, haunted and inhospitable. Fortunately, no matter how late, we were normally driven back to the reasonable comfort of the Victoria Hotel at night.

One Sunday morning in the autumn of 1943, after returning wearily in the small hours from one such expedition and stiff from the bumpy ride, Rosamund and I were catching up on the hours of lost sleep. We were rudely wakened by the clamour of the telephone, I sleepily picked it up. The voice on the other end of the line startled me out of my dreams. 'This is your husband.'

I nearly dropped the phone. 'Pat, is that really you?' was all I could manage.

'I am on my way up,' was the answer.

By now I was out of bed. Rosamund had realised the situation and was already struggling with her bathrobe. 'My God, I must get out of here.' She was grabbing at whatever she could. I rushed to the basin in the room to clean my teeth, there was no time to do anything about my face, just a quick brush of my hair.

A knock on the door. I was suddenly panic-stricken. 'Rosamund, *please* stay where you are! Take your time, please.'

I opened the door with a thumping heart. Patrick grasped me in his arms before I even had time to look at him. This was the great moment I had been waiting for since that parting at Sheffield Station in early 1941. I had come half way around the world and yet somehow it was not as I had dreamed and imagined through those long years of waiting. I would like to have been prepared and

94

given some warning, but that was stupid. He was here, that was surely all that mattered. I put my arms round him and my head on his shoulder, but he lifted my face and was kissing me wildly. Rosamund appeared at the door looking dishevelled and carrying a few belongings, saying she would collect her clothes when she had found a room. I introduced her to Patrick and apologized for the disturbance. I was worried where she would sleep for the hotel was packed, but she hurried away.

We went back into the untidy bedroom. This was not the way in which I had pictured our reunion. We looked at each other properly for the first time. He was better looking than ever, tanned, sporting a moustache and handsome in his officer's uniform. He was based in Tripoli, but said he had been given leave as soon as I had notified his headquarters of my arrival in Cairo. I insisted he must be longing for a hot bath and a shave, indeed I wanted a bath and would go first while he ordered breakfast. I was still in my nightgown but he grabbed me again and started kissing me passionately all over. I had the feeling he was going to make love to me there and then. I disentangled myself. What was the matter with me? I couldn't respond, perhaps it was the surprise. Common sense told me we had to get to know each other again, we needed more time. Saying I was a mess I made for the bathroom, firmly closing the door. Pat called out that he would fetch his kit from downstairs and order breakfast.

I lay back in the bath and as the warmth went through my body it began to become alive again – that was better. How wonderful to be together again after all this time. The plans I had of looking my best, the romantic clinch. Oh well, all plans went astray, at least mine seemed to. The unexpected was always my fate.

I dried myself and searched around for the French perfume to which I had rather expensively treated myself – the shops in Cairo were full of such temptations. Then Patrick was grasping me again in the bedroom. I wafted expensive scent and was more relaxed, yet couldn't escape a feeling of shyness. I felt as though Pat was someone I'd just met, not my husband. I was especially embarrassed when the Egyptian servant entered with the tray bearing our breakfast and Patrick continued kissing and nuzzling me in the man's presence. He averted his eyes. When Patrick spoke to him in Arabic he hurried away.

What to do with the day? It was Sunday so I was free. Patrick was on the first day of a long leave and was the one who knew Cairo, so I thought we should go out and he could show me around. After all the room was a mess and had to be cleaned and the beds made so it was best to get out.

We wandered out into the warm sunshine, it was early autumn and hot and dry. Cairo was a beautiful city; trees lined the streets, there were open air cafes and all the hotels had terraces filled with tables and chairs for leisurely drinks. The desert wind was thick with sand, making everyone's throat as dry as dust, and thirsty. We walked arm in arm and I began to feel the pleasure of having my own man with me. I had forgotten that feeling, in fact hardly known it. He steered me into a very English bar called Tommy's and at last we began to talk, to exchange news. An officer walked in, Patrick gave him a big hello and they fell upon each other as old friends rediscovered. He joined us and Patrick rather proudly introduced me as his wife. Patrick's chum leapt to his feet, obviously feeling he had intruded, but both of us insisted he stay, I think we were glad to have a third person. Soon others joined us and by lunchtime we had a full table and I was swept off with them to eat. By this time we were all drinking and having fun. As usual I was the only woman.

When we finally returned to our hotel I was relaxed. The drink had submerged my inhibitions, which was just as well. My husband had returned from the desert with an insatiable appetite for sex.

Roz very kindly said she would play our shared role of Amanda all the following week, which would give Patrick and I much needed time together. We spent a day out at the Medina Hotel near the pyramids where there was a pool, and booked tickets for a concert by the Palestine Philharmonic.

I was changing for the concert when the telephone shrilled. Patrick answered, it was a friend on leave who wanted to meet him downstairs for a drink. I said I would join them shortly when I had changed, but by then they were thoroughly engrossed in conversation with large whiskeys in hand. Patrick's friend regarded me with a mixture of amazement and approval. They agreed we should get together for dinner after the concert, and as we hailed a taxi Patrick said he hoped I didn't mind. Secretly, I was hoping we might have an evening alone with a quiet dinner, but it was not to be the entire time we were in Cairo.

The days were full of great gatherings of young men, always drinking. There was a large table every morning on some hotel terrace or bar. I would either join the fray late, or leave them and return in time for lunch. I understood they were enjoying a badly needed leave, and supposed this was their way of trying to forget the past and not think about the future. Freed from the threat of German occupation, Cairo seemed to be enjoying one long party. There was constant movement of Forces personnel – but to where? Italy, it was assumed.

I began working again. As this meant leaving early, often in the heat of the afternoon, sitting through morning drinking sessions was out for me. Some nights Patrick would come with me to the theatre, otherwise he would stay in Cairo with his cronies. This was preferable to him hanging around while I was performing, but I then I returned to a drunk husband. There were twin beds in the room but Patrick was always in mine. That was fine; I expected that, although it was close quarters and hot, but late at night when I returned from working, longing to relax in bed, he would ring for room service. The waiter would knock and enter, visibly shocked at Patrick's naked body so close to mine. I would settle for tea and lemon while Patrick always ordered a large brandy, though he was so full of booze he hardly needed more.

I began to dislike his behaviour towards the Egyptian servants. Although he always spoke Arabic, I knew by the tone of his voice he was being rude, even insulting. When I once asked him not to speak to the Arabs with such disrespect, he answered sharply that I didn't know them as he did. I thought about this, also his general behaviour. The war had a lot to answer for, it had certainly toughened his personality, but I had changed too, I had grown from a girl to a woman. The last few years had matured me, my whole outlook on life had changed.

Patrick had arrived with leave and back pay which was fine for a while, but not for long. He began to borrow. I'm sure his friends loaned him some money and he visited his headquarters with a request for an advance on pay. I received a small allowance as his wife which was paid into a bank at home. I never touched it, anyway it was impossible to get now. Money, or the lack of it, was a normal state for me but I always managed. My keep was provided for, the small amount paid for my other needs often remained uncollected, in fact in remote places it was often not available. In Cairo there was an ENSA headquarters so pay was regular.

Patrick's leave was rapidly passing.

*   *   *   *   *

The subject of post-war was briefly raised. One breakfast, which we always ate upstairs, Patrick mentioned that he had thought of joining a Colonial Police Force, possibly in Hong Kong, because the pay and life were good, although everything depended on the outcome of the war. He then suggested I return to Tripoli with him, he was certain he could find a job for me. I thought he was living in some sort of dream world.

'What would I do?' I asked him. 'My life has been spent in the theatre. I know no other kind of employment and what would happen to me when you were transferred? Anyway, you know I have a contract to go to India.'

Patrick knew I had promised Henry Oscar when I signed the ENSA contract in London that if I should see my husband I would not break it to join him. Secretly I was relieved. That his leave was nearly over filled me not with the sadness that I would have expected, but a longing for a normal life again. I wanted to be on my own, to get on with my job and my life. These were thoughts that I dared not admit to myself until that morning. The drinking had now become too much – as had the sex. His constant demands were not prompted by love, it seemed I was to be used at any given moment. I made my excuses for him, but we had now been re-united for well over a month. I tried not to show my feelings, always acquiescing, but I was becoming weary of it, and resentful. Did I still love him? Had I ever loved him? Was it my fault? Had I changed?

Patrick broke into my thoughts. 'By the way I have something for you.' He walked to his drawer and pulled out a small handgun. I was not just astonished but horrified. 'It's a Beretta, just right for a woman, small and easy to handle. You should carry a gun for your safety, especially if you are going to India.'

I drew away from both the gun and Patrick. 'Take it away, I couldn't even touch a gun.' My first instinct was to try and laugh it off, but then I decided to humour him. 'Listen darling, I am well taken care of by whichever Force we're attached to. Also I'm classed as a non-combatant, so can't carry a weapon.'

He was upset. 'I bought it for you in Tripoli, it cost me a lot of money.'

'Well sell it again, we could do with some cash.' I finished the conversation by going into the bathroom, closing the door behind me.

Lying in the bath I tried to put my jumbled thoughts into some sort of perspective. A colonial policeman's wife! I wasn't in the least suited for such a life, nor did I want it.

We had never discussed our plans for after the war. Back in June 1940 when I accepted Patrick's proposal I never thought there would be such a time. War was still being fought in Europe with great ferocity. I knew little about the Far East where I was being sent next. We had heard of the awful suffering of the prisoners, of the atrocities and the way the Japanese had swept through the Far

East. Then Pearl Harbour and the Americans fighting in the Pacific – oh, there was a long way to go yet.

I came out of the bathroom tightly wrapped in my bathrobe, and with a plan. 'Lets go to Alexandria for a weekend, I've some free time before we open at the Opera House during your last week. I've never been to Alex and it would be heavenly to lie on the beach and swim.' Secretly I hoped it would get him away from his drinking pals in Cairo and I might even re-discover the man I thought I was so passionately in love with. Patrick agreed.

We arrived about lunch time. The room was much larger than in Cairo and with a double bed. Wonderful. Being squeezed into a single bed each night was beginning to pall. I unpacked swiftly, putting on my swimsuit, hoping we would have some lunch and then lie in the sun and swim. The climate was perfect, the sun beautifully warm with blue sky during the day, followed by a cool evening.

When Patrick said he wanted to visit a bar he knew, my heart sank, and rightly. As we entered there was a great shout of welcome, and sure enough along the bar were several of Patrick's fellow officers. There were introductions and drinks all round. I made my half lager last whilst they exchanged news, Army gossip and 'in' jokes. Suddenly I decided to make a stand. 'It's great to meet you all, but I didn't come here to spend this beautiful day in a darkened bar. I came for sea and sand – and anyway I'm hungry.'

Patrick put his arm around me. 'She's right, I did say I would take her swimming.'

'We'll all go.' was the united reply. 'Someone arrange sandwiches and beer.' Everyone had another round. 'Wahid for the sharia' – the usual one for the road.

Eventually we emerged into bright sunlight and made for the beach. It was now October, but blue, blue sea, and sand. In no time we were in the water, it was bliss. I had not been in the sea since South Africa. Patrick was a great swimmer, I watched him as I swam around and later as I lay in the soft sand. He had a magnificent body. They were all swimming, splashing about like a bunch of schoolboys. I was happy I had been able to drag them away from that bar Smiling, I stretched out to enjoy the warmth of the late afternoon sun.

It was at least five o'clock when we returned to our room. I stood under the shower washing away the salt and feeling refreshed and relaxed. Pat joined me under the jet, rubbing my body with soap and his hands, but my senses no longer responded. I longed to just stretch out on the bed and fall into a heavenly sleep. The sun and swimming had given me a healthy exhaustion – it had the opposite effect on Pat.

Later he was dressing while I dozed. He never appeared to be tired and expected me to be ready for the next – whatever – sex, drink. I turned on my side saying I would sleep for a while. He said he would go down to the bar, and I fell asleep as soon as the door closed behind him. When he woke me at nine o'clock I sat up in bed trying to pull myself back to consciousness. He said he'd met some Egyptian friends who wanted us to join them for dinner. It was the last thing I wanted to do, but I knew I must make an effort, so I told him to go on down, I would dress and be there as soon as possible.

When I joined them half an hour later I could tell that Patrick was well on his way to being drunk. There was good French wine on the table, and although it was not his to pour, Patrick was splashing it into my glass, totally ignoring the wine waiter who was hurrying over to our table. I talked to the Egyptian couple, who were curious to know about the play opening at the Opera House in Cairo the next week. We talked about theatre in general, they had spent time in England and France before the war. The dinner was progressing enjoyably, but unfortunately Patrick was becoming increasingly drunk. Our host was watching him warily. I don't know what he had been drinking before dinner, but whatever it was it must have been strong. Towards the end of the meal things became rockier. Patrick was trying to press me to more wine, but I refused. The Egyptian couple rose to bid us their goodnights.

'You can't go yet, there is plenty of wine left,' said Patrick, getting to his feet with difficulty.

Our host smiled. 'Just leave it or drink it.'

I felt ashamed as I thanked them, but I hoped they understood. When they left, I sat there and watched Patrick finish the remaining half bottle of wine. We were the only people left in the restaurant. Waiters were hovering around waiting to clear. Eventually he lurched to his feet and we wove our way out of the dining room.

I decided it would be better to return to Cairo in the morning. The weekend was not at all what I had hoped for. The next day Patrick leapt out of bed as fresh as if he had spent the evening on plain water, he never appeared to suffer a hangover. He told me we were out of funds. I didn't have to query where the cash had gone. We had only brought enough for the two of us, which would have been quickly swallowed by several rounds in a bar. Fortunately I had kept money back for the hotel bill.

Returning to the hotel in Cairo that afternoon was perfect. There was much to be done before the first night at the Opera House: rehearsals, all kinds of preparations and work again – my salvation.

*   *   *   *   *

What a pleasure to be in a real theatre again, in a proper set with all the furnishings. We had got used to working with the minimum either on hastily constructed platforms, or, if we were lucky, in some local building with a podium and a roof.

It was a while since I had seen all the company. At the Opera House we were playing *Private Lives,* Roz and I were sharing the lead, Amanda; Pamela and Joanna shared the second lead, Sybil, alternating as the French maid. We were still a reduced number from the original cast as several of the older members were waiting for transport home or had joined the ENSA pool, which meant you were available to be sent anywhere if needed for some show.

Pam and I were playing together on the opening night. She said she missed seeing me because I was always with Patrick. She thought I looked tired, was I okay? I told her Patrick's leave finished that week, and about the gun episode. I asked her what she thought. She fixed me with her large eyes, looking at me very directly. 'He's mad of course. Why ever did you marry him? He's certainly not for you.'

I began to bluster excuses in his defence: I thought he had changed, it must be the time spent in the Middle East. 'I simply don't know,' I finished lamely.

'That's no excuse and you know it. Many have been through far worse. He drinks too much.' There was no answer to that one.

Once the play opened friends we'd made on the voyage from South Africa came to see the show. When they came round to the dressing room afterwards I began to realize how much I'd missed other company. We met for dinner one night in the hotel where they were staying, somewhere entirely different from the usual rendezvous with Patrick's chums. I kept trying to draw Pat into the conversation, but my friends were not part of his group. He was rather silent, almost surly. Gradually it dawned on me he was jealous.

The commanding officer of Patrick's company of the Intelligence Corps had invited us for lunch. I was to be the honoured guest and a few of his friends were to be there. Patrick took special care, polishing his Sam Brown belt and buttons and brushing his desert boots. I dug out the pale turquoise dress in which I had been married. Patrick announced we would meet in Shepherds Hotel first for drinks with several friends, so I suggested he went ahead as I had a show to do that night and didn't want to drink too much. When I got there, there were about six of them grouped around a table covered with glasses on the terrace. They leapt to their feet at my appearance, pulling up a chair and paying me many compliments. They were in a festive mood, judging by the full glasses of pink gin on the table. When it was time to go there was the usual argument over the drinks bill, then they quickly swigged down their gins.

Patrick and I were the last to leave. He was swallowing as many gins as he could. 'We can't leave all this,' he was saying. Someone else said, 'Oh do come on. Leave it.' He took my arm and led me to the waiting cab but I could see Patrick still pushing back as many gins as he could. I was disgusted, and anxious – I knew he would soon be very drunk. There were about five of us crushed into the taxi, all in a party mood and looking forward to a special lunch. We were the last to arrive, but it was of no consequence, more drinks were served before lunch. Sitting next to the CO at table, he told me how much he was looking forward to seeing me at the Opera House.

I was uneasy. I was the only woman present and Patrick was obviously drunk. The first course was eaten without incident. I was making small talk with my host, then, to my horror Patrick suddenly lurched to his feet. He knocked over a glass as he leant across the table in a verbal attack on the friend who had earlier escorted me to a taxi.

'Stop looking at my wife,' he slurred, 'I've been watching you, you're after her, just waiting for me to go.'

There was a deathly silence. He shook my hand away. Someone told him to shut up. There were voices from the other end of the table telling him to sit down. Patrick was turning ugly, he repeated the accusations. The CO tried to remonstrate with him. It was turning into a bar room brawl. I suddenly leapt to my feet, apologising to my host as I fled from the room, I just couldn't stand any more. I ran down the stairs two at a time, jumped in a taxi and told the driver to go to my hotel. I lay back in the seat shaking from head to foot.

By the time I reached the Victoria I was steady, but cold with fury. How could he? I went to the bedroom to change my dress, then tried to find Roz. Since she had been shot out of the bedroom that Sunday I had seen little of her. I knew she was temporarily in a small room nearby and went down to the desk to ask. While I was there Patrick's CO phoned, I took the call in the kiosk. The CO was being kind and soothing, he asked me to forgive Patrick and to try to understand because the boys had been through a bad time. I replied I fully understood what havoc war can create, apologised again for my abrupt exit, and hung up. I stood still for a while in the dark phone booth. I knew I had run away from an embarrassment that I could no longer suffer. God knows what went on after my departure. As I was standing there I saw Patrick stagger in – going up to the room I supposed. Could I face him? I had to sometime, it had better be now.

When I opened the door he had his back to me vomiting into the basin. I stood still, disgusted. Eventually he turned, swaying and wiping his mouth with the towel.

'Thank you,' he managed to slur, 'for making me look an absolute idiot in front of my CO and all my other officers.'

All I could say was 'You revolt me.'

He was in front of me now and hit me full in the face. The impact jerked my head to one side, the pain almost brought tears, but no, I just turned and walked out of the room shutting the door. Then the tears came – holding my face I rushed to Rosamund's room. She was on her bed having an afternoon siesta and leapt up when she saw me. 'Darling what has he done to you? Has he hit you?' She removed my hand from my face and put her arms around me. 'The brute, you've got to leave him. He's in no way right for you. We've all noticed how you have become more embarrassed and unhappy. But this –'

We sat on the bed. I stopped sobbing and tried to blurt out the whole story. She soaked a towel in cold water and I held it to my face. 'You were quite right to leave. The situation is impossible. You mustn't go back to him – when's he leaving?'

'Tomorrow, early evening. You're playing so I suppose I'll see him off.'

Rosamund was against that. She tried to persuade me to squash in with her that night. I looked at the tiny cupboard of a room that Rosamund had been given to allow Patrick to share mine. The bed was hardly big enough for one let alone two.

My brain had gone into overdrive, as it does in a crisis when there is a decision to be made. 'I know what I'm going to do,' I said. 'I've only got twenty-four hours to get through before his train leaves for Tripoli and I shall get through them as quietly and amicably as possible. I shall mean it when I say goodbye at the station. I know I should be honest and brave and have a confrontation, but his behaviour is so irrational.' I thought about the guns in the room. I knew he would protest and even plead with me. I also had to admit that I was scared of him when he was drunk.

Roz said she would play for me that night, but I refused. The theatre was what I needed. Not only would I be away from him for a few hours, but once in the theatre I could only think of my performance.

Patrick came to my dressing room after the show and several friends joined us for a drink, but I declined a supper date for us. Patrick said nothing. When we were alone he made no mention of the traumas of the day. No apology – nothing. I was getting used to this convenient amnesia. I was looking in the mirror removing my stage make-up. Still no comment, not even an enquiry, 'was it tender?' I was glad he hadn't punched me, I'm sure he could pack a hefty one.

The last day was full of grim sadness. He said he was desolate to leave me and hadn't we had a lovely time together. I made non-committal remarks. He had to collect his travel pass from headquarters, I had to go to the ENSA offices. When we met again in the hotel, there was the usual group round a table full of drinks. On the surface, all was normal. Nobody made any reference to the day before. In fact Patrick asked the others to take good care of me for him!

When we finally took a taxi to the station, the train was already in, so there was no uncomfortable wait. We went through the usual sort of conversation that one has in moments of strain. Writing – of course. No, I didn't know when I was India bound or for how long, so no address as yet. There was a shriek from the engine. I thanked heaven. He was clutching me, then the train moved. I thought of the goodbye that dismal morning in Sheffield. What did I feel now? A deep sadness. I was sad for a marriage that had never been, but I knew that I could not spend my life with him. We had nothing to keep us together. I had come all the way to Egypt to discover this, but it was better than waiting until the end of the war to find out what a dreadful mistake I had made. I blamed myself. I had gone against all advice. As the train disappeared I felt as though the weight of the world had been lifted off me. I turned and walked away.

* * * * *

I walked through the swing doors of the Victoria Hotel. Standing at the bar was the actor Anthony Quayle of all people, a much-decorated Major. He hailed me and I joined him for a drink. I knew he was in Cairo because we had lunched at a party given by mutual Egyptian friends in the film industry. Pat was with me and it was one of those occasions when he had felt left out. Rosamund, also a friend of Tony Quayle's, was there, as were some other English actors now in uniform and passing through Cairo, including Michael Denison. The conversation turned to all of the latest gossip from London, theatre friends, plays, films which Patrick had no part of.

I told Tony that I had been at the station saying goodbye to my husband. 'Oh, you must feel miserable – for long?'

I took a deep breath. 'For good.'

Tony gave me that quizzical look that I came to know well in the years ahead. 'You'd better have another!'

Finally I went upstairs. The bedroom did not feel empty or forlorn. It was somehow comforting to see Roz's clutter once again strewn around. When I flopped into bed I felt no loss or loneliness – only the pleasant sensation of being alone. My body was my own again. I stretched out and was asleep within minutes, so soundly I did not even stir when Rosamund returned from the theatre.

* * * * *

I gazed at the minarets through the windows. The gold was dazzling, hypnotic, obliterating all the dark thoughts of the departing train the night before. I dragged my eyes away to concentrate on the conversation.

Colonel Dunstan had invited myself, Pamela and Joanna, to lunch with him. He was in charge of ENSA in the Far East. A formidable task as it was a vast area, deprived of entertainment from home for too long. He wanted to hear at first hand of the state of the India Repertory Company. The Company had effectively gone missing for nearly a year, and he now listened intently to our potted version of our strange seven months in Africa.

'As usual, a complete cock up,' was all he said. 'We intend to be very different in the Far East. I know you've done splendid work wherever you've been, but *we* need you. The 14th Army has had nothing in the way of entertainment, except what they've arranged for themselves. They call themselves 'the forgotten army' with good reason. Are you ready to join us?'

I looked at the two girls, and said I had a contract to fulfil and didn't intend to break it. I knew Jo and Pam would agree, but we couldn't vouch for the rest of the company. Indeed there was hardly anyone left. 'You'll open with *Private Lives*,' the Colonel stated. 'I've seen the production at the Opera House, and it's just what's needed. We'll take it from there. Your departure will be arranged as soon as we have a ship.' He bade us a courteous farewell, saying he looked forward to seeing us in India.

We three gazed at one another. It was a momentous decision, but it was the reason for our leaving England, and it was also a welcome change to feel really needed. Little was known about the war being fought so desperately in the Far East. Everyone had been concentrated on what was happening in Europe. As far I was concerned, the more distance I could put between Patrick and myself the safer I would feel.

Practically speaking we had little to offer. The original company appeared to have disintegrated. We had not seen Jean or Charles in ages. We thought they were awaiting transport home, if they hadn't already left. Godfrey, our juvenile, had just disappeared. We had seen Roy, the partially deaf actor, apparently he was coming to India. He made up the fourth in the cast of *Private Lives*, which was the only play the repertory company could still perform. Our manager, Maurice, played the lead opposite myself and we presumed he would be there.

Sadly, I knew Rosamund wouldn't be joining us. One evening she had come into our room with stars in her eyes, whirling round ecstatically. She didn't have to tell me, I knew her too well. She had fallen in love with a Canadian major with whom she had become absolutely besotted. I had never seen her like this before. His name was James, and his peacetime occupation was centred on politics. An intellectual and well read, for Rosamund he was perfection. Could I play Amanda for her that night? It was her turn, but his last evening before being posted to some secret destination. Of course I would. So there was no question of Rosamund going to the Far East when we finished in Cairo, which left the cast of *Private Lives*, and the good-humoured and indomitable Ron, our stage manager with the tin leg.

So it was back across that grey desert once more. It was late December and cooler, but so early in the morning I was hardly awake. In fact I hadn't been to bed at all. My last night had involved so many farewells it was one long party. Social activity apart, we had worked hard whilst in Cairo, initially enduring the uncomfortable conditions of the Western Desert before performing night after night in the Opera House. I must have slept most of that long haul across the desert. By this time I was so used to being jolted around on hard seats I could sleep anywhere. When we finally arrived, I didn't even notice the objectionable smell of oil that pervaded the port, indeed I hardly remember going on board.

PART III

INDIA

EIGHT

Meeting Jack, 1944

Iwas up on deck at first light along with most of the ship's company. It was New Year's Day 1944, and we were all eager for the first sight of land after several weeks at sea. As the sun rose, India appeared as a bright line of gold, glittering on the horizon. It was breathtaking and lifted my heart. The ship slowed down as we gradually drew nearer. Buildings emerged – seemingly out of the sea – dazzling in the sunlight. It was such a magical sight I felt my life was going to be renewed in some way. We were drawing closer now. The buildings became more distinct. Domes shimmered gold and silver as the sun rose higher.

Someone pointed out the Gateway of India. We could see people, cars, taxis and gharis (horse drawn cabs) and the inevitable rickshaws. We were all so excited at the prospect of being on land again, no one thought of the unknown ahead. The war was a long way from Bombay and we had little knowledge of what direction it was taking here. When we left Cairo it had been packed with every kind of serviceman in the Allied Forces, and something important had been about to happen. We guessed the invasion of Italy was imminent. We didn't yet know it, but here in India we were about to play our part in an entirely different, but equally dangerous war.

It had been a comfortable voyage, my fifth on a troopship. I'd spent much of it lying on deck with my book and trusty Mae West as a pillow. The weather had been perfect, and the warm sun enormously recuperative after Cairo. Even my jaw was not painful. I had seen an excellent dentist in Cairo who tutted away over the gaping hole left after the extraction. I still had some infection, but he managed to remove some fragments of tooth or broken bone.

My face finally returned to normal. I hoped that would be the end of it.

We had given two or three performances of *Private Lives* on board, on a stage rigged up in the dining room. It was a bit cramped, but provided a welcome diversion. There were some other ENSA artists on board beside our reduced company. The Chinese Crackers (they really were Chinese) were a small band that played various modern tunes on not very modern instruments. A young singer called Jean Shaw shared a cabin with us. Another performer from the pool of artists in Cairo was a ruddy faced gentleman who sang rollicking sea shanties, and there was also a contortionist called Maisie Griffiths. Come Christmas Eve some celebration was called for. We had already done our stint with our play so the musical artists were called in to put on a show.

The troopship was a converted liner with circular staircases and cabins on the various levels. On this occasion, the stage was in the well of the ship. The ship's company gathered on each level, crammed together and leaning over the stair rail for a good view.

The Chinese Crackers, who kicked off, were noisy and jolly and rewarded by resounding applause. The sea shanties were not that popular, so the singer changed to well-known songs in which everyone could join in, of which *Red Sails in the Sunset* was a favourite with the troops: it was a good marching song – I think the only clean one. Then Jean Shaw came on to sing, followed by Maisie Griffiths. Maisie was wearing a red satin bathing suit with a fringed skirt, and received all the usual wolf whistles and catcalls. Her act constituted of kicks – back bends – legs over her head etc, but then came the finale when she stood on her head and opened her legs into splits! I was standing on one of the upper galleries and the view she was presenting was so embarrassing that I wanted to escape but was hemmed in. The uproarious and raucous laughter, plus loud applause, encouraged the poor girl to stand and take a bow. The evening ended with a great sing-song.

That was Christmas Eve on the Arabian Sea.

*   *   *   *   *

Now we were making our way down the gangway onto the soil of India. Awaiting us were the usual lorries, also two welfare officers from the newly formed ENSA offices in Bombay. As entertainment for the troops had been almost non existent, everyone was anxious to put on some performances as soon as possible. A Captain Donald Neville-Willing lifted the flap of the lorry to bid us all welcome. He had bundles of our mail with him, for which we thanked him joyously.

'I'm taking you to the Taj Mahal Hotel,' he announced. 'The new offices are at Greens Hotel, almost adjacent. I'm sure you will be pleased to know that Captain Jack Hawkins has been especially released from his regiment to organize all the entertainment.' I thought, thank goodness, a star actor and at last someone who knows his job. I felt confident that improvements and real professional help would put paid to the dreadful frustrations we had suffered. What a relief! I fell upon my letters.

The Taj Mahal was very grand and I wished I had some smarter clothes. When in Cairo we were issued with a sort of uniform in light khaki, which was ill-designed and not practical. We were wearing it today, but rarely did so unless ordered to.

We had a room overlooking the Gateway of India and the sea. Miraculously, we had our own bathroom with a proper lavatory and flushing water. Three of us were sharing and we felt we were in heaven. Joanna Duncan, Pamela and myself were the only girls remaining of the original company. We had shared rooms, cabins, everything since our departure from England and I only recall friendship between us. By now we were so used to being together we knew exactly how much space to occupy to retain our own territory. Looking back, it seems almost insufferable, but we were all young and could laugh most disasters away.

Our finances were a constant problem in a city. ENSA paid us £6 a week, which even for wartime was low. I for one was always short of cash. We had all our food, keep, laundry etc. The £6 was for pocket money and to buy the necessities. Thankfully I had been able to spend a little on clothes in Cairo. Cairo was like being in Paris. All the women were so chic and seemed to have escaped the war entirely. The shops were unbearably tempting and I spent my all on two outfits I couldn't resist.

When there was a tap on the door, a tall good-looking officer in charge of publicity presented himself to take us to lunch. He took us first to the Harbour Bar for a welcoming drink, then into the air-conditioned (then almost unknown) hotel restaurant, where a band was playing. My feet began tapping under the table as I looked at the menu, which was full of delicious dishes, both European and Indian. I was hugely enjoying myself.

That night Donald Neville-Willing took us to dinner in the same restaurant. Now the ceiling had lighted stars sparkling all over it and the band, under Sonny Lobo, was playing dance music. The setting was enchanting. The Indian ladies were decked out in magnificent jewellery and gorgeous saris. A mixture of English and Indian officers, the latter mainly Naval, wore their white tropical uniforms. There were Sikhs in white turbans, one with a monocle in his eye and whom I thought the most handsome and regal man there. There were some civilians, American and English, and we were introduced to several. It was a world of civilisation that I had not encountered before. The war seemed remote. It was a complete break from reality.

*　　*　　*　　*　　*

He stood silhouetted in the wide doorway. Brilliant sunshine lit his tall, broad frame. Khaki shorts, long socks, officer's cap. The uniform for the tropics. He paused for a moment, adjusting to the darkness inside and spied our small group gathered together awaiting him. He strode towards us and into my life.

He was greeted by Donald Neville-Willing.

'Jack, I want you to meet the India Repertory Company who

have finally arrived.' He turned to me for some reason for the first introduction.

'Jack, this is Miss Doreen Lawrence who is playing Amanda in *Private Lives* – Captain Hawkins.' All very correct and strangely familiar. It seemed to have happened before, or had I been waiting for this? Jack removed his cap, put it under his arm and took my hand. He bent over it slightly. His hair, that dark thick mass, the deep brown eyes that looked briefly into mine.

'We've had great reports about your work.'

That unique voice. I took a breath to reply.

'Captain Hawkins, we're so thankful you're in charge of our depleted little company. We're putting on *Private Lives* because it only needs a small cast,' I added lamely.

He smiled and turned to the others for further introductions. They were offering explanations for our over-extended journey here, and why others had left, sickness, re-posting etc. also telling him our wardrobe was in a rotten state. Jack could see the stories of our various journeys and our complaints, would take all morning, so he called a halt, saying he would see us individually later.

The priority was to get the show into shape as soon as possible. He suggested we adjourn to a nearby hall to have a run through of the play. Our wardrobe he assured us would be replaced – quickly. This was a great relief. We might have begun this adventure splendidly garbed by Drury Lane, but the periods in Africa and five troopships with the heat, humidity, packing and unpacking, had taken its toll.

The officer accompanying us was introduced as Lt. Nelson-Richardson and Jack added he would be joining us in the rehearsal room. Once out of the Taj Mahal the heat was intense, like a blast from a furnace. As we walked, the lieutenant told me that before the war he'd been an actor as well, named Philip Ashley. He was eager for theatre gossip. He had been in India, like Jack, since 1941 and was amusing, urbane and full of charm.

Once in the rehearsal hall, we set some boxes out to form the set for the first act with some rickety chairs that were lying around.

'Right – let's begin,' said Captain Hawkins. For some reason I felt nervous. I had played the part heaven knows how many times in front of an unbelievable assortment of audiences, but I just knew that I wanted to be at my best. I was thankful that I looked good: I was still tanned from the last sea voyage with my hair highlighted by the sun. I had chosen to wear my pale yellow pleated skirt and matching shirt – one of my Cairo purchases. It gave me confidence.

As the other two began the play, I noticed Jack open his briefcase and take out some paper and a pen. He was going to make notes – very professional. Once I was on, I was away. In spite of the surroundings I was oblivious to everyone except the actor I was acting opposite. I don't know if Jack made notes, but I could sense he was impressed. He thanked us all.

'It's fine, but needs some tightening here and there. A few more rehearsals, perhaps a change with some of the moves.'

We started to wander back to the hotel, Jack walked with me.

'You're very good,' he said, 'but you've all fallen into a few bad habits, which always happens when you are in a show for too long without attention from a director. But with all you've been through, the various stops and starts and changes of actors, I thought the rehearsal showed great promise, more than I'd expected. I think we should soon be ready to open at the Excelsior in Bombay. Tell me, how do you get along with the leading man, your Elyot?'

'As an actor, or a man?'

Jack laughed.

'Well, he was much better in the beginning – but then,' I added hastily, 'we all were.' Jack cocked an eyebrow at me. 'He understudied Coward once,' I added.

I told him about Roy and his deaf ear, and Ron with the tin leg. Jack laughed out loud. I don't think he believed me.

At the hotel we split up until the following day.

We were thirsty so Roy suggested we go into the Harbour Bar for a drink. The four of us found a corner to discuss the morning's events. Roy was a little apprehensive about his future, but we girls were delighted that Jack was going to direct us in a completely new show. At that moment Jack entered the bar with Philip in tow. I was riveted. What was it about this man? I had learned very early in my career how to make a good entrance. Indeed I had employed it myself to great effect on occasions. Yet when Jack entered a bar full of splendid looking young officers, almost all eyes were instinctively drawn to him, rather than Philip. They were shown to a table and were immediately engaged in deep conversation, probably about us.

The following day, instead of beginning our new rehearsals, the publicity officer rang to say he was taking us, with his assistant and a photographer, to the bazaars and various sights in Bombay. This gave us an opportunity to see more of the city than the surrounds of the Taj Hotel. We posed with fruit, lengths of wonderful silks, saris and hand-made crafts. It was a full morning's work, providing useful publicity. Although we had been prepared, we found it colourful, exciting and disturbing. The poverty in comparison to our part of Bombay with all its canopy of wealth and power was extreme. We were told we had been to the more civilised bazaars, heaven knows what the others were like. Joanna had spent a great deal of her childhood in India so she was more acclimatised. I was totally unprepared for its realities. India moved me tremendously. In due course its sounds and smells became so familiar that even now I know India will be with me as long as I live.

The next day there was again no rehearsal so our wardrobe could be renewed. An Indian lady took us shopping for materials and then on to a dressmaker to get our new clothes made up. I needed a replacement for the white evening gown for Amanda, a negligee for my first entrance and a suit for the final act in an apartment in Paris. All to be finally approved by Captain Hawkins. There were so many gorgeous materials, gossamer, fine silks and brocades, it was like being a child in a sweet shop. I finally chose white with a silver line running through it, which I knew would look good under the lights and was so sheer it would cling in all the right places.

Finally, on the third day, we were called for rehearsal. Jack was there talking to Philip Ashley and another tall officer. Jack was brief and to the point. 'Philip is to play Elyot, we've been fortunate enough to have him on indefinite leave from his regiment.' I was delighted to have a young attractive actor to play opposite after the years of war rejects.

Jack introduced the other officer. 'This is Richard Caldicott, who will take over from Roy. He's been given some leave for this production.'

Wow! Captain Hawkins certainly had been getting things moving. What had happened to the others? How had they made such a rapid disappearance? I didn't enquire.

We commenced the rehearsal. Having new blood and a director who really knew his job was like a shot in the arm. With new actors it was fairly slow going to begin with, but they were both highly experienced professionals. In a few days they had learnt their lines and we had put together what was almost a new production. Not for a long time, if ever, had I so enjoyed acting. This was as it should be. Jack was a fine director and I was learning so much. He was giving me new inflections in lines, new moves, in fact I was a whole new Amanda. Philip and I worked well together, and it was the same with Richard Caldicott. Ron was still with us as stage manager, but Roy and Maurice had returned to Cairo. Jack was obviously a man of decision, who acted quickly.

Greens Hotel, next to the Taj, had given office space to ENSA, who eventually took over the whole ground floor. For now it was make-shift, just a couple of desks screened in a corner. One afternoon after work I went over to see if there was any mail. Jack was sitting at his desk and called me over. 'Are you happy the way rehearsals are going?'

I told him I was enjoying them immensely.

'You don't think I'm giving you too many notes?'

I assured him that I was relieved to receive some good direction at last. I'd never had any for the role, having taken it over at such short notice. I told him about Roz and her illness in Takoradi.

'It's amazing that you learnt that part in twenty-four hours. I can tell you're experienced, but you're so young, where did you train?'

I laughed, 'Not RADA or at any academy, just in the theatre from childhood.'

'Incredible, so did I, we must exchange histories some time.'

I was standing by his desk. 'There's something I want to ask you, a favour,' I said, crouching down by his side.

He put his arm loosely around my shoulder – I liked it. 'Anything,' he replied.

'It's for Joanna Duncan. Her father is in Jodhpur. He's in command of the Maharaja's forces. Jo and her brother went to America when war was looming and so she hasn't seen her father in years. Do you think she could have some leave to visit him? She only has a small part with a few lines in the last act, and could be back by the opening.'

Jack laughed. 'You've no idea of the distances here. Jodhpur is several days away, but of course she must go. Tell her to come and see me so we can get on the wires to her father and get some transport arranged. Anway, he should be told she's here.' Jack paused. He wondered if I would be around one evening so we could go over certain scenes together. I readily agreed and left with my heart high with hope that it might be soon.

In due course Joanna went on leave. One evening, sitting alone at a table in the hotel studying my script, I was about to give up when suddenly Jack was standing there.

'I hoped I'd catch you. I had to stay for dinner but managed to make my escape afterwards. May I join you?' My face had suddenly become alive at seeing him. I nodded towards the vacant chair. He ordered some drinks and for a short time we chatted about the play. Inevitably the conversation came around to us. I longed to know more about him, and he seemed interested in learning something of my background. That evening we began to discover the great pleasure we had in being together. We had so much to talk about, with such fun and laughter. Jack had a wonderful dry sense of humour and wit. He was also quite unconsciously a great mimic. He seemed to know everyone – there certainly wasn't anyone in the theatre past or present that he had not met or worked with at some time.

I asked him how he began in the theatre. 'King Elf,' he replied – in a Christmas production of *Where the Rainbow Ends*, put on by Italia Conte. Italia was a famous children's agent and proprietor of an acting academy, who had been persuaded by a family friend to see young Jack in an amateur production of *The Pirates of Penzance* out in North London. Despite Jack being dressed in a grey wig and women's clothing, Conte was impressed by his talent and singing, and asked his father's permission to let Jack appear in her Christmas show. King Elf gave Jack a taste for the footlights. Though he returned to his studies briefly – he had won a scholarship to a higher school – when Italia came knocking at the door again to ask him to attend an audition at the New Theatre, for Sybil Thorndike and Lewis Casson, the theatre won. It was for Bernard Shaw's prestigious new play *St Joan*. None of this meant much to the Hawkins family. The extent of their knowledge of the theatre was music hall – Jack, being the afterthought of the family and quite unlike his grown-up sisters and brother, was often taken along on these outings.

Jack told me he went to the audition accompanied by his father and Italia Conte, who had been coaching him in the part of Dunois' page. He walked out onto the stage and delivered his lines in a clear confident voice, and then waited, looking out into the darkened auditorium, without any sense of the importance of the event. Suddenly a figure mounted the steps to the stage, grabbed Jack by the arms, and in a broad Irish accent patted his head and said, 'That's my boy – that's my page.' Jack had no idea who this was except that it was a tall man with bright red hair and a flowing beard. So it was with the approval of George Bernard Shaw that the career of Jack Hawkins was launched.

In his review of *St Joan*, the eminent critic James Agate praised the thirteen-year-old boy's talent, predicting a great future for him.

All of which came true – greatly assisted by the Casson family.

During the General Strike in 1926, they learned that 'little Jack', as they called him, had been walking from Wood Green to the Lyceum Theatre for rehearsals: there was no public transport. Sybil Thorndike insisted he move in with them. Staying with such a family and working with them over several years gave him a unique knowledge and background in theatre. Already a rising star of the London stage in his teens, he was acclaimed for his performance in *Journey's End* on Broadway at the age of eighteen.

Jack's career was unstoppable until the war came and changed his life for good. Sent to India with the regiment he had volunteered for, he soon fell to organising troop concerts, entertainments, many of which he performed in himself. Resourceful and always popular, he was fated to take charge of ENSA in the Far East and turn it into a huge success. He was to be away from the footlights of London for six years – a gap that not many careers would survive. But not Jack, who was to go on from theatre to films, and an entirely new audience.

The following day after the rehearsal had finished, Jack asked me if I would go with him to Eric Dunstan's for dinner. We had been invited out to the villa that Colonel Dunstan had been loaned by Prince Aly Khan. I was flattered and somewhat surprised, but accepted with pleasure. Needless to say, I took a great deal of trouble getting ready for the evening, and more than anything looked forward to being collected by Jack. The villa was outside Bombay by the sea. We entered through large well-guarded gates. I was excited and curious. It was a small group, if there was another woman there I can't recall who it was. Music wafted through from the terrace: Jack was all ears. 'Prince Igor,' he said, and made for the gramophone, eagerly exploring the selection of records.

'I love this ballet it's so full of action – Borodin,' I added.

Jack turned and looked at me with mild surprise. 'You like music?'

'I was brought up on it – I love all music – classical, modern. I miss it so much.' I did not have a radio; it was forbidden, and of course no gramophone or records.

He regarded me with a new interest. 'Music is a great part of my life too.'

Drinks were served by a sergeant, but the food was served by the Prince's staff, who were beautifully turned out in livery. The meal was delicious and of many courses. In those days I was always shy in non-theatrical company, not having spent much time away from it. I was unused to such grandeur, but situations such as this were not infrequent in India and gradually I grew more confident. I hoped no one but me knew I was acting, and that beneath the sophisticated exterior of the worldly woman I was always vulnerable.

The conversation was flowing. I was next to Eric at the head of the table. I was to discover he could be the master of the put-down. He suddenly in a loud voice remarked on my nail varnish. 'What a disgusting colour, Doreen, do not wear it again, it is enough to put everyone off their dinner.' I looked at my nails – the polish had been bought in Cairo and was considered the latest colour. The vogue then was a very dark colour – not red – more the purple shade. I found my voice. Loud and clear I replied, 'You are absolutely right, it is the first time I have worn it, it will be the last.' Jack came to my rescue saying that here in India little was known of the latest colours, then changed the subject.

Sunday was our last free day before we opened The following week would be a hectic time getting into the theatre. An invitation to the cast was issued informally by Aly Khan – would we join him for a picnic on Juhu Beach? He had arrived for a short stay and would enjoy meeting us. Most of us went together in the lorry, clutching our swim suits. When we arrived we found the beach transformed. Two tents had been erected for changing. A third was a beautiful canopy with golden tassels at each corner and a table underneath on which were flowers, silverware, and plates with his crest emblazoned on them.

Eric and Jack were already there in their swim suits. He was the perfect model for an actor I thought. Everything about him was right, his legs, waist, broad shoulders, even his feet weren't too big! We girls all went into the tent to change. It seemed unbelievable that we were here among glorious sand and palm trees by the sparkling blue Indian ocean. Within moments Prince Aly roared up in a sports car, he jumped out and we were all introduced. He clapped his hands 'Martinis,' he said, and within moments trays of the most delicious iced cocktails arrived, served by servants wearing the Prince's colours on their turbans and sashes. What a way to live!

We all swam before lunch, splashing back through the shallows to find rugs and tablecloths spread out under the palm trees. We dried almost instantly in the hot sun. An informal lunch was served, and we all sprawled about eating. We had time for a final rush into that beautiful sea before leaving. I noticed that Jack had almost always been by my side during that magic day – he was now as we waded out of the sea.

He invited me to go with him to a circus act he had to vet for ENSA the next day and perhaps have dinner afterwards. A date together – nothing to do with *Private Lives*. An unexpected pleasure, which I accepted although I have to admit to a lack of enthusiasm for circus entertainments. As well as being scared of horses, performing animals make me feel guilty, and high wire acts uneasy and nervous. We were ushered into the ringside seats of honour. So anxious were the artists to please Jack that every act was played straight towards us. I managed to restrain myself as the lumbering elephants came to a halt in front of us, rose up on their great haunches and pushed their trunks into our faces. When the horses galloped around the ring, beautiful though they were, with the girls in tutus dancing on their backs, my composure began to fray. I tried to concentrate on other things, but alas, the finale when the whole team of horses rushed straight at us, then reared up, hoofs in the air inches away, proved too much. Jack dutifully applauded madly, and turned around to find an empty seat beside him. His companion, pale green, was hiding underneath it.

He was still laughing when we reached the Chinese restaurant.

Although sympathetic, he found it highly amusing. He ordered some drinks and as he was more acquainted with Chinese food than me, I asked him to order the meal. He introduced me to the art of chopsticks, which I soon mastered.

For the first time he began to talk about his marriage to the actress Jessica Tandy. In 1940, just before the Blitz, he had evacuated Jessica and their five year old daughter, Susan, to America. The Oliviers lived next door to them in Hampstead. Larry and Jack had both volunteered for active service. Whilst awaiting call-up, aside from the men digging an air-raid shelter in the garden, it was decided that Jessica and Susan, and Jill Olivier and Tarquin, their son, should travel to the USA on the last available civilian boat. Jack sold the house and everything he had to pay for the voyage and provide them with money to live on.

When he was finally called up to join the Royal Welch Fusiliers, he began at the bottom as a private, which must have been tough after living the life of a West End star, though he did not say so. He was soon commissioned as an officer and was sent to India in 1941, by which time disturbing letters were already arriving from America: Jessica had met another man and wanted a divorce. He was very funny about this. Training deep in the jungle for action with the 2nd Division, a runner reached him with an urgent communication from America. 'Greetings from Nevada,' it read, 'your divorce was granted on [date] in your absence.' He laughed when he told me the story, but then said, 'The trouble is she's free, but the divorce isn't legal in England, by our laws she's a bigamist. It has to go through the English courts for me to be free.' It was all in hand he said, but slow going. He looked at me, 'I suppose it doesn't matter at the moment, but I will be free.'

There was a silence, then Jack spoke again 'Where's your husband?'

Taken unawares, I stammered, 'Not here.'

'That's obvious,' he said, a trifle testily.

I took a breath, 'He – I have left him – for good.' Silence. 'He's in the Western Desert, based in Tripoli I think.'

We both raised our heads at the same time. He looked into my eyes and must have seen the bitterness and desperate unhappiness in them.

*　　*　　*　　*　　*

We had a dress parade for Jack to vet the clothes. It was a pleasure to be working for a director who took as much interest in this production as he would for a West End show. Luckily we had the use of the theatre during the mornings for rehearsals. One day when the lorry collected us from Green's Hotel I had some difficulty getting up into the back. Either I was wearing a tight skirt or the lorry was higher than usual. Jack put his arms around me and lifted me high into the air, planting me inside, then jumped in himself. I felt as if I had been hit by a bolt of lightning. I have never known such a dramatic sensation of two bodies touching. I sat on a box – silent. He sat on another staring straight ahead of him. I knew he had felt the same wild effect that I had, so I did not look at him either – it was too deep for that. I suddenly realised that we were in for something far more involved than the lighthearted relationship we'd been enjoying. What's more, I knew he'd sensed it too.

After rehearsals, Jack suggested we meet later at the Harbour Bar to talk, and then have dinner. Talking about my marriage was not what I wished to do. I'd had plenty of time to regret my impulsive error, which had turned into a nightmare of incompatibility. I had tried to bury it – to drag the whole story out now was impossible – but obviously, he needed to know something more.

Finally, I said, 'When I saw him in Cairo it wasn't right. Actually, it was torment. So after he returned to Tripoli from leave, I wrote to him telling him I wanted to end the marriage. That it was finished.' I felt Jack holding my hand.

'Something went very wrong between you in Cairo?'

I nodded, but I did not intend to enlarge upon it. I never did. We hardly ever spoke of it again.

*   *   *   *   *

Pam, Jo and I decided to throw a drinks party for a few of the officers who had been squiring us around. Our room had three beds in it but it was quite large with a lovely view. We were all used to having drinks sitting on beds or bunks or whatever, so there was nothing unusual in asking a group of men into the bedroom for a get together before dinner. We made a quick list and I said I thought we should invite Jack and Philip. The others agreed.

We dressed early so we would have all the clutter out of the way. We covered the beds – the dressing table became a bar – someone had sent flowers. All was ready. We were certain to be invited out to dinner afterwards. I was secretly hoping that Jack might ask me. We had invited about eight people and it didn't take long for the party to warm up. No sign of Philip or Jack. I hoped he hadn't changed his mind.

A knock came at last. I was standing right by the door so I could open it. He was there, looking more handsome than ever. He was wearing his correct evening khaki uniform: long trousers and the jacket with all the Royal Welch Fusilier flashes with his regimental fore and aft cap on the side of his thick dark hair. He looked magnificent, but he always wore clothes well, especially uniform. Over the years ahead he was to appear in films in every known form of military uniform.

Introductions were made and Joanna handed out drinks. Jack and I seemed to be keeping our distance. Suddenly he was beside me, 'This isn't a bad room, with a really splendid view.' We moved to the window together. Soon there was no one else there – or so it seemed to us. I can't recall our conversation, but I know we were oblivious to everyone, so deeply were we involved with each other.

'Can you have dinner with me? I'd like to take you somewhere away from here where we can dance. I long to dance with you.' I accepted at once, When Jack makes an exit he knows how to do it and I found myself waving goodnight and out in the corridor in seconds.

I don't remember where we went, or ever going there again. The band was in full swing. Although no table was reserved we were shown to one immediately. I'm sure dinner was ordered, but I have no recollection of eating it. All I recall is going into the firm clasp of Jack's arms, then dancing together in such perfect unison as if we had been doing it all our lives. It seemed almost an impossibility to stop. When at last we did, it was to look around at an empty room and a rather weary looking band. It was time to go.

We moved out into the warm Indian night and Jack hailed a ghari. The horse had a garland of flowers around its halter. We travelled slowly through the streets, looking up at the velvet starlit sky. I was happier than I could believe possible and I knew he was too. 'Let's dance some more. I want this night to go on forever.' He held me close, my head on his shoulder. I had no idea of the time, I certainly did not care.

I was vaguely surprised when we finally halted outside Greens Hotel, but even more so when we took a lift to the top. As the doors opened a burst of dance music greeted us. Within minutes we were on the floor again.

Because at night the breeze off the sea made it so much cooler and fresher, Bombay was alive with groups of Indians walking to and fro. After closing the dancing at Greens Hotel, we joined the throng. We leant against the huge archway of the Gateway of India. We kissed for the first time and stayed in an embrace unaware of the milling Indians around us. Finally we walked across to the Taj Mahal Hotel, where we sat at a window table for most of the night. It was almost dawn when we reluctantly parted at my door. It was obvious to both of us that not only was there the most vibrant sexual attraction between us but, more seriously, we were falling deeply in love.

*　*　*　*　*

It was the morning of the dress rehearsal. We were opening that night at the Excelsior Theatre and there was the usual rush and panic getting into the theatre after the Indian dancer, Ram Gopal, had vacated the previous week. Ron, with the aid of servicemen with ENSA, had been working most of the night moving in scenery and furniture and all the props and paraphernalia of a new production. Jack was out front directing the lighting and making sure that everything was in the correct position. I was called for a lighting check, walking from the darkness back stage into the bright lights. I heard an exclamation and moved down to the footlights, shading my eyes so I could see into the auditorium. 'Is something the matter?' I was nervous anyway, and now was anxious that something was wrong with my appearance. 'No, no, nothing at all.' It was Jack's voice from the darkness of the stalls. 'In fact, it's just perfect. Stay where you are in the spot for a moment while we light you.'

I stood on the balcony set for the first act of *Private Lives*. The ENSA workshops in Bombay had done exceedingly well, the two adjoining balconies, with foliage in between, were quite authentic South of France. As the electricians tried out various lights I felt the old atmosphere of the real theatre once more and knew how much I had missed it.

Coming off stage in a hurry to change, Ron limped through the pass door from the front of house. 'What happened when I came on, Ron?'

He grinned. 'Only that the way you looked seemed to shake the Captain. You'll probably start a riot in that white dress.' I laughed and hurried off.

I had a dressing room to myself, a great luxury. When I heard Ron tap on the door and call the quarter hour, I was ready. For me this was a special first night. I wanted to give the best performance to please the audience, but most of all for Jack. He had done so much to give me confidence in myself and my future. Ron had said to me once during rehearsals, 'You were good in this before, now you're going to be great.'

The audience was packed and enthusiastic. After Philip and I made our first exit we received an encouraging round of applause. I recall Jack's delighted face as he rushed through the pass door and the three of us hugged each other. 'It's going just as I'd hoped. Keep up the good work.'

We did. In 1944, in far-flung Bombay, we had a real success on our hands.

Eric Dunstan was the first into my dressing room with congratulations, followed by Prince Aly, who told me he had arranged a surprise party for us at his palace, to which we were all invited; finally Jack, who had been rushing round seeing the others. I was worried because I had only the cotton dress to wear that I'd put on that morning. Jack told me it didn't matter but to hurry as there was a car waiting for the cast.

It was one of the most glamorous parties that I have ever enjoyed. Above the terrace there were tuberoses – on wires presumably – creating a ceiling of intoxicating scent. The garden stretching to the sea was beautifully lit, and the tables were laden with food and drink. A band on the terrace, our old friends the Chinese Crackers, were playing the latest tunes on new instruments acquired for them by Jack. I wished I was wearing something worthy of the surroundings, but all of us from the theatre were the same, and as we were the reason for the party it was not important.

Jack and I had a moment to wander down into the garden. After the two weeks at the Excelsior Theatre I was to be off with the company to begin our tour. Time was on no one's side during the war. I was used to that, but now it seemed horribly short. Jack and I agreed to spend one night of that time together, dancing and dining to the music of Sonny Lobo in the Taj ballroom.

NINE

The Beginning of the Tour

Before leaving Bombay there were many changes. The tour had been organised by ENSA's head office with Army personnel to accompany us on our travels. This meant Ron had to leave us – sad but necessary. Looking back it would have been impossible to make these long tough journeys without the help of a sergeant in charge of the scenery. He had to set up on a procession of different sized stages, then take it all down and load up, plus the props, furniture and the wardrobe, with the assistance of a corporal and extra help recruited wherever we were playing. The officer in overall charge was Richard Caldicott, one of our actors. It was obvious to Ron, as to us, that it would be more than he could manage. He was fine about leaving, saying it was time to return home. We felt great affection for him, a young man with a disability, never mentioned, whose courage and stamina had never deserted him long after the others had left. We could only wish him luck.

We were issued with a bedroll each, with linen, towels and our own mosquito nets with collapsible poles. Despite our reluctance, we three women were given a bearer called Vallabh: the men had one of their own. Apparently everyone had their own bearer when travelling by train. We travelled first class, which sounds grand but simply meant that bunks were lowered from the walls of the compartment at night. Vallabh was also responsible for a multitude of other tasks, such as boiling drinking water, brewing tea, carrying all our hand baggage on a long journey (as they all were). We also had a dhobi (a laundry boy) who had an assistant because they did everybody's washing. There was a cook boy, mostly for the bearers and other Indians who were with us, who had their own diet. Terrible rows would sometimes ensue when they were of different religions.

Jack had found some fine carpenters and craftsmen who helped him design an entirely new set that would expand and retract to fit any stage. We, as actors, had to be completely adaptable in performing as well – we were to be the guinea pigs on this tour. With the run at the Excelsior Theatre over, our caravan took to the road, or rather, the railway.

Our first booking was in a garrison town not more than five or six hours away from Bombay. Jack wanted to try us out nearby so he could keep a watchful eye on our first few performances. As the train approached our destination after a dusty jolting ride – my first encounter with Indian railways – we noticed an appalling odour. Philip had the answer, 'Bombay Duck'. The railway followed the coast and the stench came from acres of fishing nets festooned with thin slices of fish drying in the sun. Vultures and seagulls hovered overhead, trying to snatch pieces of fish. The sight has prevented me from adding that delicacy to a curry ever since.

We were allocated basha huts which kept out some of the heat, but not the monsoon. Vallabh unpacked the bedrolls, placing one on each cot, or charpoy. Next he erected the mosquito nets. Already I realised his worth – he was to become invaluable. As this was a garrison there was a sense of permanency. Our basha even had its own thunder box and shower, quite a luxury we were told. We inspected the entertainment hall as soon as we could, since our first show was the following night. We found the sergeant and his helpers already setting up. Miraculously, there were proper footlights. Once we'd found the dressing rooms, we unpacked our clothes for ironing and put out our make-up.

We spent about five days there. We were right by the sea, so could swim in that lovely Indian Ocean (well away from the Bombay Duck). Jack arrived on about the third night and watched the play with the colonel in command, whom he knew. Afterwards the colonel and officers gave us a welcoming party. Jack suggested

minor adjustments to our performances for the troops, who were
a rowdy, but lovely, audience. Their whistles and remarks helped
the whole evening go with a swing.

Jack and I had only a brief snatched conversation and farewell. I
had no idea when I would see him again and felt quite desolate.

*   *   *   *   *

We were off once more, this time to Karachi, then just a small but
colourful town with few hotels, so we found ourselves billeted at
the airport, and very comfortabnle they made us too. We used the
airport lounge and ate in the excellent restaurant. We were only
there four days, performing nightly in a local hall. Troops were
brought in from nearby camps.

Soon we were making our dusty way across the Sind Desert,
miles and miles of hot, humid, nothing. It appeared to be never
ending. It reminded me a little of our journeys across the desert
in Egypt, but whereas that had been dusty and dry, this was dusty
with heat and humidity. Philip and Richard were more used to the
climate and the length of the railway journeys and stocked up on
bottled beer – and an opener. I soon followed their example. Even
today I never travel without a corkscrew, a can opener, a small
sharp knife and a tiny bottle of brandy for emergencies. Several
fellow travellers have been grateful!

Whenever the train came to a jerking, grinding halt, Vallabh
would appear with welcome mugs of tea, the beer having long
since been drunk. Eventually there was a halt at some minute
station in the middle of a plain. We all climbed out and walked
along the platform till we reached the so-called dining car, passing
the second-class carriages with their wooden benches. We then
clambered up into the dining car, remaining stranded there once
we'd eaten until another halt allowed us to return to our carriage.
There was no corridor; therefore whatever existed in the way of
a lavatory in the dining car became a pressing necessity. It was a
long time between stops.

I had time to reflect on my stay in Bombay. I was suffering from severe withdrawal symptoms and the long dreary train journey gave me time for reflection and soul-searching. My mind retraced every minute of the time Jack and I had spent together. Did it really happen? Was I the victim of some imaginary romance? No, it was much more than that. He was older than I, older than any man I had been close to before. Early in our association, before it had become serious, he had remarked that he was too old for me. When I told him I was twenty-four, he replied 'Heavens that's so young, I'm thirty-four.' I said how wonderful it was to be with a man who was so self-possessed and experienced in life. Looking back on our time together, he not only provided safety and care, but he also formed my life. With his wide knowledge, he virtually educated me and I was an eager scholar. I suppose it was a two-way exploration and enjoyment of life. Anyway it was lovely.

Philip was sitting opposite me. He was hot and fed up and decided to have a go at me. 'Missing the captain are we?' he remarked. Of course he had hit the bull's eye. I jumped out of my reverie.

'Oh, shut up, Phil,' I answered. I knew that would get at him: he hated being called Phil.

'Well I must have been right, *Dore*!' He said, knowing I loathed being called Dore more than anything. We were about to continue in this childish way when Joanna interrupted with the news that we had reached the outskirts of Jodhpur, where her father was in command of the maharaja's troops. The train came to an abrupt shuddering halt.

After a few seconds Vallabh opened the carriage door, bowing again and again at the sight of such splendour. There, in the middle of nowhere stood Brigadier Duncan, covered in gold braid and the blue flashes of the Maharaja of Jodhpur. He was followed by retainers wearing pristine white turbans, with the blaze of Jodhpur blue on them. Joanna kissed her father fondly, but before we could be introduced he insisted we all get out of the 'cattle truck', as the Maharaja's private three-carriage train was waiting for us. This wonderful creation was the cause of our abrupt halt.

A blue coloured carpet was placed on the steps and two soldiers in the same blue livery came to a smart salute as we climbed on board. It was like being in another world, on Queen Victoria's royal train or the one belonging to the Russian Czar. Soon I was sitting on a blue, beautifully upholstered seat, my bottom recovering from the previous ill-treatment of Indian railroads; in front of me was a real crystal glass, a bottle of the best Scotch and a large bowl of ice. The Brigadier was opposite with Jo next to him, Philip was beside me, and the others were across the gangway. As the drinks were poured we sat back and relaxed – huge smiles stretched across our grubby faces. I had even forgotten Jack for the moment.

I stayed with Joanna at her father's house, where we shared a room and were waited on for everything. I soon came to understand that in India it was not an unnecessary extravagance to have so many servants, because six were needed to do the work of one. Strict rules governed the household; no one encroached on another's territory. There was a chef with assistants; a butler, more of a major domo, with two or three to wait table under him, and a dhobi in charge of all the laundry, with extra helpers. Apart from the household linen there were endless uniforms to be washed and ironed; khaki drill was changed daily in that climate. Then of course there were the personal bearers: Vallabh was accommodated with the rest of the staff. The gardens were large, and one never saw the same gardener twice.

The 'untouchables' as they were known (for what ghastly reason, I could never understand), cleaned the floors, washed the tiles, emptied all the thunder boxes and were never permitted to associate with the rest of the staff. Outsiders could most definitely not question or interfere – they had their own rules. Most of those in good positions had their own small houses on the compound, and were looked after in old age until they died. Whole families stayed in the same houses for generations. The cause of most major troubles was religion, rather than caste.

Our stay in Jodhpur was definitely one of the 'up' times. The theatre was the cinema, so the stage was rather shallow. Because there was no space behind the screen, dressing rooms had been made for us on either side of the stage. They were adequate, but below stage level which meant a hazardous exit down temporarily erected steps. Joanna pointed out the curtained boxes at the rear of the theatre, which were for the wives of the Maharaja who were not allowed to be seen. Apparently purdah was still practised in the more far flung states of India, in spite of the European education, polo playing, apartments in Paris and country houses in England, where I suspect there was only one wife on show, it was not so in Jodhpur.

The social life laid on for us was delightful. The Maharaja attended the first night and gave a splendid dinner for us afterwards, presiding over the whole event in his gorgeous finery. I was honoured to be seated next to him, with an amusing American colonel on my other side. It was an evening of pure pleasure, combined with satisfaction that the play had been so well received.

The next day the mail arrived and amongst it was something I had not dared to hope for, a letter from Jack, which I couldn't wait to open. I took it aside to read away from Philip's amused gaze. Two full pages, written on both sides. I didn't know how fortunate I was, Jack was no letter writer. I suppose in twenty-five years of marriage I probably received only the same number of letters.

We must have remained in Jodhpur for at least two weeks. There were many military units stationed in the enormous state, and all those within travelling distance were brought in lorries to see us. As we had a theatre with a stage and a good-sized auditorium, it was more practical that way and much better for us. But it was becoming hotter. The Indian winter had ended, and Jodhpur is situated in the centre of the desert.

The quick changes for Philip and myself in *Private Lives*, particularly after the fight scene in the second act, left us both exhausted with our clothes glued to our bodies with sweat. Rushing off stage one night, trying to tear off my clothes and get myself down the rickety stair, I missed my footing on the top step and was hurtling towards the stone floor when Vallabh broke my fall by throwing himself underneath to cushion me. He was only a small man, slight as most Indians are of his age. I think he was about twenty. I was tall, if slim, but I must have been two of him. What had I done to him? When he crawled out from under me, his only concern was for me and my injuries. We had no time for anything but my wardrobe change, all the time he was fussing over me. I had twisted my foot and banged my head, but without his quick thought I would have had a much more serious accident. I felt I must have crushed every bone in his poor little body. He never thought of himself.

When we left Jodhpur it was late March and it becoming hotter by the day, with the humidity as high as the temperature. I have forgotten where we were playing, but it was not long before Philip became ill. The doctor thought it a recurrence of his amoebic dysentery, a tropical disease that burrows into you intestine and is debilitating. To be completely cured it is necessary to leave the tropics. *Private Lives* relies heavily on the two main actors, and is not the play to be in unless you are fit. I had also begun to realise that it would be a difficult play to tour in the extreme heat of summer. We had all lost a considerable amount of weight. I couldn't afford to lose any more as I was a lightweight for my height and already only eight and a half stone.

Matters were resolved with orders to return to Bombay, as requested by the medical officer. Philip was to go into hospital there. It had been six weeks since I had seen Jack. I was happy and excited, but I did worry about what we could do without Philip? We needed another play. I racked my brains and ran through the selection we had brought from England.

Jack was there to meet us as we steamed into Bombay Station. I wanted to shout with delight and jump into his arms. Impossible of course, one had to be circumspect (Jack's words, not mine). There were enough rumours before I left anyway.

After the baggage, scenery and bearers had been loaded onto the trucks by our sergeant and his helpers, we made our way to the headquarters at Greens Hotel, which had been transformed.

There was a large office for Eric, mainly used by Jack, and the rest had been divided into small offices with swing doors. 'Cattle pens,' Jack said. There was no room for us at the Taj, but a small apartment had been found for the three of us further along the sea front, which we would inspect later. Pam made for the telephone; Jo said she was going to join someone, and Jack invited me for lunch. 'But first come to my new abode and freshen up.' Wonderful! He had found somewhere to stay in town, several floors up in Greens Hotel. It was a pleasant room with a bathroom and, best of all, a terrace with a table and two chairs, which looked onto the inner courtyard of the hotel. I had longed to be with him again, we had so much news to exchange. While I was cleaning up and combing my hair, Jack sent for some ice and drinks so we could sit on his terrace and talk. After lunch together, we strolled down the sea front to the small hotel where we three women had a large apartment on the first floor with two bedrooms, a bathroom and a sitting room. Vallabh was sent off to buy anything we needed – he always produced tea and ice and plenty of fruit and looked after us well. He slept outside our door at night.

Jack had told me over lunch that many new artists had arrived. A large concert party had returned to Bombay from a successful tour and was awaiting a ship for England. Jack said that Stafford Byrne, their manager/director, indeed writer of most of their numbers and sketches would like to meet me. He had run a good quality repertory company near London, and had been connected with the Webber-Douglas acting school before the war. Stafford knew a great deal about the theatre and Jack had asked him to stay on to become his assistant. Stafford and I and hit it off immediately. We knew the same people, and only stopped reminiscing because Jack felt left out. His theatrical friends were a rung or two higher and more famous. We became a terrific trio and Stafford was to prove invaluable, both as assistant and friend.

There was a question hanging over the future of the company. Richard Caldicott had returned to his regiment and Philip was still in hospital, with no date given for his discharge. Jack decided we should meet at our apartment, as the next move mostly concerned us.

When Jack arrived and we'd given him some coffee he asked how we felt about continuing with *Private Lives*. I said I thought it would be impossible, partly because of the heat, but also because I thought we needed something less sophisticated for touring. We didn't even know if we would have Philip back, and if so, for how long? *Hay Fever* was unsuitable, needing a large cast and an older leading lady. Now we had experienced playing to Forces audiences, we knew what they needed and liked, plenty of laughter. What else had we in our repertoire?

I had an idea at the back of my mind that I thought might be the answer. I asked Jack if he had the collection of scripts we had brought from England. There was one called *Love in a Mist* that had been on our list but never rehearsed, and which I had read on board ship. I had never played in it, but knew it might be just what we needed. It only had one set, two young couples and a character actress to play a Gorgon of a landlady, plus her husband, a duck farmer. He makes an entrance, occasionally crossing the stage, but never speaks. Jack was laughing already.

'Where is this set – what are the couples doing?'

'In thick fog in the middle of Dartmoor. They're lost – one on honeymoon and the other on an illicit weekend. It's all about them trying to get to bed, and there is only one bed.'

'That's it – that's just what we want.' Jack went off to hunt through whatever plays our manager had left behind.

Naturally we didn't mind being in Bombay. I hardly ever saw Pam or Jo. We all had our own friends. At the same time we felt guilty about not working. Though we were entitled to some leave, we would be glad when a new production began. We found out that a ladies' welfare group in Bombay had started a 'caff' for servicemen. Egg and chips, or bacon and egg, with of course, tea, seemed to be the extent of the menu. We volunteered to do so many hours a week, which was gratefully accepted. Jack arranged for transport and we went off to the Shandy Tavern, to practice our cooking. It was something new and fun, though somewhat exhausting in the heat.

Jack and I had dinner together almost every night, either in the Taj Mahal Hotel, or more often up in his room in the cool of his balcony. *Love in a Mist* was dug up but as there was only one copy, scripts for the actors had to be typed. We would be rehearsing before long.

Jack asked me if I would care to do a day's filming. Delighted – when – where? He took me along to meet an actor, John Warwick, at that time a Wing Commander, temporarily making propaganda films for the Forces. We discussed the part I should be playing. The scene was a bar and I was the publican's daughter with a cockney accent. I remember little about it except the message for the Forces was 'Careless talk costs lives.' It was only for one day, and I had what I needed to wear. I was to be taken to the studios for make-up by 7.30 a.m. There was nothing difficult about the work. I followed the directions, camera angles, without problems. John Warwick told me he had worked with Jack in a film before the war.

I later went to see Philip in hospital and took him some cigarettes. They were all smoking like chimneys in the ward. I told him about *Love in a Mist* – not nearly as strenuous as *Private Lives,* and asked him when he thought he would be fit for work. He looked fine. He hoped he would be out in a week.

Jack had found a character actress from the Cairo pool, who was on her way, and a new officer arriving at headquarters who was a peacetime actor. Dominic Roche – did I know him? Of course I knew Dom, he was with Manchester Rep, in fact used to be director of the company.

'He's not the best looking, and not a juvenile, but what he doesn't know about comedy you could write on a postage stamp.'

Jack was very happy. 'He can manage the company as well, that's great.' I didn't add that he would probably get through most of our NAAFI booze.

We had a read-through of *Love in a Mist* without Philip. I

decided I would prefer to play the secretary away with the boss for a dirty weekend: it has good lines and I could have more fun with the part. Also Pam was good casting for the honeymoon wife. She had a talent for playing silly, naive girls. The troops loved her. Her wide innocent eyes and pouting mouth, the long brown curly hair set them all stamping and whistling. Casting the men was more difficult. Philip would play my boss. Dom, who had been hoping for a peaceful office job, was to play the bridegroom. Hardly ideal, he was probably the same age as Jack, but what he could do with a comedy line was to be envied. He was a master of the double take and the slow burn-up. We would certainly get plenty of laughs.

We opened just outside Bombay where there was a garrison and a theatre. Jack was busy helping with the setting up. I sat in front watching with Elsie Orf, our new character actress beside me. She might have been created by God for the role of the duck farmer's wife. She was almost square, with thick legs and straight mousey hair pulled back into a knob. Her face was round, and by nature pleasant, but when she stopped smiling, she was the Gorgon of a landlady we needed. She was a person of indeterminate middle years, with more strength than most of us put together and nothing fazed her – discomforts were unmentioned. She tramped everywhere to see everything when sight-seeing and took endless photographs. As Dom once remarked, 'No ancient monument or revered religious statue was safe whilst Elsie was around.' He swore she chipped souvenirs off everything. She was always good humoured and never missed a performance.

As to her husband the duck farmer, Jack had the inspired idea of asking our sergeant to walk on in the part. He was not only thrilled to participate, but to our astonishment almost walked away with the play! Put into baggy old corduroys, a sweater full of holes at the elbows, mucky wellington boots, a flat cap and with his face well dirtied and stubbled, he shambled across the stage not having to utter a word. He was so proud to be one of the actors it was suggested that he might like to stop centre stage and give some sort of a glance around at the antics going on in his living room, but he did more than that. He would stop with a gormless blank expression, take us all in, then shamble off the stage. He was a riot. Every time he made his entrance and crossed the stage he was rewarded with roars of laughter.

The show was just what the troops wanted. We opened to tremendous laughter and applause. Both Jack and Eric were delighted

Philip was really not fit. Though he was loathe to admit it he really shouldn't have been working. Jack had the foresight to grab an actor who had arrived from Cairo with Elsie Orf to understudy the two men. The third night, or rather during the day, Philip was too ill to work and was in hospital by mid-morning. What to do? We had a massive audience waiting to see the play, as we were to be there for several days.

'Jack, you play tonight.'

'Darling I can't. I don't know the lines for one thing.'

After much persuasion he agreed. I pointed out that most of his scenes would be with me, and I could help him through. As director, he knew a considerable amount of the part plus the moves. He spent the day swotting away with me. Come the evening he had the inspired idea of playing the man with a stutter, so if he dried he could stutter away until he remembered the line again. This resulted in one of the funniest performances I have ever seen. With the stutter he pointed and timed lines so that each one produced a roar of laughter. He was wearing Philip's suit, which was too small and disguised his natural elegance. Now I knew what it was like to play with a star actor. It was the best evening, and the only time we ever worked together.

Jack simply could not play another night. He had to return to Bombay – also, acting with us at all was against Army regulations. Alec Hall was rushed in with his one-man show to fill the theatre for the final two nights. We packed up and made our way to the next stop, during which time we hoped our new actor would learn his lines. Jack would join us to rehearse him with the company before opening.

*   *   *   *   *

Poona – I didn't really believe it existed – but it did, and we were there. To me it was Rudyard Kipling and Memsahibs. It had always been a garrison town with proper quarters for men and officers, as well as a theatre and clubs. We were installed in a bungalow with a degree of comfort. There was also a palace belonging to an Indian prince who had wisely left long since. This was where the British had imprisoned Ghandi for some of the time he was incarcerated, and was where we were to rehearse with our new member of cast.

Indian palaces were often filled with everything that could be squeezed in; a strange mixture of antique furniture from Europe, combined with Indian and Persian ornaments, hunting trophies, and the inevitable tiger skin rug, head and all, spread out on the floor. We tried to make enough space to work but it was not easy. Jack's stutter had now become a must for that role: it raised laughs and made the part more fun. Elsie insisted on taking a picture of us all. We posed, and I mean really posed. Pamela stretched herself out on the tiger rug, draped over its head like a 1920s film star or Norma Desmond in *Sunset Boulevard*.

Jack stayed to see our new actor through the opening in Poona which was, thankfully, a big success, but that was the last I was to see of him for many months.

TEN

Trains across India

We were eternally on trains trundling across miles of seemingly deserted Indian plain, punctuated by the occasional small shack-like halt, hardly big enough to call a station. During one of these endless journeys, Vallabh came to my rescue once again. It was hell hot and humid. We'd stopped at a halt in the middle of nowhere so the engine could take on water and we could walk along the track to the dining carriage to eat. Once there we were trapped until the next stop.

On this particular day it was dark before we halted again. We all piled out and began going back to our carriage, the last one on the train. Indian trains were high off the ground and one had to be fairly agile to climb up into them. The others had gone ahead and I was with Elsie who, with her stout frame and short legs was having difficulty mounting the steps. I helped her by pushing, while the others began pulling.

It was only when Elsie was safely on board that I realised that the train had begun to move. I hung on to the door, but the train was gathering speed and the ground had dropped beneath me, so I couldn't get my feet on to the steps. Vallabh's frightened face appeared – 'Mis-sahib Lawrence *please* quickly.' He was frantic and so was I. Terrible thoughts flew through my mind – left alone in the middle of India – no money on me – very little grasp of the language.

To my horror we were rapidly approaching the water tank used to fill the trains. It protruded most ominously and I had a vision of my legs being amputated. 'Hold on! Hold on!' Vallabh was pulling with all his pitifully light strength. By a supreme effort I managed to get a foothold on the last step, Vallabh hanging on to my arms and dragging me, joined by the others, who suddenly realised my plight. I was heaved inside the carriage with a split second to spare as we passed the water tank. Vallabh and I lay in a heap, panting with exhaustion. It took me awhile to stop shaking, both with the effort and from fright. That was a moment when I was grateful for the little emergency bottle of brandy in my knapsack.

We were on our way to Secunderabad, a large town in which we were put up in the Government Rest House. While there I received a letter from Owen Feldman, the officer I'd met on the voyage between Takoradi and Accra. He had been badly injured and was in hospital, would I go and see him. Of course I went immediately.

It was my first visit to a hospital full of badly wounded soldiers and it was profoundly disturbing to see row upon row of beds with so many ashen faced men, obviously in pain and suffering silently. Owen was heavily bandaged across his chest and one arm. He didn't want to talk about it – to spoil the visit – he wanted news of the world outside the hospital. I told him of our many adventures and journeys since we had last seen each other in Accra, and he was much amused at our misfortunes in ENSA. There was an unfamiliar odour that I remarked on to Owen. He said, 'It's the fellow next door. He's had several operations on his leg, but it doesn't get any better.'

'Will he lose the leg?' I asked.

'Probably.'

There was also a Sikh officer in some distress who wandered about the ward muttering to himself. He'd lost one arm and the other was bandaged in a sling. His hair was matted and tangled hanging down his back. I enquired about his unhappy state.

'It's his religion,' Owen explained. 'No one's allowed to touch his hair. It's sacred.'

Owen quickly changed the subject and said how anxious he was to see the play. I had an idea. Why couldn't we come to the hospital to perform *Love in a Mist*? He thought it a marvellous plan and that a performance would boost everyone's spirits, including the nurses. The sister and matron were equally enthusiastic, and the cast were more than happy to give up their day off to provide laughter to a group of people who needed it more than anyone. Our sergeant cum duck farmer and the corporal would deal with setting up the stage in a lecture hall. The glory of that ridiculous comedy was that it had only one set, no change of clothes and very few props. In fact, as we travelled further and the going became rougher, more and more things were discarded, including the antique piano. It was the ideal play.

It was the first time we had performed for a hospital audience and it was enormously rewarding. All those in wheelchairs, with nurses beside them, were near the front. I could see Owen laughing away. The hall was packed with patients. The hospital staff, orderlies and porters gathered at the back. The laughter that evening was special. Matron was grateful to us for creating such an unexpectedly happy evening, a chance for many to forget their wounds. We only wished we could have done more.

*　　*　　*　　*　　*

Our first town in the south was Bangalore. After the flat plains the colourful trees and streets were a pleasant change. We stayed at the unlikely named West End Hotel, but at least it had beds and running water. It was high summer and the heat was intense. Those who could had taken to the hills to escape the appalling humidity. From Bangalore we also went up into the hills of southern India. At Wellington, there were trees, lawns, gardens full of flowers, and it was so blissfully cool that we had even a big log fire at night. I was grandly staying at Flagstaff House with the C.O. and his wife. She was the first white civilian woman I had met since my arrival in India. She had a two year old toddler. Since her other children had been returned to England and then stranded by the war, to be brought up by grandparents, this little golden-haired boy filled a painful gap in the her life. He was adored and indulged by all, including me. There were several other officers' wives who looked on this prized child with some envy; all their children were far away too.

The great, long awaited, D-Day happened while we were in Wellington. We all gathered as close as we could to a small wireless set, ears straining to hear every piece of the momentous news through the crackles and atmospherics. They had landed! The Allies were fighting on the beaches and going inland. They were in France at last. We could imagine it all – the frightful battles – could they progress inland – could they hold on? Tears of excitement were flowing. I thought about the war at home, so far away and felt homesick for the first time. I longed to be there and be part of it. D-Day cancelled the show. Instead the regiment in nearby Ottacamund threw a party and dance where we could all celebrate. We were high with the hope that at long last we were going to win this dreadful war.

We departed once more on the never-ending train journey across India. We found ourselves stranded in Ahmedabad in central India, a great junction where we should have changed trains, but when we arrived we found that there were only bookings for half our number. Obviously old Elsie had to go, protest as she might; also Pamela, who we had always considered fragile. Our sergeant/stage manager went along to look after them and our scenery, and to get the show ready. The rest of us had to wait for the morning train, which would arrive at our destination, Madras, in time for our first show.

I lay on my back staring at the roof of the railway station and the myriad of stars beyond. The night was humid, mosquitoes were attacking and the stench was unbelievable. The discomfort did not bother me particularly, I was used to the misfortunes and vicissitudes that came with wartime travelling, and grateful when a little luxury or a lucky break like an airlift came our way.

The railway stations in India were a pitiful sight at night. Row upon row of sleeping figures wrapped in rags, some clutching babies. The very old and the very young of both sexes side by side with nowhere to go, and considering themselves lucky to have found a place to lay their weary half-starved bodies. I had been horrified when I had first come upon this heart-breaking scene, but I had walked through so many stations in the past months that I had acquired an outer shell of some kind.

My companion on my right, Dom Roche, nudged me, handing me a flask. 'Help you to sleep and keep the mosquitoes at bay.' I took a gulp and passed it to Joanna on my left. I wondered what her father, the Brigadier would say if he saw his daughter in these unlikely circumstances. I was exhausted but couldn't sleep. What on earth was I doing here, I asked myself. I longed for a bath, clean linen and a bed – any kind of bed that would allow me to stretch and relax. A bedroll is hardly luxurious, although without them on trains, in basha huts and Rest Houses we would barely have slept at all. They were reasonably bug-proof and we did have our own sheets, towels and mosquito nets. I was so thankful for Vallabh. He always slept outside my door on his own bedroll and now he was lying at my feet. We had great respect and affection for one another. He had saved me from possible injury, and there was great courage in that small frail body. His loyalty was beyond question.

Joanna was whispering to me something about daring to try the lavatory. I replied that I intended to give it a miss as we were hoping to get on a train at 6 a.m. I closed my eyes and thought about Jack. Where was he now? Bombay perhaps? Or whisking about the place getting more shows together. I knew he would not be visiting us. We were doing well and off his mind. *Love in a Mist* was a huge success. Communication was so difficult and anyway we were on the move all the time. Was I 'off his mind', I wondered.

I was finding it more and more difficult to sleep and the constant movement from one place to the next didn't help. However, it was always rewarding to play to some unit gathered in a small town or village, training and getting ready to be sent to war. We were made so tremendously welcome that it made all the hardship bearable.

There was the usual chaos when the train arrived. Two thirds of the carriages were covered with Indians clinging to the outside – heaven knows how many were crammed inside. Many of the inert bodies sleeping with us had optimistically rushed towards the crowded carriages. We made our way through the crush to the reserved compartments, hoping, at least, for space to sit. Without reservations there was no chance of sleeping accommodation, but we had to make it to Madras. Finally we forced our way into seats, Vallabh squeezing in our luggage before vanishing into one of the packed cattle trucks at the rear of the train. I tried not to think about the discomfort ahead, how to pass the time and endure the heat and sweat. I knew the temperature in Madras was going to be even higher, but took my mind off it by trying to imagine the hotel and a bathroom with running water that awaited us. Most of all I longed for that bed.

It was the middle of the afternoon when we finally arrived. Madras resembled the interior of a furnace in which the Connemara Hotel was a blessed oasis of cool. The others were already installed. Incredibly, Joanna and I had a room to ourselves, as the whole place was bursting with airmen on leave. We had two punkahs, a bathroom with flushing toilet and a small balcony. Most definitely one of the 'up' times to be enjoyed.

Youth is wonderful, and all too short, as my mother was always telling me. She was right. After Jo and I bathed and changed our clothes we were in fine spirits once more. After that appalling night journey we rushed downstairs to be greeted by members of our company, then joined a throng of airmen eager to meet us and looking forward to the play that night.

There had been a delivery of mail awaiting our arrival. I was counting on it, in fact that was what had kept me going. When my bundle was handed to me I saw immediately that the envelope and writing for which I longed wasn't there. I was utterly miserable. I had endured all those long weeks of silence, but I had hoped on reaching a city once more there would be some word from Jack. I suppose I just had to swallow my pride and write to him.

We stayed in Madras for a week or ten days, playing either in the theatre or the famous fort. Most of the airmen were on leave but waiting to return to action, so there were many after show parties. We had not known – how could we – of the dreadful struggle they were having to hold back the Japanese from their attempt to invade India.

Our next destination was Ceylon, which we reached in four hours. Through the kindness of the RAF we had been given a prized airlift to the island. The Dakota, fitted with tin bucket seats, was so much more comfortable and quicker than a never-ending train journey, jogging and jolting through the heat, already breaking into monsoon.

I fell in love with Ceylon, it was so utterly refreshing after the dust and dryness of India. The lush green with the beautiful white sands, coconut palms dipping towards that bluer than blue ocean. Everywhere and everyone appeared cleaner. The people were elegant and lovely to look at, their movements graceful. We were fortunate to be billeted in the Mount Lavinia Hotel, situated outside Colombo on a point looking directly out to sea. Beside it was a sheltered cove, just made for relaxing and swimming. In peacetime it was a holiday hotel, but now it was for Forces only, used, I think, for leave or convalescence. We had plenty of space in our shared rooms with running water and baths, whilst the beach made it seem almost a holiday.

We travelled all over the island, which then was entirely undeveloped. From a bus or a jeep on unmade tracks, we saw elephants in their natural habitat. Sometimes they were working, pushing along great logs with their trunks, guided by their mahoots sitting high astride their backs. In the evening we watched them bathing in a pool, or waterfall, the mahoots scrubbing their huge backs while they blew water out of their trunks. There were brightly coloured birds, monkeys everywhere, leaping from tree to tree, their babies clinging tightly to their mothers' necks. Sinister flying foxes, asleep in the daytime, hung like black rags from trees stripped of bark and leaf. As dusk approached they let out an unnerving screech, unfolded their black wings and flew off into the night.

Some journeys took us to the concealed airfields that were dotted around the island, and which were almost impossible to spot from the air. One was a Fleet Air Arm base south of Colombo whose camouflaged seaplanes were hidden on a lake. We were billeted in basha huts nearby on the beach. Jo and I used to swim naked in the sea every night after the show, then dry ourselves and fall into bed. At last I could sleep. By day we wandered along the beach, which as far as we could see was totally uninhabited.

There was a small island off the shore, which, when the tide was low, we decided to wade out to. Several of us had spotted a villa or bungalow through the trees that made us curious to explore. When we stepped ashore, out of the trees appeared a 'chokidah' (minder-concierge), who amazingly spoke French as well as Urdu. We explained we were only sightseeing and he asked if we would care to go into the villa. It was empty, and apparently had been since the start of the war.

It was strange and almost eerie. It had to have been an unusual person to build a villa on this minute isolated island. The shutters flapped in the breeze. Decaying curtains hung in shreds from a four-poster bed. The dining room furniture was rotting antique French. The tropics are not kind to any possessions left unattended. We wandered out on to the terrace. What a view! Straight out to miles and miles of beautiful blue sea; steps leading down to a small beach. I walked down to the edge and found I was standing on a stone slab. It had writing on it. Pam and I cleared away the muck of seaweed and moss. We read, 'As you stand on this stone there is nothing between you and the South Pole.' Underneath was a signature that looked like 'de Maupassant'. Could it be, we wondered, the French author? Later we found shelves of damp, disintegrating books, some by Guy de Maupassant.

The tide was fast rising. We took a last look at that incredible terrace, its view and its rotting rattan furniture – the termites would soon take over the whole place. We tried to give the old housekeeper some money, but he would not take it, so with thanks we waded ashore.

One day before leaving a Captain Hugh Latimer roared up in his jeep. A peacetime actor, a splendid attractive young man, he was the officer in charge of the Ceylon area for ENSA. He handed me a signal, which had arrived from Colombo. His excuse for his visit was that he wanted to make sure that we were all right. We reassured him that we were fine and I retired to open my signal, thankful not to have to listen to snide remarks from Philip.

Unable to stand my unhappiness and insecurity any longer I had written to Jack from Madras. He must have received the letter unusually quickly. His reply went something like this. 'You silly gosling. No time for anything but work. Hope to see you soon. I will then tell you all you need to know. But I thought you already understood.' Sending a signal on open wires was very public so little could be said, but this was enough. I got the message. I suddenly felt juvenile and silly, but all the same the mention of possibly seeing me again lifted my heart. How this was going to be achieved I couldn't imagine, but I felt a different person.

*　　*　　*　　*　　*

We travelled from one airfield to another, staying in their camps. Occasionally we would be lucky with an air hop from one place to the next in a light aircraft, while our sergeant and the gear followed by road. On one RAF station the men had relieved their tedium by creating an imaginative miniature of London's West End. There was Regent Street, Piccadilly, Leicester Square, even parts of Soho off Shaftesbury Avenue, all accurately placed. The huts were named after first class hotels: we were staying at The Ritz and playing our show at Drury Lane. We had enormous fun. One bright spark had rigged up an ingenious bath-shower with a hot and cold water system. The sun quickly raised the water to the right temperature; you pulled a lever and, hey presto, warm water descended.

Apart from Colombo, Kandy was the only town of any size we visited. It was Mountbatten's headquarters as Commander-in-Chief in the Far East, therefore a hub of activity and full to capacity with men and women from all three services. We were somehow squeezed into the Queens Hotel, right next door to the Temple of the Tooth. Every day worshippers, who had hardly sufficient nourishment for themselves, left plates of food as offerings. We visited, removing our shoes and admiring the extraordinary interior with the ornate casket containing the tooth. Whose? Buddha's perhaps, or maybe the sacred White Elephant's. I must have known, but alas have forgotten. Elsie Orf was naturally in her element taking photos, though I'm sure it was forbidden in that holy place.

From Kandy we went north to Anuradhapura, an ancient city, the relic of a long lost and forgotten civilization. I don't know why we were there, but we must have been en route to some camp or other. We stayed in a Rest House in the middle of the ruins. Ellsie, camera at the ready, was in seventh heaven among crumbling statues. I'm ashamed to admit I remember very little of its historical origin, only that it was a place of unexpected beauty that we wandered around at will.

The Eastern Fleet was in at the port of Trincomalee, in full force. Visiting different ships each night to perform *Love in a Mist* was one of the highlights of our tour. Early in the evening we would set off from the harbour in launches to board the destroyer, aircraft carrier, or whatever was to be our theatre afloat on that particular night. We were made enormously welcome by the Navy. The ingenuity they used to build the stages was marvellous. We were almost always able to use the full set and furniture – even the ancient upright piano. On the aircraft carriers *Victorious* and *Indomitable* the flight deck became our stage. It was lowered like a vast lift to within about eight feet of the floor of the area below deck, creating a huge auditorium. This makeshift stage was one of the best we had to play on and open to the sky, so blissfully airy.

Disaster struck the night we were playing on *Indomitable*. We had the first act going with wonderful laughs and the audience were enjoying it enormously, then suddenly – a loud clap of thunder. Before we could take cover the heavens opened and the monsoon descended on us. Sheets of rain like a screen cut us off from the audience; they, of course, were under cover. In no time at all the stage was awash and we were soaked to the skin, our hair hanging down and plastered to the make-up running off our faces. We were guided off the stage by sympathetic sailors to the cabins we were using for changing, but what to do? We had abandoned an audience of disappointed sailors who had not seen a live show in ages. They sat there patiently waiting, singing songs to pass the time. Our clothes were taken from us and ironed dry. We repaired our make-up and did our best with the hair towels. The stage was swept dry and the furniture was mopped as soon as the torrents of rain ceased. Fortunately the sudden bursts of monsoon rain seldom last for long. Our audience gave us a huge round of applause when we reappeared to carry on from where we had been so deluged by the elements three quarters of an hour earlier.

Some years later, Jack and I were in Malta when he was filming *Malta Story* with Alec Guinness, and among a harbour full of ships was the *Indomitable*. During a ship-board party to which we were invited, I met some officers who remembered me from that wet and unforgettable night.

One night when we were performing on the battleship *Renown*, across the water came the strains of Noel Coward's music. The Master himself was performing on a neighbouring ship. I wished that I had been one of the audience. No wonder Jack was so overworked. Arranging tours for Noel, who was an old friend, must have taken time. I had heard there were many other stars on the way, also big companies, all to be routed. We had been in 'Trinco' for nearly three weeks. Apart from two or three performances at the theatre on shore, we played nightly to the Fleet, and were afterwards entertained by the Navy. The Senior Service certainly lived up to their reputation for hospitality. Some of our members found difficulty at times negotiating their departures. It was necessary to be both agile and moderately sober when jumping into small boats in the dark after climbing down ladders from large ships.

During the free days I enjoyed sailing, collected by a meteorological officer with a suitable craft.

One day the admiral, no less, invited us for a picnic. He was on board, so his launch was crewed by splendidly turned out sailors, and a canopy rigged to protect our soft skins from the sun We made for an island, beached there and swam. The sailors had thoughtfully brought masks and goggles so we could see the tropical fish among the coral.

* * * * *

A large grey rat and I stared at one another balefully. He gazed down at me from a rafter without particular interest. I viewed him from the comparative safety of my mosquito net with much the same sentiments.

I lay on my bed drenched in sweat. I had one towel around my neck with my hair piled on top of my head, the other round my middle. There was no punkah or fan of any kind: as a visitor I did not qualify for one. The heat was devastating. I was in a cubicle at the WREN compound at Trincomalee. I felt terrible. Several rats, like the one twitching his whiskers at me were gnawing my insides, and the sweating was not only the result of the humidity.

Oh God, had it caught up with me at last? In Africa every member of the company was ill at some time with malaria or dysentery, but I never missed a performance. It was the same in India, and now here in Ceylon. Call it luck, or an extraordinarily good constitution – my only misfortune had been the wretched impacted wisdom tooth. I *cannot* be ill. I must be better by tomorrow. Try to sleep and forget about it. We were almost through our tour of the island. We were due for some sort of leave or re-organisation, and the possibility of returning to Bombay where I would see Jack. Even that happy thought did not make me feel better. Oh *please* don't let me be ill. Where would they send me, or would I be left behind with the WRENS? I prayed not. They had been polite, but offhand when we were billeted with them. Our routine was quite different to theirs. We may have disturbed them by getting to bed late after the show, but it was impossible for us to sleep through their early noisy reveille.

If only I felt better. It was now late August and we had been going flat out for months, travelling all the time. I finally had to succumb to the Medical Officer who was called in by Vallabh. I was carted off to the WRENS hospital. The prognosis was dysentery, but of which variety I wouldn't know until the test results came through. Fortunately I'd become too feverish to care about being left behind in a strange hospital, of being separated from my companions. I had never been in hospital before. Having a bedpan thrust at you, then being told to sit on it, is a shock when you have never set eyes on one. Dysentery is a great leveller, and most had the beastly bug.

When my pain eased a little and I became less feverish, I took in my surroundings. We were only three girls in cots in this part of the ward. No one spoke, we were all in the same condition. The nurse had given me some magic potion that eased the awful stomach cramps, but I was so dehydrated I had to drink pints of liquid placed beside the bed. The following day when I was more alert. I was told I had bacillary dysentery. I had been terrified that I had succumbed to the feared amoebic variety, but apparently the symptoms of that disease were very different. This particular bug I had burrowing inside me was less serious, in fact a hazard to most in the tropics. Rest, plus treatment with one of the sulphur drugs would clear it up in a week or so.

When I protested that I could not stay in the hospital and must rejoin the company, no one appeared either to understand, or care. The company had left without me and I felt bereft. In all my time in the theatre I had never missed a performance. Now I felt like a prisoner.

The girl in the next bed began to talk to me. She was curious about our travels and way of life. She had seen and enjoyed the play. To pass the time I began telling her of incidents from the tour and my career as an actress. She was riveted. To my surprise so was the girl in the other bed. After several days I acquired quite an audience of WRENS. They teased me and called me 'glamour girl' or 'fancy pants' – an allusion to my French knickers, which were the fashion in those days. It did not worry me, I told them it was only sour grapes because they had to wear those frightful bloomers, and we laughed. In truth they thought my life much more exciting than theirs, with less regulations and more variety. They knew we had been playing aboard all the ships and entertained by the admiral and his officers. I did not blame them for feeling envious.

In a few days I was feeling strong enough to sit out outside in the beautiful garden overlooking the sea. I was really relieved at not having to work. But the days passed slowly listening to all the WRENS chatter.

Back in my bed one evening depression and desperation had really set in when suddenly one of the jolly nurses announced, 'Miss Lawrence, a Wing Commander to see you.'

Who? All the girls sat up in their beds as the desperately handsome film actor, John Warwick walked in. Powder compacts were brought out from under pillows and there was much combing of hair. I was amazed and delighted.

'John you are the best sight I have had in ages. What brings you here?' He laughed and sat on the bed producing a bottle of Scotch. 'Any glasses?' Several were produced.

He had brought the propaganda film he had made in Bombay, in which I played the part of the publican's daughter. He thought I would like to take it home as it might prove useful as a test for a film job. He wrote the name of his agent on a piece of paper. 'Do go and see him, say I suggested you should.' I thanked him profusely. It was wonderful to be with a fellow actor who talked the same language as me.

I asked John to rescue me from Trincomalee. I didn't know who to approach to arrange my departure. I had lost all touch with ENSA. He said he could organise a flight for me to Colombo for the next day. 'Will the hospital give the OK?' I didn't care, I was over the moon, and breathless at the prospect of release. He promised to pick me up the next morning between eight and nine, and would signal Colombo to meet me. 'Wonderful, I'll be ready and waiting.' At last my luck had turned.

Captain Hugh Latimer was there to meet me when I landed in Colombo. I enquired about the company. Apparently they had returned to Bombay. We had covered many miles and performed many shows since we had opened *Love in a Mist*, and we were all entitled to some leave.

'I thought I'd take you to headquarters for some lunch.' There was a pause. Then he added, 'There's a friend of yours visiting for a few days.' My heart thumped.

When we turned into the drive I saw him at once through the window. He rose from his chair then he was coming out of the door to meet me. I couldn't rush to him and hug him with all those officers around, but he put his arms around me in an embrace, then held me away to look at me. 'Amazing, I thought you were a very sick girl.'

I laughed, my eyes alight, I could hardly have looked better. 'I'm fine, much better now, it was nothing too serious.' Inside there were a few young officers, delighted to have a visit from Jack and eager to learn of plans and instructions for the future. I noticed the all-important pip on his shoulder. 'Many congratulations Major Hawkins.' He thanked me, his eyes sparkling with humour.

After lunch Hugh said, 'I have put you out at Mount Lavinia again. I know you like it. You can be quiet and relax and recover.' He added he had put Jack out there as well. I could have kissed him, the kind thoughtful man.

My room was large, overlooking the sea, but with a heavenly breeze gently lifting the curtains. It was wartime shabby, but so was everything. To me it was luxury. Within twenty-four hours my whole world had tilted from misery to most unexpected happiness.

I took off my clothes and hung up the few I had with me in the creaking old wardrobe, then stretched out on the bed with a deep sigh of contentment and was instantly asleep.

I awoke with Jack bending over me. It was evening. Oh, there was so much to say about ourselves – all our news – just to be together. We dragged ourselves away from each other to bath and change into something for dinner. I had loved Mount Lavinia before, but it was an entirely different place now. I noticed everything: the waiters in their long robes with their hair twisted into a knot enclosed in a tiny net on the top of their heads, the windows onto the ocean, the down-at-heel furniture – it all appeared beautiful to me now.

Jack told me how he had been rushing all over the place. Many artists and companies would be arriving in the New Year, for Jack had numerous contacts, all good friends from the theatre. John Gielgud was due to arrive with the company of *Hamlet*. His Hamlet was hailed as great, there have been many fine ones since but his performance remains a theatrical legend. Jack had been in the original production and had played Horatio and later Claudius with John. He told me that when war was declared and the theatres closed, all actors were left with nothing to do. Being thoroughly frustrated John decided to perform *The Importance of Being Ernest*, and gathered together the most incredible cast. Jack played Algernon, Edith Evans, Lady Bracknell, Peggy Ashcroft, Cecily and Gwen Ffancon-Davies, Gwendoline. Margaret Rutherford was Miss Prism. With such a cast how could it fail – it was the definitive production. It was such a riotous success in the provinces it was later brought into the West End. That was Jack's final appearance on stage until 1946.

Jack was naturally looking forward to John Gielgud's arrival. Much preparation was necessary for the company to play at the Excelsior Theatre. Jack had also been kept busy with Noel Coward, who was a true professional, so easy and no trouble, the ideal one-man show. Noel only needed a piano, and would go anywhere to entertain the troops and improve morale.

Joyce Grenfell was expected, another fine comedienne and singer, as was Vera Lynn. Edith Evans was due to arrive with her own play company.

'Wonderful, you really have got things moving.' It was incredible how after such a dearth of entertainment in the Far East, there was now a constant flow of talent arriving.

'But,' said Jack, '*Love in a Mist* is one of our most successful shows. You can go anywhere with it, which is great. I know you must be sick to death of the show but that comedy has the perfect ingredients.'

I agreed with him. 'Perhaps we could do some reorganising when everyone has had some leave,' he suggested.

I didn't know about the others but I was sick of moving around and would stay in Bombay for any leave due to me. all I needed was to be in one place.

Three days of tranquillity followed, lying on the sand during the day reviving my tan, which had turned yellowish-grey in hospital, and swimming in the sea, my favourite exercise. It was the first time I had been alone for so long, able to relax and read. I had lunch alone, then dozed away the heat of the afternoon. Jack returned in the evening with his longed for presence.

I returned to Bombay, flying with Jack.

Everyone in our company had already taken whatever leave they wanted. Pam and I were in a room at the Taj Mahal Hotel. Joanna had managed to return to her father and was nowhere to be seen. There was much activity at headquarters, the Gielgud Company was arriving shortly. Jack was hardly ever available except in the evenings. We always managed to have dinner together, whatever the time.

But the moment to leave for our next tour was fast approaching. We were already being kitted out and measured for Burma Greens, as well as Bush hats, boots, warm capes, blankets for the bedrolls. We were thankful to be in some sort of uniform, the practical trousers and cotton shirts were so much easier for travelling. I asked if we could also have triangular headscarves to keep the dust and dirt away from our already ill-treated hair.

I saw Vera Lynn sitting on the steps of Greens Hotel, looking a touch forlorn. She had only recently arrived, by air. She was wearing a khaki uniform of a sort, one supposed from Drury Lane, they must have at last got round to it. I sat beside her.

'What's it like?' she asked.

'Oh not too bad. You'll be absolutely fine. With no scenery or props to cart around you'll probably be flown to most areas. The troops will be wild with joy to see you and hear you sing. You'll have a great time.' We exchanged gossip. I was eager for news from home.

She was, of course, an enormous success.

The Gielgud Company arrived and the night they opened at the Excelsior Theatre Jack and I went together and sat in a box with Eric Dunstan. To hear Gielguid's magical voice was a theatrical treat. The Hamlet company were going on to play at the Garrison Theatre in Calcutta, which is where Jack was also bound.

Before he departed we needed to come to a decision about *Love in a Mist*. Because it was so popular we had to continue with it, but in order to freshen it up Pamela and I decided to swap roles. Jack said he would re-rehearse us two or three times before we set off and we would probably start with a few nights at the Garrison in Calcutta. I would play the bride and Pamela the part of the secretary. I felt that might save my sanity! Only actors know what it's like to be in the same play saying the same lines every night. If you're in a show for too long your mind can go suddenly blank because you know your lines too well. You don't know where you are in the play, which act, which day!

ELEVEN

Calcutta & Burma

Calcutta was a whole different world. To begin with there was no accommodation, everyone had to take whatever was given and be thankful if it had a bed. I was put into a cupboard-sized room in the Grand Hotel, which was far from grand, but it had a roof.

I have never seen so many men in uniform even in Cairo. They were either on leave or going to a new posting. I was told very soon after arrival by one of the officers that there were numerous rats, especially in the roof, and not to drink the water. It was rumoured there were drowned rats in the water tanks. This officer, full of good cheer about the state of the hotel was kindly seeing me through the heaving, perspiring, thirsty mass of men and overworked waiters in the so-called lounge. Every table full, day and night, with others standing by to grab any chair vacated. The whirling punkas were not able to compete with the atmosphere. The officer negotiated a path through a crowd of men pressing their offers of drinks on me; he steered me through the doors into the street, and hailed a taxi. He said he was a War Artist by the name of Richard and hoped we would meet again. I waved from the taxi and I was off to rehearse at the Garrison Theatre – used by Indian Companies in peacetime, now become the headquarters of ENSA.

I walked in and there was Jack, a leap of the heart and the feeling of relief and joy. As promised, he was getting a rehearsal together for Pam and myself, in the roles we had exchanged. It was just the change I needed, it was fun again. We were to have one more rehearsal and a dress rehearsal, as we were to do two or three nights at the Garrison. We finished work quite late, so Jack took me for dinner to a splendid restaurant called Firpos. Stafford Byrne joined us.

Well fed and content, I returned to my tiny room at the Grand Hotel but had difficulty in opening the door. To my horror I saw another bed had been squeezed in on which an Indian lady was already asleep. Though I was left with scant space to get into my own bed, my unexpected roommate was not the reason for my distress. That was caused by a large parrot – in a cage, thank heaven. As soon as I entered the bird flapped its wings, squawking and chattering in one of the many Indian languages. Feathers and seed were everywhere. It occupied the only remaining space in the room, on top of a small chest. The lady muttered some form of apology for the bird, turned over and went to sleep again. With my ridiculous phobia of flying wings and feathers, sleep was nearly impossible. I reversed my pillow to the other end of the bed so the parrot was not directly over my head. In a moment of desperation I recalled one of my grandmothers owning a parrot and when it became too talkative she placed a cover over it to shut it up. I did the same, covering the cage with some bedding. It worked – I slept.

We opened at the Garrison Theatre in Calcutta to much laughter and applause. The changeover had worked well and Jack was delighted. As the bride I had an entirely new outfit with a rather over the top going away suit crowned with an inane little hat. Dom and I got our laughs.

*   *   *   *   *

Once across the Hooghly River in East Bengal you are in another land. Even the change in trains – from bad to worse – came as a shock. No dining car at all, not even the grotty ones in which we whiled away the hours across the plains of central India. This was our first experience of being utterly alone in rather strange inhospitable territory and we soon realised the importance of travelling with our own supplies. We had been in the train all day, heading for somewhere called Comilla, with no idea where it was. Occasionally when we came to a grinding halt at some out-of-the-blue station or hut, Valhabh and the other bearer would rush in with tea. At some of the stations there would be an Indian with a tray offering flyblown food, Indian beer or soft drinks. It was growing dark and we had no idea where we were. Suddenly, at a halt, who should jump into our carriage but our friend the war correspondent, Stuart Gelder. He was never given a more grateful and effusive welcome. He was bearing cold drinks and sandwiches. Stuart was well acquainted with the area we were now entering. He knew it would get worse, but was kind enough not to tell us. Talking to him livened us up, and the rest of the journey quickly passed.

When we arrived, Comilla proved to be nothing more than a wayside halt. A wavering lantern guided us off the train and onto a short platform. Torches lit the way to waiting trucks. Our sergeant and helpers were, with difficulty, unloading our scenery and props, assisted by a lantern bearer. When our truck was found, we scrambled aboard, while seemingly endless numbers of soldiers disgorged from the train into the unwelcoming darkness.

We set off in the truck, bumping along the rough track past undergrowth and palm trees. This really was out in the wild. There was no sign of lights anywhere, just the comforting smell of Indian cooking fires – so there was life out there.

We jerked to a stop. Peering out of the tail of the truck we saw a bungalow with lights, so out we jumped. After the journey a thunder-box and refreshing wash were a priority. We found ourselves in some kind of general mess. There was not much in the way of home comforts, just trestle tables and chairs and a makeshift bar. The NAAFI was here, so if nothing else we knew we should be adequately fed on a steady diet of egg and chips.

Later that night we found ourselves at another dilapidated bungalow where Pam and I shared a room. We hadn't seen Joanna since Ceylon. I wasn't sure if she was in Jodhpur, or England, or if we might see her again in Calcutta.

Calcutta, I longed to be back there. With all its smells, dirt and sweltering millions it was preferable to this. The silence was creepy, broken only by the occasional shrieks and wails of predatory animals in the outer darkness. I realized we had left civilisation behind and shuddered.

I thought of Jack. How long before we were together again? Whatever, it would be too long.

A theatre had been rigged up by the Forces. It was certainly needed – entertainment was all the men had to look forward to – there was absolutely nothing else. I guessed Comilla was a place for re-posting after leave. A short stay before being sent on to some rotten foxhole to fight.

Every night the comedy played to a packed theatre. The audience joined in with wolf whistles and funny remarks – 'get up them stairs' – being a favourite. I enjoyed acting with Dom. He had a naturally gloomy face topped by his bright red hair and we always received a huge laugh when the landlady opened the door to the obvious newly-weds.

Sadly we were to lose Dom, He had received the welcome news that he was to return to England. He had done his time in India and would most likely be de-mobbed on his return. I would miss him.

Before we left Calcutta Jack had asked me if I knew a Captain Wilson. 'He claims to have known you at the Lyceum Theatre in Sheffield.' I looked puzzled. 'His full name is Donald Manning-Wilson.' Recognition came at once. 'Don Manning'. He was the first member of our Sheffield company to receive his call-up papers when he was nineteen.

When we finally met we looked at each other and just laughed and hugged. I could hardly believe that this Captain with a moustache was the same boy we bade a sad farewell to back in 1939, and that he and I were about to be in the same company again.

Jack told me he was to replace Dominic Roche as manager. 'As you said he was good in light comedy he can take over my role –

the stuttering lover.' We laughed at the memory of Jack's one night performance. I knew our 'ulcer' actor was hoping to be relieved. He had been immensely stoic, but the Indian diet was doing him nothing but harm.

Jack explained that Captain Wilson had been in Imphal, a dangerous area and had earned his leave. Jack thought it essential that we have an officer with us who was familiar with where we were to be travelling. There was to be another change. A Canadian peace-time actor, Robert Ayres, was on extended sick leave after severe fighting. He would play Dom Roche's role.

We were still in Comilla and the theatre was crammed every night because Forces were arriving and leaving constantly. We formed brief friendships over music played on Jack's wind-up gramophone, and records that he had given me – then the next moment it was all change and a whole new load of soldiers would arrive. Stuart Gelder had already disappeared, to where we had no idea.

One day our two new faces appeared – Captain Wilson and Lieutenant Ayres. Robert Ayres was good looking, though from rehearsal I soon realised he was not experienced in comedy, nevertheless we were fortunate to have our two new male acquisitions, both young experienced officers who proved perfect companions during the arduous weeks ahead. They brought with them Peggy Margolis, who lived in India, and remained with her parents throughout the war. As an amateur actress she had appeared in troop concerts. She joined us as the understudy, with the great asset of being fluent in Urdu.

Chittagong, a quaint name, but there was nothing quaint about the place. If there was a town I have no recollection of it, only the reddish mud churned up by so many vehicles and boots that it was difficult at times to manoeuvre a way through it. There was a depressing all-pervading damp about the area.

We were in the Arakhan, an area of India on the eastern side of the Bay of Bengal and billeted in a basha hut divided into cubicles. I remember I had one to myself, but I spent so little time in it that it gave me no pleasure. Everything was temporary, with a constantly changing population who were all on the move. There had been some awful recent battle with the Japanese, but we were kept in complete ignorance of the war. We were so used to this, so conditioned by the need for security, we made no conscious efforts to ask for information – anyway, it wouldn't have been given. I seem to recall that the Japanese either tried to make a landing south in the Arakhan, or they appeared out of the jungle. There was never a front in this war. This had been one hell of a battle, which we had won. It was difficult to imagine any sane people fighting over this unpleasant piece of land. But how can you think of sanity during a war.

Entertainment was desperately needed in Chittagong. There was a hall with a platform that was reasonably dry and *Love in a Mist* was on as soon as we could unpack and get the set up. The welcome was warm and we were glad to be there. There was a great camaraderie between us all; there were no barriers. Lack of reading matter was one of our greatest hardships, and mail hardly ever arrived unless you were in civilisation. Folks at home had learned to send newspapers and magazines, which sometimes arrived, to be passed around until they were rags. Some fellow lent me a book of verse, and I lent him a copy of *The Stage*. It was something to read.

* * * * *

Our next venue was surely a joke – Cox's Bazaar – could it be true? Yes – and to get there it meant a journey on a paddle steamer down the Brahmaputra River. The call was for 4.00 a.m.! I don't know why, but all wartime travel, air travel especially, commenced with the dawn.

I had managed a few hours sleep. We had worked hard under uncomfortable conditions at Chittagong but they were so sad to see us go we had been given a farewell party – a liquid farewell. The morning was cold and damp and I was wearing my uniform cloak for the first time. The boat seemed far from seaworthy, but as we were going down river I supposed we might make it. It was overcrowded, as most transport was, with people hanging on to anything they could hold. The river looked disgusting. Through the humidity and mist I could see beyond the water to the dunes and mud banks, and some vegetation in the far distance. 'Paddy fields,' someone volunteered. I looked into the filthy waters – a bloated baby floated past, drowned. We gazed in horror and sadness. Was it deliberate – an unwanted girl? Or just washed away from its mother while she was breaking her back, toiling?

We were by a door. Pam opened it. Inside the cabin were two bunks and we were in like a flash. We slept for the remainder of the long river journey, and were only roused from our stupor by the clank of a chain and padding of feet overhead. Pam and I struggled out onto the deck, breathing in the humid air. It was late afternoon.

The paddles of the ancient boat had ceased revolving so we were gently rolling. An anchor had been dropped though there was no jetty, or quayside. Coming towards us was a flotilla of flat rafts, each with a tattered sail, though their main progress was from poles and oars. It dawned on us that this was to be our final transport to Cox's Bazaar.

When we finally set out we were in a fleet of about eight rafts, all struggling to reach the shore. How they managed to load our scenery I can't imagine. Some foliage was visible through the prevailing mist, then a wooden jetty. The War Artist I'd met in Calcutta was on the same trip and on our arrival he drew a cartoon of me leaping ashore clutching on high a bottle of Heinz tomato ketchup: I always travelled with a bottle to help make the food edible.

We were now with an RAF unit hidden away in the undergrowth. Some we had met in Madras. We all slept under canvas in camouflaged tents. There was one basha for the mess and another for showers and thunder-boxes. I wondered where on earth we were going to perform the play, but I should have known how resourceful these men were. The stage they erected was just about big enough. I'm sure we could have performed *Love in a Mist* on anything by now, even a billiard table. The stage had lights and somewhere for us to dress behind the scenery. Audiences sat on benches or whatever could be found in the open. We were told that the area had been sprayed with an insecticide, but it seemed to have little impact on the droves of mosquitoes in this sweaty and humid jungle. I cannot say how long we were there, but the wind-up gramophone was a popular item during free time, and men would gather round it to listen. Beethoven's Pastoral Symphony was played so often I'm surprised the record survived. With the performances and the music, it was easy to forget how close to the fighting we really were. One night as I was taking the gramophone across to our tent, an officer ran up to help me.

'I thought you should know that Blackie bought it . . .' That was all he said. I was silent, so was he.

I longed to ask where and how he 'bought it', but all I said was, 'He was here with us, yesterday.'

His comrade nodded. 'He'd been lucky many times, and it just ran out.'

That had to be their attitude to death, none other. It could be the man at my side next time. I thought about Blackie as we were playing the music: so young, so full of life – they all were. Here we were buried in the jungle with the 14th Army, like them we felt lost to the world.

'Blackie' – I wondered why the nickname, brown eyes, glittering with fun. I thought of his parents.

* * * * *

We had to return to Chittagong. The very thought of that river journey filled me with dread. My friendly War Artist was also travelling back. He wanted to take photographs of the area that had been so much fought over. Instead of the rafts and boat he was taking a jeep. There were two spare places so I asked Pam how she felt about joining us. She was delighted to avoid the unsteady raft and overcrowded paddle steamer. When we informed the others, Don Wilson, our new company manager, merely raised his eyebrows and wished us luck.

After an hour of bumping and swerving to avoid shell holes and rutted tank tracks, I began to wonder at the wisdom of our choice. This had never been a road, just a jungle track, scarred by vehicles and tramping feet. But we pressed on, shaking and jolting. At one point I feared we might turn over, but jeeps are reliable and the mud had been baked hard by the heat. Conversation was limited, the driving needed concentration, and also Pam and I had to hang on in order to avoid being thrown out. I did gather however that the camp we had been staying in was quite close to the airstrip, which had been hectically busy transporting men, mules, vehicles and equipment. It was strange that we had not heard the roar of the aircraft. Perhaps the density of the jungle deadened the noise. The strip was heavily guarded by Sikh gunners, whose aim was said to be deadly. After twelve hours of being thrown around in the jeep, we longed to be back in Chittagong! We felt as if we would never be able to walk or sit again, all we wanted was to lie absolutely flat. Our belief that the jeep would be quicker than the boat proved unfounded. The rest of the company were there to greet us, looking a little smug.

We left Chittagong with no regrets for another unknown destination: the Arakhan behind us, we emerged into the foothills of Assam. It was now late November and the climate was perfect. There were beautiful trees, amongst them the giant and colourful Banyan, green grass and pretty villages, the land was completely different and lovely. We even enjoyed the luxury of staying in well-appointed Rest Houses, a clean and welcome change from the basha hut. Our base was an army camp of some permanence with a theatre, from which we made sorties to other camps. It was great. We could walk among the trees, admire the many small temples or enjoy a buying spree in the bazaar. It was like a holiday.

*　*　*　*　*

'Where is Shillong?' I asked Don Wilson.

'Very high in the mountains,' he replied.

There was no point in pressing for more information, he possibly knew no more than his instructions to transport us there. Since our departure from England this had become one long mystery tour. We played in an RAF station, whose commanding officer kindly offered us a Dakota aircraft to take us to a nearby USA base, saying that from there the Americans would transport us to Shillong. It seems Shillong could only be reached by road – and that usually meant a mule.

At the first streak of daylight we were squeezed into a dilapidated Dakota. Weight was a problem, so after an aborted trial run the pilot suggested we squash ourselves as far forward as possible, while the sergeant and corporal in charge of the scenery were instructed to lean against it to prevent it slipping. Someone else was told to hang on to the door in case it flew open. We took off with a sigh of relief, then went through the same procedure for landing.

We received a warm welcome from our Yankee friends. Whilst willing hands unloaded the aircraft we were escorted into the officer's mess for 'a real American breakfast'. For a while now food had become unimportant to me, you just ate what was on offer, either because of hunger or because you didn't know when you might have another meal. It was mostly unappetising, but I always thought of the shortages at home – one egg a month, a piece of cheese the size of a postage stamp and so on. The Americans always had the best food and were very generous with it.

Over the meal, and many cups of excellent American coffee, the journey up to Shillong was discussed. They would provide a bus and three-ton lorries, but two splendid young men had attached themselves to Pam and myself, who offered us a lift in a jeep. Apparently, it was a steep climb up a narrow winding road, uncomfortable in a bus and awful in a truck. They wouldn't take no for an answer and assured us that the views were spectacular.

I will never regret or forget that hair-raising magnificent drive. Looking out at a grey damp London I often remember the four of us on that glorious morning driving round endless hairpin bends, going ever higher. The drop below us became deeper and more dangerous but we did not care. We sang our hearts out, mostly from *Oklahoma* 'Oh what a beautiful morning – oh what a beautiful day.' It was, and the scenery was breathtaking.

Pam and I had no idea why we were heading for what seemed liked the top of the world, we encountered nothing – our convoy must be well behind. After we had been climbing for several hours we came across a lone building hanging over the precipice. Men are fortunate in that they can urinate against or into anything; we women have a more difficult time. Pam and I leapt out to enquire what was available in this odd building, leaving the fellows to it. The door was eventually answered by a strange old woman with almost Mongolian features. Somehow we managed to explain our urgent need. She beckoned us in and took us to a room, which was empty except for a hole in the floor. The stench of urine was so strong it was obvious for what it was intended. Desperation can overcome squeamishness – it was really a question of a good aim. Pam forced herself to use the hole after me. We gave the old crone some annas, and reeled out into the fresh air. Our waiting companions were grinning, they knew about the facilities on offer. Another time I vowed I would forget modesty.

As we climbed ever upwards we began to see signs of life: mountain goats with great horns and shaggy coats down to their hooves. The people were short and stubby with flat features and wore blankets with skin or fur boots tied round their legs. It was so cold we stopped to wrap up: the men in their flying jackets, us in our capes. We arrived in Shillong in near darkness, after driving since early morning. We were stiff and cold, but it was an experience I would not have missed.

Don Wilson had given me the address of our billet and we knocked on the door, it was difficult in the darkness to tell whether we were in a village or a small town. The fresh mountain air was freezing.

An English lady of uncertain age welcomed us politely but eyed the two men with suspicion. She showed us into a bare room with a heavenly log fire, which we clustered around immediately. Our driver produced a bottle of Scotch – glasses were found, and we had a wonderfully warming drink. Going to investigate the accommodation, a bedroom with two beds, not cots, we broached the subject with our hostess of our American friends, and where they might sleep. 'Not here,' was the flat response. They could stay for the meal, which was to be served shortly, but they must sleep elsewhere. We had hoped to let them have our bedrolls to grab a few hours sleep by the fire, before they faced the descent back to their base. I could sense it was useless even to suggest it. The woman probably assumed we wanted a night of sex – after that journey! I am sure she lived an unworldly isolated life. We never did meet the husband, a civil servant, or anybody else in the house at all. I was thankful to be there only briefly. Both Pam and I felt like unwelcome interruptions in their dull but untroubled lives.

The Americans were not surprised to discover that there was 'no room at the inn', but happily enjoyed the dinner. When Don and the rest arrived at about ten o'clock, I explained our dilemma. He took our companions away with him, and promised to arrange something. I hope they managed a few hours kip and a safe journey back. There was no way of knowing.

We had no performances in Shillong as there was no one to entertain, just a few English, presumably tea planters or government officials. The compensation was the locals, who were both friendly and fascinating to look at. It was a beautiful location with spectacular views of the distant Himalayas and the slopes of the tea plantations, but intensely cold, especially at night. I was glad of the blanket provided with the bedroll and also of the Burma Green cloak. When I was given it in Bombay I couldn't imagine what use it would be, but it proved to be one of the most versatile garments.

I realised that going all the way up to Shillong was merely for the purpose of descending the other side. The journey down in the bus was very different to the upwards adventure, but neither was the route – it was much shorter and not so steep. We were on the lowlands once more and thankful to be warmer.

*   *   *   *   *

All these weeks and no word from Jack – he was in everything I thought and did, always at the back of my mind. I realised that communication was impossible. If Don had received a signal from him he would have told me. We finally reached what we hoped would be our last destination before leave, a place called Dimapur at the end of the India Railway. The town had been evacuated of all the women, children and civilians, leaving it empty save for a large garrison to defend it from the Japanese. If they had succeeded in their aim to capture Dimapur, the Japanese would have gained access to the railway and thus perhaps India itself. I looked around aghast. 'What stopped them?' I asked Don.

'Just a few very brave, desperate men in the battle of Kohima.'

He added that he had a signal from Jack. He read the usual brief wishes and thanks to all, but more importantly a signal from Bill Slim, the popular and revered general in command of the fighting forces on the India/Burma border. Jack had intended to withdraw our company for much needed leave and reorganisation, but his plan had been overruled by a signal from Slim himself. The gist of it was that on no account was *Love in a Mist* to be withdrawn. It had proved a great morale booster for his troops and he wished the company to advance from Dimapur as far forward as possible, and continue performing so popular an entertainment. There was no way Jack could refuse such an order. We were disappointed about Christmas leave, but proud that our efforts had been appreciated and received such praise.

We played at Dimapur for several days. The soldiers there seemed to have been left behind in the aftermath of furious activity. Field hospitals had by now almost been emptied, the wounded moved further away. An air of boredom hung over the garrison. To refresh ourselves, and the play, we rehearsed daily, as Pam and I had swopped parts again.

Our next destination was Kohima, high up in the peaks. It meant little to me, but Don filled me in on the way up. He had fought on the other side of Kohima, so had Robert Ayres, endeavouring with everything they could muster to halt the Japanese advance, who, after crossing the Chindwin River, had eventually surrounded and laid siege to Imphal. Neither of them wanted to talk about it. I was just amazed that they were both so calm about returning to a scene of such fierce fighting. I suppose playing in a farce would be an antidote. Don was driving the jeep and I was beside him, Pam and Robert were in the back, the rest of the company following. Don knew the route well and advised us to have warm clothing ready as we were going up to five thousand feet with very low temperatures at night.

As we climbed, leaving the stubble and rubbish behind, the terrain became more lush and finally jungle. Then came the first Bailey bridge. All the bridges across the ravines had been blown up to hinder the Japanese advance. Their simple steel and timber replacements seemed unsteady, and I wondered how our lorries would fare. I was in my Burma outfit, with boots, and bush hat to keep the blinding sun out of my eyes. About noon we stopped for a sandwich and a stretch, by now we were in dense jungle. Don and Robert made for one side of the road, Pam and I the other. Don shouted at us not to venture into undergrowth, it was full of leeches. They peed happily into the jungle and looked the other way while we tussled with our trousers and boots. Military uniform and female anatomy do not go well together.

On and on we drove. The sun climbed higher, the jungle became less dense, the track well worn by Army vehicles.

Then, suddenly we noticed a tiny wooden cross on the roadside. I drew in a breath.

'They become more frequent from now,' said Don quietly. He

was right. I could hardly bear to look at them, knowing that the soldier beneath each home-made cross of twigs had been buried in a hurry. No one had time to weep for him. What about the family and friends at home who loved him, but who would never know about these makeshift graves? The heroism of those men, too many of whom lay dead, had prevented the Japanese from descending out of the jungle to that bloody railway.

The sun disappeared behind the vast brooding hills. Our destination was a camp just below the summit, which had to be reached before dark. We wrapped our cloaks around us and drove on.

From our reception and greeting on arrival, we might have been royalty. There were cheers as the men followed us into camp, willing to help in every way they could. They were so thankful to see us. Hot tea was produced and thick sandwiches, anything to make us comfortable. Sadly, we couldn't put on a show, we were only there for one night, but the officer in charge told us his men would be able to attend the show in Kohima, one group at a time. Apparently a treat awaited us there: a theatre had been constructed and we were to open it. The anticipation was immense.

The camp was under canvas and not large. There was a tent for the women and one for the men, but we lacked warm clothing. Headquarters could not have realised the extremes of climate we would meet, or that we would be away so long. We mentioned this in the mess and when we retired to our tent there was a collection of blankets for us. The corporal who brought them asked if some men's vests would help – oh yes please, anything. The next morning the corporal brought the vests, which were enormous. The sleeves were well over my elbows and the length reached to my knees but, my heaven, they were warm. No one cared how bulky they looked, we wore them most of the time from then on, and they were wonderful in bed.

We left camp after breakfast, climbing once again. Don hoped to be in Kohima by midday, unless there was trouble with the road. It had been in a rough state when he had last seen it. As we drove it appeared to have been well cleared. Just more little crosses, one

The Gateway to India: first seen on arrival, last on departure. This photograph, with the British fleet in the background, was taken by war correspondent Stuart Gelder.

The depleted *Private Lives* company in front of the Taj Mahal Hotel – digs for we three girls. Standing between Joanna and myself, our wonderful A.S.M. Ron.

A detail from the poster for the Concert Party. Jack Hawkins, now a Captain in the Royal Welch Fusiliers, had been asked by the commanding officer of 2nd Division to provide entertainment for his troops, which he did so successfully that he was soon transferred to organise ENSA throughout the Indian subcontinent.

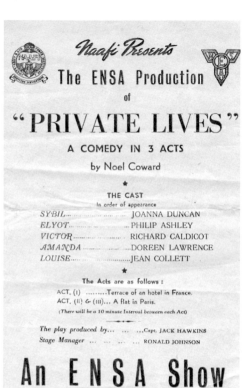

Above Once we reached India, Jack directed and revitalised *Private Lives*. Playing the lead, I had the benefit of most of the attention.

Above right Jack liked this picture of me, which he carried around.

Below A Bombay beach party hosted by Prince Ali Khan. Left to right: Philip Ashley, Col. Eric Dunstan (reclining), Prince Ali, a Turkish prince, Joanna, Pamela, Jack and myself.

Crossing the plains of India in trains – a station halt with a rather fed-up looking company and clobber.

With the RAF in Ceylon, and one of their amazing inventions: a solar heated shower in the middle of the jungle – Pamela, Elsie Orf and myself patiently waiting our turn.

A hazy shot on the foggy Brahmaputra River en route for Cox's Bazaar with our two newcomers: in the foreground, Robert Ayres, and behind Don Wilson.

Above The cast of *Love in a Mist* (minus myself), our hugely popular comedy: Joanna, our 'Duckfarmer Sergeant', and his corporal assistant, Pamela, and Dom Roche, who's had more than enough.

Right A faded shot, my only one of Vallabh – my constant companion, helper and friend.

Below After a day's filming in Bombay Studios, visiting Phillip Ashley in hospital, I was unaware I was being photographed by Cecil Beaton.

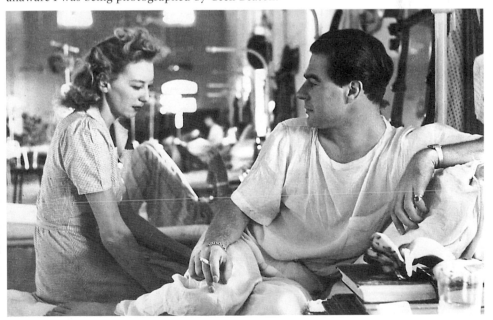

Two photographs kindly provided by the Imperial War Museum (IND 3698, IND 3430).
Above The blasted trees on the hill of Kohima are a terrible reminder of the destruction
we encountered arriving soon after the dreadful battle that laid waste to a once peaceful
hill-station, yet proved decisive in the outcome of the war in the Far East.

Below Down the dusty and cratered road from Kohima to Imphal, or what remained of
the town after a siege and so much fighting. Many of the bridges had been blown up by
the Japanese, others were booby-trapped.

Burma: myself and Angela in a wet and ruined Rangoon, thankful for our Burma Greens.

Angela and I trying to look as graceful as the Burmese dancers (girl on the left unknown). The photograph was taken by a publicity officer.

Last visit to Juhu Beach, Bombay, early 1946 – waiting for a passage home to an uncertain future in post-war Britain.

All uncertainties behind us. A sadly water-damaged but favourite photograph of my husband Jack and myself in 1954. We had returned from New York, and looked so happy because our two little boys were on the platform to meet us.

with a pathetic tin hat on it. Then we came to the trees and my blood began to run cold. There was not a leaf on them, the trees of a battleground. Pictures I had seen as a child of the Western Front in France flashed through my mind. These trees, blasted leafless, stood stark against the skyline, with twisted broken branches, stripped of bark and burnt black. Finally we drove into battle-torn Kohima, once a pleasant hilltop tea plantation town with a District Commissioner, a club and tennis courts. To me it was haunted and so it should be. Many men, both Japanese and British, had fought here to the death: the cost in lives was appalling.

We drew up at a group of tents and were given a warm welcome. They were anxious to meet us, but most of all to show us the theatre they had built, of which they were right to be proud. It was a theatre anyone would be happy to play in, with a real proscenium arch – not seen since Calcutta. There were dressing rooms and an ample stage from which you could glimpse the distant Himalayas beyond a line of valleys and snow-capped hills. Why had they built it? An officer said that when the aftermath of battle had been cleared, a depressing job, the soldiers needed a more uplifting and constructive activity. 'Building this theatre I suppose was a therapy.'

I told him how delighted we were to be opening it.

*   *   *   *   *

I gathered most of my information about the Battle of Kohima from Don Wilson. The objective of the Japanese Army was to invade India. After Burma they succeeded in crossing the great Chindwin River and then made their way through dense jungle to the only road over the mountains to Imphal. They surrounded the town, cutting it off and completely isolating the garrison. Having taken Imphal, a crack Japanese division, huge in numbers and sensing victory, fought their way through the jungle to Kohima, which one imagines they considered a push-over. Once captured, they could easily advance down the mountain road to Dimapur and the beginning of the railroad to India. But the Japanese had not reckoned with the few hundred men hastily sent up to hold them at bay, mostly West Kents with some Sikhs and Rajputs. Later they were joined by Gurkhas and Assam soldiers, who had managed to make it through the jungle from Imphal, all trained and tried, but exhausted fighters.

Out of the five hundred men who were first faced with holding off a whole division of fanatically driven Japanese, only a few remained alive after the siege of Kohima. They were near to death from wounds or sheer exhaustion. Food ran out as the sixteen days of hell passed; water was rationed to half a mug a day for each man. Sleep was impossible except for naps snatched in cramped, damp foxholes between bombardments and vicious hand to hand fighting. The so-called hospital had been an enlarged dug-out with only a dim hurricane lamp for light. The wounded men were placed in slit trenches cut into the earth to try and protect them. There they had to suffer the pain and discomfort, but most died or were blown away. The few who survived were finally taken to the ambulances when relief came. They must have been at the utter limit of their endurance.

Two Victoria Crosses were won at Kohima, but the British and Indian forces lost 4,000 men, dead, missing and wounded during the battle. It was to prove the turning point in the Burma Campaign and brought to an end the Japanese offensive into India. Mountbatten was later to describe it as one of 'the greatest battles in history.'

Being in Kohima was an experience I will never forget.

*   *   *   *   *

We were under canvas, everyone had to be, there were no buildings left standing. The tent that Pam and I occupied was more of a bivouac, and so Arctic at night we were grateful for our army vests.

The opening of the theatre was an event. We were proud to be playing on the site of what had been the scene of so much courage. The auditorium was full of soldiers, apart from those stationed at Kohima, others had appeared from hidden jungle camps, by jeep or three-ton lorries. It was a joy to hear them laughing and forgetting, joining in the amiable fun of the farcical *Love in a Mist*. Afterwards we would get-together over mugs of coffee or beer. We spent well over a week there and were cheered every night.

During the day we walked cautiously about, and always accompanied. Although the ground had been cleared of mines and booby traps, no one wanted to take risks. We saw the desolate ruins of the District Commissioner's bungalow, once surrounded by beautiful shrubs and flowering trees, with the tennis court at the front where some of the worst battles had been fought. The once well cared-for court had been left strewn with bodies. All the surrounding basha huts were burnt out or demolished.

A favourite ploy of the Japanese was sniping from the trees. They would bind themselves to the branches and pick off targets. If they were shot in return they didn't fall, they just hung there. They were more fearful of being taken prisoner than death, and their numbers dropped as more were killed and the trees became blasted and bare. Wandering through the mud we came to a tank on its side. Shuddering at the thought of the men trapped inside I turned away to fall straight into a foxhole, which contained a boot. Japanese? For an awful moment I wondered if there was anything inside it. They pulled me out and I ruefully rubbed my ankle. The debris of war was all around us, tin hats, even the occasional Japanese sabre. For me Kohima was full of desolation; there were ghosts in the atmosphere.

Before we left the headman of the Naga tribe and some of his people emerged from the bush and were warmly welcomed. The Naga tribes had lived nearby in their villages in peaceful isolation until 1944. They were silent and invisible and proved wonderful allies as their life of hunting, using traps and jungle weapons, was often more effective than modern equipment. At the height of the siege their knowledge of the jungle had enabled some of the walking wounded to be evacuated during one desperate night. The Nagas guided them along tracks in the jungle to below the 42nd Milestone, which had been blockaded by the Japanese when they surrounded Kohima. From there they limped the long route to Dimapur. Remembering the pathetic crosses we had seen on our way up, I wondered how many had made it.

The headman spoke little English but some Urdu, sufficient to thank the officer for his kind words and for the relief the defeat of the Japanese had brought his tribe. He then gave us women Naga cloths of beautiful heavy woven cotton, black with wide borders of orange and green. The Naga men wore them over the shoulder, the women wrapped theirs around their bodies. It was indeed a special gift for which we gave thanks as best we could. Mine has remained with me and always will.

Before we left we were taken to a clearing to see the memorial that had just been erected. The stonemasons were still working on it, carving the names of the men who had died defending this tiny spot. They had just finished the inscription, which has since become world famous as the Kohima Epitaph:

> When you go home
> Tell them of us and say
> For their tomorrow
> We gave our today

Tears welled, my throat choked. We stood there silently with our own thoughts. I saw some names from Jack's division, the 2nd Division (the Cross Keys) amongst those being engraved. He could have been with them. I felt guilty at my immense relief that he was safely in Calcutta. Fate had chosen otherwise for him.

*   *   *   *   *

Early next morning in the jeep with Don, Pam and Bob in the rear, we bade a warm farewell to the friends we were leaving behind. As the sun rose, I looked at the unforgettable sight of the distant Himalayas covered with golden mist. A bird began to sing, and another answered. So, life was returning.

The way down to Imphal was less steep than the road up to Kohima, but it was much rougher with a great deal of bumping and skidding trying to avoid shell holes and great lumps of mud. The jungle was less dense, and the surrounding trees not blasted and burned like those at Kohima.

Presently Bob spoke. 'You see that tree over there?' We all looked to where he was pointing. 'I was holed up there behind it with a Jap firing at me from that bush.' I hadn't realised that Bob Ayres had been involved in the desperate battle to prevent the Japanese taking the road up to Kohima.

'What did you do?' asked Pam.

'Peed myself with fright and fired back.'

'Whatever happened in the end?' I queried.

'I'm here, thank God.'

We all fell silent again.

Imphal was of course a shattered town; it had been heavily bombarded, though as it was almost dusk when we arrived it was not easy to grasp the state of our surroundings. We women were installed in a bungalow. It had been damaged, but it did have a roof, also a sitting room with a fireplace. As it was so cold at night and Christmas was almost upon us we had visions of lighting a fire – there was enough debris around to feed it. We had a bedroom and a bathroom, though no running water – we could ask for no more.

The welcoming Entertainments Officer told us there was a theatre cum hall waiting for us, where they had previously shown a few old films. They were looking forward to *Love in a Mist*, which had, apparently, become famous among the Forces. Some had even seen it before.

We opened the following night and the event was made more special by General Slim himself attending. He was wildly popular with his men, who would do anything for him. He had his own headquarters in well-camouflaged tents a little away from the others. After the show he came backstage to greet and thank us, say how delighted he was we had finally arrived in Imphal. He invited us to take tea with him in his tent, which we gladly accepted.

In due course our bungalow became a home from home, specially once we had the fire flaming merrily away. Many of the officers and men we had met before on our travels, a few I even remembered from *The Athlone Castle*. They would come in for tea, or bring bottles of beer. They had been through a lousy time and there was more ahead; some had been away from England for years. It helped to sit around and talk of home news – although we had very little. There was still no mail, though by Christmas 1944 we knew that the Allied advance was slowly pushing back the Germans towards the Rhine. But Europe was so far away. We had no details.

Just before Christmas we took the show to the 97th Milestone – the furthest point we were allowed to go. We were told it would be rough and cold, so out came the army issue vests to wear under our flimsy stage costumes. It was about an hour's journey and Don suggested we dress and make up before we leave. We set off in three-ton lorries. The stage was a temporary affair in a jungle clearing, but with a tarpaulin roof and footlights. As soon as our lorries arrived the soldiers started cheering and running towards us, eager to help in any way they could. There were hundreds of them, many from camps scattered in the jungle. We were shown our 'dressing room' by an apologetic captain, who guided us into what was a chilly foxhole with a Kerosene lamp and a cracked mirror hanging from an earthen wall. We were thankful we had taken Don's advice about make-up.

We were ready to begin. Although it was freezing, the audience sat outside on ground sheets or whatever was available. The stage was set, the curtain made of army blankets. Cheers and clapping greeted us as we raised the curtain. We got off to a great start with whistles, laughter and general letting off steam, just what was needed. Then disaster. Midway through the second act all the lights failed. Yells of fury and frustration from the audience. What to do? Hurricane lamps were seen waving about in the darkness, there was a flurry of activity around what one could see was a generator. We all stood still on the stage, wary of falling into that foxhole in the darkness. To disappoint these wonderful men would have been unbearable. An officer with a torch groped his way towards us. 'Wouldn't you know, it's a bloody Jap generator that we captured.' Getting its own back? I thought.

Mugs of tea were produced to warm us – I had long since lost any feeling in my feet.

Suddenly there was a blaze of light, so strong it was impossible to see out front, and cheers from everyone, including the cast. We were asked to restart from where we had been interrupted, but needed no prompting. Incredibly, the blaze of front lighting was coming from jeeps. Our impatient audience had lined up every jeep they could muster and aimed all their headlights at the stage. We proceeded happily to the end with laughs louder than ever. Afterwards we were taken to a basha hut where some precious whisky was produced and, my heavens, was it welcome.

The next day I awoke aware that something was not right. I felt unwell, but worse, the glands in my neck were swollen so much I could hardly swallow my morning tea. As the day progressed so did the lumps. My temperature rose and I wheezed and coughed; my neck was agony. I didn't think I could play that night, and it was decided that Peggy should replace me. The Medico said I should stay in bed. I felt lonely, ill and depressed. I wanted to be working as usual, but I could hardly utter, let alone swallow. It would be Christmas in two days. One year ago I was on a ship in the Indian Ocean nearing Bombay – could it really be only a year? It was unbelievable – so much had happened. I thought of Jack – was he in Calcutta? He had changed my life, my whole outlook, my future. How I missed him, he was never far from my thoughts, but no word of course. I wondered where we would be sent to next. I got out of bed and staggered into the living room. It was empty, but I wondered who had once lived here and how they had escaped when the Japs advanced.

Surely we were at the end of the road, literally, and due some leave. We had been working and travelling non-stop for about five months.

The following day was Christmas Eve. My neck was still swollen but not so painful. On Christmas Day everyone joined in for the big open-air service. I stayed in, lying on the ancient horsehair sofa. After the service I had several callers, who all brought either food or drink so we could celebrate. I was relieved to have company and began to feel better.

With Christmas behind us, my future seemed uncertain. My temperature was now subnormal. One of the quacks called with a jeep to take me to the field hospital for a chest x-ray. Whilst I was there the senior Medical Officer spoke of my returning to Calcutta. My heart leapt – Jack was there. He said I was not only overdue for a rest, but needed a proper overhaul by a civilian doctor. 'It's time you returned to a more civilized area, I will write a chitty for you.'

The more I thought of New Year's Eve, the more determined I was to fly to Calcutta. But how? I asked Don what was to happen to the company. He said they would leave as soon as they had finished there and could get away, though transport might be difficult to arrange.

TWELVE

Calcutta, Rangoon & Bombay

Sitting alone whilst the others were working, who should leap up the steps but my very own knight in shining armour, my old friend Richard the War Artist. He had heard where I was and that I'd been ill. We exchanged news, and then I asked him how I could get out of Imphal. 'I can't work and have been ordered to return to Headquarters for leave, but no one knows how.' He did – apparently the best way to get on a plane was for the two of us to go together. He needed to get back to Calcutta urgently and said having a pretty girl with him would help.

We agreed he would collect me to be at the runway at dawn, which is when most flights took off and, literally, hitch a ride. I told Don of my intentions. He agreed I needed a thorough check-up to find out what was ailing me, and added I should give his regards to the major. I crept out at 4.00 a.m., trying not to disturb the others. I was ready when the jeep drove up.

The airstrip was busy. Planes were being loaded in the half-light. There were troops with mules being coaxed or pushed up ramps at the rear of the aircraft, along with supplies and machinery. We stayed in the jeep for a while. The light was becoming stronger, a vivid streak of red across the sky heralding the dawn.

As soon as the planes were loaded and the wretched mules coaxed aboard, they careered down the runway and were suddenly airborne. A silence after so much din. Richard went off to make some inquiries, returning with news of a small plane flying to Calcutta, dropping down at Mandalay to refuel and deliver mail, then further deliveries en route for Calcutta. The pilot would squeeze us on board if we would help drop the mail. We were delighted. We waved to our driver to let him know, then embarked with our kitbags. What luck – we were swiftly on our way.

About two hours later we descended into Mandalay to deposit the precious mail. The landing was bumpy, just a makeshift wartime airstrip in a jungle clearing, but the pilot knew how to find it.

'You've time for some tea while we refuel,' he told us.

There was a queue outside the field kitchen. I joined it. So this was the famous Mandalay. It did not look in the least like Kipling's Mandalay to me. But we had landed in the aftermath of bitter fighting. A cheery soldier was mixing the brew: a large jerrycan of water was bubbling away on a charcoal fire. First a packet of tea was tipped in, followed by the contents of a large can of Nestles milk, and well stirred. I was about to remove myself from the queue, but being the only woman there I was conspicuous.

'Here you are, Miss – lovely cuppa char,' he said, handing me a mug-full. As they were all watching me with faces wreathed in smiles, I was forced to take a sip. My stomach heaved. I had eaten no breakfast, and heaven knows when I would eat again, but I could not force that sticky sweet dark brown concoction down my throat. Smiling my thanks, I edged away to a convenient bush to empty the mug.

When we took off again it was with a second airman, who sat up front with the pilot, while Richard and I crouched among the mailbags. The pilot's skill was amazing. After spotting a tiny remote clearing in the jungle, he flew around until a sheet was laid out or some other marking. The other airman joined us in the rear and with Richard's help pulled open the door – no easy job, after which we heaved out the mail sacks, trying not to follow them. We then flew low over the clearing to make sure the precious cargo had landed safely, then banked and flew on to the next camp. I thought of all the men cut off down below in that dark, dank, unfriendly jungle. One hoped our delivery did not give away their location. We were kept busy for the whole flight, which was just as well: Richard was beginning to look pale green.

I began to wonder where on earth I should stay when I arrived in Calcutta, I had given it no thought, I just wanted to be there. What if Jack was not there? I didn't have time to ponder, it was now late afternoon and we were making our descent to Dum Dum airport. Once we'd landed, we found a taxi into town. My first task was to contact our headquarters, who didn't even know I was coming. Richard suggested we head for the Great Eastern Hotel, where he knew the manager; there would be no room, but he might be able to squeeze me in temporarily. The taxi pulled up at the hotel and Richard made for the desk. I was looking around for a telephone, also longing for a wash and clean up. It had been a long time since four o'clock that morning. Richard came back. 'All they can offer you tonight is a bed in the Transit Room. I'm going up to the men's dormitory on the top floor. They can find me a cubicle later as there's an officer leaving tonight.'

'What's the Transit Room?' I enquired.

'Pretty awful but it has a bathroom. Tomorrow I *might* be able to find a room for you.'

A bearer came to collect my kit bag and knapsack and take me to the Transit Room, which in peacetime was possibly a banqueting hall or luxury suite. Now it had as many beds as could be squeezed in with just room to walk between them. My belongings were dumped on a bed. I've never seen so many women in one room, and their din and chatter reminded me of a chorus dressing room.

I spied a telephone – in use of course – I'm sure it was all the time. At the far end of the room was an ironing board, also in use, and there was a bathroom where I could hear water running. I discovered there was a waiting list for that so I suppose it was rarely cleaned, oh, don't be fussy, but where was the lavatory – another queue. Need was great so I was forced to join it. That achieved, I set out to find a telephone. When I told the manager behind the front desk I needed to make an urgent telephone call to my headquarters before 6.00 p.m. then only five minutes away, he took me into his office and indicated the phone.

My heart thumping, I found the number of the office at the

Garrison Theatre and dialled it, afraid I might find that Jack was not in Calcutta. When the secretary answered, I asked for Major Hawkins and gave my name. 'A moment, please.' He must be there – but even before relief flooded through me he was on the line. 'Darling where are you?'

'Calcutta,' I replied.

'But how for heaven's sake? This is wonderful. Are you alone? Did you fly? We must meet at once.'

I interrupted to tell him where I was and that I would explain everything when we met. I also hoped he was free for dinner, and soon, because I hadn't eaten all day. By coincidence he was installed in the officer's dormitory upstairs in the same hotel, and said he would be back as soon as he could close up the office. I asked for time for a bath and a change and we agreed to meet in an hour. Bravely, he said he would call for me at the Transit Room.

'God, it's wonderful, I can't believe you're here, there's so much to say, see you soon, so very soon.'

I walked out of that office on air. Gone was the fatigue that had plagued me with the mystery illness, gone was the hunger, I was in a heaven of my own. I was suddenly alive. I must hurry, what can I wear, my hair, my face, must have a bath. Back into the hen house, through the din I spoke to the girl in the camp bed next to mine about the bath. 'Hurry now,' she urged, 'the two booked to follow me have received their call to go.' I didn't know what she was talking about but flung myself into the bathroom, claiming it by turning on the taps and slamming the door behind me.

Singing away, I luxuriated in the warm water until a banging on the door cut me short. Five minutes was the time allotted. I pulled out the only dress I had, now screwed into a ball, and prayed that the iron might make it wearable. Sitting on the bed, the only place, my chatty neighbour informed me that the rush was slowing a little. The girls that were here for the night, or part of it, all had dates so they had either left or completed their turn with the iron. She advised me to keep a watchful eye on it, which I did whilst trying to fix my face and hair – not easy on a camp bed with only a small hand mirror. My dress ironed, I discovered a long mirror on the back of the bathroom door. When at last I found my high heels hiding at the bottom of my kit bag, I began to feel quite glamorous. I was ready and waiting. I looked around the Transit Room, already several of the other women had departed and others arrived. All were in the Forces of some kind but wearing mufti, so we were anonymous. Everyone was awaiting a call to a train, plane or to rejoin a unit. No one spent more than one night in here, if that. All night there were constant calls, so there was no sleep for anyone.

There was a knock on the door and the nearest girl answered and went outside. She came back 'Anyone by the name of Lawrence?' I stood up. 'My, there is a gorgeous Major out there for you.'

There he stood. We looked at each other, just took hands, and walked away. There was no need to speak just to hold his hand was enough. He guided me down to the dining room where he had a table. Drinks arrived and then we began to talk. It seemed as if we could never close the floodgates over everything that had to be said between us.

Although I had been hungry, now that I had food in front of me my appetite had disappeared – excitement and emotion had taken over. Jack urged me to eat, he was concerned about my health. He knew I wouldn't have deserted the company and returned alone without a good reason – this was true, no matter how desperately I wanted to be with him. I reassured him, telling that I had recovered but had been instructed by the M.O. to return to civilization if possible. He told me how happy he was to have me there, whatever the reason.

'Tomorrow is New Year's Eve,' I reminded him, the anniversary of my arrival in Bombay – our fateful meeting on the second day of 1944. We talked of how we might spend the evening. Right here in the hotel seemed the best choice; there would be dancing and, most importantly, Jack knew he could get a table.

We wandered slowly along the hotel corridor to the Transit Room. The lights had been dimmed and it was late, the time had flown. Jack took my face in his hands.

'You must be exhausted after such a long day.'

'I'm so happy, I don't think I could go to sleep, not that there will be much opportunity tonight.'

He put my head on his shoulder and stroked my hair, 'You know I want to give you everything in life. Everything you desire you shall have. I shall work just for your happiness.'

I looked up at him, 'I only want you, that would be my happiness.'

I opened the door and entered with my head and heart singing. I hardly noticed the many bodies, some trying to sleep, others trying to dress or undress depending on whether they were coming or going. I sat on the narrow camp bed and undressed trying not to disturb my neighbours, though all around me girls were packing or unpacking. I just slid into the bed in my own blissful cocoon.

Before rushing off to the theatre the following morning I called at the desk. There was a message from Richard, he had tried to contact me the previous evening to suggest dinner (I felt guilty), and it was all right about the room, he had been able to arrange one for me. I couldn't believe my good fortune. I raised my eyes to the manager, Richard's friend, who merely said, 'Your room will be ready after midday Miss Lawrence. I'd be obliged if you wouldn't mention this to anyone else. You realise how pressed we are. It's a private room for you only.' He handed me the key.

I was flabbergasted. I hadn't believed that this mythical room would ever materialise. What should I do about Richard? I hastily scribbled him a note of thanks in case he was still installed in the men's dormitory and left it at the desk. I was bemused by the situation. What if he was hoping I would join him for the New Year celebrations? When I had explained to Jack that we were only casual wartime friends, of course it was true. No more than the many others with whom I'd shared the good and bad times.

I took a cab to the Garrison Theatre. It was great to be back and to receive such a welcoming hug from Stafford Byrne. Stafford had become such a valued assistant as well as friend to Jack. I retrieved the clinging white and silver evening gown I had worn in *Private Lives*, which Jack loved.

Returning to the hotel, it was difficult to believe this room was mine: spacious with windows and a punkah; a bed that was a real bed, not a charpoy or a camp bed, but a bed with a proper mattress, sheets and a coverlet. I felt the pillows and they were soft and did not smell of the usual mustiness. The bearer stood waiting for my orders, so I gave him the white gown for pressing, and as an afterthought asked for tea at five o'clock. A wise precaution, for when I lay down, the fatigue and exhaustion that had gone unheeded during such an exciting forty-eight hours, overcame me and I passed out. I would have slept for at least twelve hours but for the persistent knocking on my door – tea and my dress for the night. I sipped my tea, savouring the delight of my very own bathroom waiting for me.

*　　*　　*　　*　　*

We had a splendid table on a balcony overlooking the dancers. For a fleeting moment I thought of that night on board ship looking down at the Chinese Crackers and poor Maisie doing her contortionist act. It seemed so long ago – though it was only a year. Now here I was with Jack. It didn't seem I could feel more happiness than at that moment.

Just before midnight we were watching the dancers, holding hands across the table. Jack spoke,

'I forgot to tell you my important news. I'm a free man: my divorce came through only a week ago. It's as well for Jessica, she and Hume Cronyn have produced two children since their Reno 'quickie' which wasn't valid in Britain.'

I was silent for a moment then congratulated him warmly. I knew what his real feeling had been. The legal papers had been endlessly delayed because of the difficulty of wartime mail between the three countries, India, the USA and England. It had taken three or four years. Yes, Jessica must be relieved that the divorce was now

191

legal in Britain, and Jack too. He had been hurt and angry in the beginning, but was now just thankful to have it behind him.

The drums rolled – the moment of midnight was with us. We all stood for *Auld Lang Syne*; balloons came down from the ceiling, it was all very festive. We descended to the floor below to join the dancing. We were oblivious to the balloons and streamers all around, we were just dancing in our own little dreams for 1945 and the future.

The last year had been the most eventful in my life – what would this year bring?

Jack held me close, kissing me. 'Happy New Year darling, it will be the first of many together, God willing.' I wished the same, but my heart was bitter. Jack was free, I would not be for a long time; I had yet to face the trials and traumas of divorce. The sadness I felt contrasted with the gaiety going on around me. I was the one who was tied – I was still married.

*   *   *   *   *

Someone was brushing the hair from my face and gently kissing my forehead, it was Jack to tell me he was off to the office and would I meet him at the theatre at 12.30.

By the time I had breakfasted and bathed I was feeling myself again and looking forward to the day.

I walked out into the morning sunshine. The sky was azure blue. Surrounded by the clamorous sound of Calcutta's streets, I felt happy, and at home. I decided to walk through the market. I made my way through the noisy colourful crowds, looking away from the wretched dancing bears – knowing there was not a thing I could do – avoiding the prone bodies, either asleep or ill. I knew better than to touch them. Beggars were following me, holding out pleading hands, patting the swollen, starved bellies of their babies. Over the past year I had become hardened to their plight: I knew if I showed sympathy or gave money to one I would be surrounded in a second. I walked slowly, looking at the stalls and their brightly coloured wares. Not for a moment did I feel unsafe. I was content on this beautiful morning, with no desire to be anywhere else. Though it was just a year since I had landed in Bombay, I felt as if I had been in India a lifetime.

I joined Jack and Stafford for New Year's Day lunch, at the invitation of their host Angus MacGillivray. Stafford had struck gold in being billeted with Angus, an affluent and influential figure in Calcutta, who became an invaluable friend to all of us. The lunch was given in the holy of holies, the Bengal Club, but his generous hospitality was more often provided at home, where the food was cooked by the best chef in the city.

He also provided me with his doctor, who diagnosed my swollen glands and other symptoms as glandular fever. The only cure was plenty of rest. As I was due for leave, we all were, I was able to obey his orders.

The next day Vallabh appeared, having succeeded in getting himself on to a plane with two or three of the company. He immediately busied himself doing whatever he could for me, and dismissed the room waiter. Gradually the rest of the company returned from Imphal.

Four days later, I was still in my heavenly solitary room. I hoped they had forgotten me. Jack would join me in the evenings, often bringing a friend we both knew who was passing through Calcutta. One evening Stewart Guelder joined us for a drink. He had succeeded in getting an exclusive interview with Chiang Kai-Shek in China. We congratulated him. Then he produced a copy of *The News Chronicle*, opening it on a page with an article he had written on Pam and myself. I was amazed the editor had given us the space, and horrified at the pictures: they were our passport photos! Drury Lane had probably dug them out, astonished to receive an enquiry about a couple of actresses they had long forgotten about.

By the next mail from home came the cutting from proud but anxious parents with the headline 'TWO GIRLS AT WAR'. They had no conception of the war in the Far East, had never heard of the

14th Army. The grim struggle for Europe filled the two pages of the daily newspapers. Air raids were less, but had been replaced by Hitler's latest toy, the buzz-bomb. I heard from Irene. She had been in Oxford Street in London when one of these monsters had 'cut out' directly overhead. Everyone flung themselves down on the street fearful of the dreadful explosion that would follow, resulting in utter devastation. Kohima and Imphal were unheard of – too remote.

My tenure of the cherished room came to an end in an unexpected way. Jack arrived as usual to take me to dinner. He seemed restive. My intuition told me he wanted to tell me something, but didn't know how to begin. I waited.

'George Formby and his wife came in by air this morning. They're being difficult.'

'That pair,' I expostulated, 'are always difficult. It is the ghastly Beryl. He's no trouble, just obeys her.'

'You know them?' Jack was surprised.

'Darling, they *are* northern music hall – everyone in the provincial theatre knows about them.' After Beryl had stopped performing, she had become George Formby's manager. He was the talent with the ukulele, while she was officious and jealous and made trouble.

'Well, they're making trouble already,' Jack said. 'Insisting on going "up front". I have tried to explain that there is no "front". The war here is fought in jungles and swamps, constantly moving. Anyway, I'll sort that out. He'll be great entertainment for the troops. We mustn't waste him. But his wife insists while in Calcutta that they must have a room in the best hotel. You know very well there's no such room available in Calcutta.'

I could see what was coming.

'Darling, I hate to ask you – but you have just the room needed.'

'Jack, I asked you not to tell anyone. The manager made me promise to be discreet. We could land him in trouble.'

'Not a problem. I have already sorted it out with the manager.'

That was Jack: success in the job came first. It always would.

'Where shall I go?'

'They'll find a room for you at the ENSA Hostel. I promise you won't have to go back to the Transit Room again.'

'Thank you,' I responded dryly. 'When am I to get out?'

'Well, darling, I'm afraid as soon as possible. They have nowhere to go. They are already making unpleasant noises about it.'

'Vallabh,' I called. He appeared immediately. 'Start packing. We are moving.'

Soon I was sharing a room in the ENSA Hostel with a young actress who had arrived with a new repertory company. Calcutta was filling up with artists from England or the Middle East. More arrived daily. Jack was at his wit's end as to where to house them or route them. In the evenings he took me to dinner, then a visit to the Garrison Theatre to see the current ENSA shows on offer. There was a ballet, which was surprisingly popular with the troops – full houses every night, with, of course pretty dancers in tutus. The other surprise hit was Soloman, the concert pianist, playing a programme of Chopin in the morning: he had queues round the block waiting for the doors to open. Jack and Stafford had won the battle to bring culture to the troops.

We needed to separate our social life from ENSA. Jack and Stafford did all they could to help the visiting artists. But after work, in an attempt to avoid the endless problems and complaints, he avoided coming to the hostel. Almost all friendly gatherings were at Angus MacGillivray's flat.

As I had little to do during the day I scanned the papers looking for accommodation so Jack could escape the officers' dormitory at the top of the Great Eastern Hotel, where he had been holed up since his arrival. I spied a promising ad. in the paper, and rushed to get there first. By the evening, he had moved in.

Once I'd recovered I wondered what might be suggested to me in the way of work. Grateful for his new accommodation, Jack broached the question.

'Darling, I know you will hate this but could you do just one month of *Love in a Mist*?' He hurried on, before I could say anything. 'Eastern Bengal – up to Ranchi where there's a big garrison. There's not much travelling. It'll be the very last time, I promise. The old company will be going up, and then most of them intend to go back to England.'

I said I ought to go home too, I'd been away so long. Jack interrupted me, saying to leave things as they were, *please*. I was needed in India. So I agreed to go to Ranchi and play in *Love in a Mist* – one last time, and for one month only.

Jack kissed me 'You're an angel and I love you.'

There was nothing more to be said.

As we left Calcutta I received a bundle of mail. The envelope postmarked Tripoli had been following me around for some time. I left it unopened for days, knowing it would make me unhappy whatever its contents.

Ranchi was pleasant enough but what I remember about that tour occurred on the journey up there. In the back of a jolting three ton lorry, I found myself sitting next to an unusually handsome officer, whose pale khaki uniform was different: there were no pips on his shoulders. He was presumably a performer, and though aristocratic in appearance his khaki drill was worn and shabby. His hair was going prematurely grey. I asked him what he did in the way of entertainment, and to my surprise he replied in broken halting English. 'I am pianist.'

The accent to my ears was Italian. 'Concert pianist?' I inquired. He nodded vigorously. I looked at his hands. They were the delicate hands of an artist, though I could see they had been subjected to rough work.

'I am a prisoner of war,' he added, staring straight ahead. 'Your Major Hawkins, he get me out. I am ever in his debt.'

'You mean you were in a prisoner of war camp in India?'

He nodded. I had known there were camps in Northern India where many displaced persons from Middle European countries languished. Jack had been able to obtain the release of jugglers from Yugoslavia, dancers from Romania etc. But this man was a prisoner of war, apparently taken during our invasion of Italy. His hands had worried him. He feared he might never again be able to play the piano, as a result of the lack of practice, and the manual labour he had been forced to do. Jack had engineered his release. I suppose he was under some form of unseen guard, but he was hardly likely to escape. Jack was his hero.

When we reached Ranchi, we were greeted by an entire orchestra, again Italian, who had been captured or capitulated en masse along with their instruments. As well as a tuneful and joyous welcome, they also used their culinary skills to our advantage, managing to produce a variety of Italian dishes from unlikely NAFFI ingredients. They did not appear to be under any special jurisdiction, except they had a curfew. But as they were always playing music at night, it hardly affected them, and like the pianist were too thankful for their good fortune to want to escape. These encounters endorsed the feeling – generally held – that the majority of Italians were the least eager participants in the war.

When I finally did open Patrick's letter, its closely written three pages were to remind me of the happy times we spent in England before he was posted overseas, and to say how passionately happy we had been. True, but that was not a normal life. Sex seemed to be the priority – there was little time for anything else. It was not real life. I knew I could never live with him, or build a future. As I watched an Indian mother bathing her beautiful brown-eyed baby, I knew I did not want Patrick to be the father of my children.

In time he would try to blame Jack, but he wasn't the reason. I had written to Pat asking for a divorce before meeting Jack, but he could never see any fault in himself.

* * * * *

When we returned from our month in Ranchi, Calcutta was hot and steamy. Cholera hit the city, soon becoming an epidemic. We had to be re-inoculated. People were dropping dead in the streets. The garbage trucks, always a revolting sight with dead dogs amongst the rubbish, now contained human beings, even dead children, like rag dolls. It was heartbreaking.

Several of the company left for home as boats became available. Soon I was the only one left, but I did not want to leave India or Jack. Indeed, I had a desire to see through the war there, but I knew I ought to begin thinking about returning to London. I hated to leave Jack. Our relationship was closer than ever. He told me it was a small miracle that brought us together. I agreed, but realised we must be on home ground before being one hundred percent certain. I would have to set about re-starting my career and doing something with my life and future.

As always, the decision was made by events.

Sitting alone in the hostel thinking on these things, Jack joined me. He was grinning from ear to ear as he dumped a fat script in my lap. 'It's Terence Rattigan's latest play *While the Sun Shines*. I have been in touch with Terry and he has given me permission to produce the play out here. It's still in the midst of the London run.'

Jack was already on his way out. 'See you at about 6 o'clock. Read the play before then – Mabel Crum's for you.'

I laughed – suddenly life was wonderful again.

We gathered on stage at the Garrison Theatre for the first rehearsal. The mood was cheerful. The play was written with a wartime audience in mind. Hugh Latimer (who had become a friend when in charge of the Ceylon area) had been made available to play the male lead. He was a peacetime actor who specialised in light comedy and was a natural for the part. Jack was also using two actors from a repertory company that had concluded its tour of India, one of whom I had already met. Her name was Angela Dowding. I had seen her act and knew she was good – and pretty. I was sure we would get along. In fact we became close friends for life. We had all read the play and were eager to begin working. Jack was directing, a treat for us, and for him an escape from the office for a few hours and a chance to use his own talents.

The first night was soon upon us. There was a packed house and a great buzz of anticipation, peering through the curtains we could see many top brass out front, which was unusual, but so was a new Rattigan play still running in London. We had a great success and enjoyed a three-week stint at the Garrison. It became hotter and more humid nightly. When Hugh and I embraced to kiss the sweat sprayed from us, unnoticed we hoped by the audience.

The play had only been on for a few days when the incredible news came through: the war in Europe was over! The excitement spread like wildfire, drinks were splashed out, champagne was brought out of cellars. We were all crying – laughing – hugging – kissing. It was an end that we had never dared hope for. We felt deprived not to be there. I longed to be at home, jumping with sheer delight and shouting with the crowds. Hitler was beaten.

All work for the day was abandoned, except for the evening show, which was packed as usual. News was coming through all the time: Hitler's death in the bunker, and his intimates with him. Pictures began to appear in Calcutta papers of the horrors of the concentration camps. The discovery of Belsen shocked everyone beyond belief – then the others – the unspeakable conditions. We had no knowledge of such camps or of the atrocities to the Jews.

Simultaneously with the news from Europe, great events and successes were taking place in our own war. The Irawaddy river had been crossed, we were racing ahead. Rangoon had fallen and been recaptured – we held our breath. When Jack told me he would be away for a few days I sensed he was about to be involved in some way.

He returned dishevelled but triumphant, and I was relieved after four days to have him back. Where had he been? To Rangoon, to find a theatre for us to play in. He had managed to talk himself onto the first plane going in, among a crowd of high-ranking officers all squashed together and squatting on the fuselage floor. The seaplane was so overloaded that the first take-off had to be aborted; on the second run they rose into the air like some overweight bird. When it landed the plane skidded over the water until finally coming to a halt in the shallows, where the officers had to wade ashore. Jack had beaten a brigadier off in order to get us the Town Hall.

'A big coup,' I laughed.

'It's the only building with a roof. I insisted that entertainment was the highest priority for the morale of the Forces.'

'What did the brigadier need the Town Hall for?' I asked.

'Oh, some bloody administrative offices. He had to give in.'

We were to fly down as soon as a plane was available. The accommodation, Jack explained, 'is a little rough, I'm afraid.'

So, out with the Burma Greens once more. Boots were essential, also an injection for bubonic plague as Rangoon was infested with rats feeding on dead bodies. It was clear that this was going to be an uncomfortable tour, but we all felt honoured to be the first company to open in Rangoon.

Don Wilson met us at the airport when we arrived. It was cheering to see him; the right man for a tough job. The last time we had worked together had been in Imphal. We were travelling in a lorry. Out of the back we could see the remains of what had once been a beautiful colonial city, now putrid with decay. Don said the monsoon had washed away some of the debris and the rats were busy dealing with the rest. He warned us that the Japanese had performed their usual goodbye – booby-trapping everything they didn't have time to smash. He warned us not to use a lavatory, any that still worked would be lethal. Thunder-boxes would be provided.

'Here we are.'

We clambered out of the lorry, picking our way through the rubble. 'The Silver Grill – your billet.'

It was an erstwhile nightclub, though it had been many years since the doors were opened to pre-war clubbers, and now there were no doors. As we entered we could see where the dance floor had once held swirling couples in evening dress. In one corner there was a band platform, even an ancient piano leaning against a wall. Don said we must find our own accommodation. There were cots – that was about all – so it had to be bedrolls. Angela and I firmly stuck together. There was not any light, no electricity or gas. Water could be collected but only for washing, definitely not for drinking, for that, bearers had to collect boiled water from the cook.

The building was a mass of narrow passages with rooms leading off and stairs to the upper storeys. Angie and I decided to make for the upstairs as we thought it might be more airy and quiet. It was dark and spooky. Vallabh produced a Kerosene lamp he had found. We clicked on our torches, wary of the stairs, some of which were missing.

When we arrived at the top floor we kicked open a door, making as much noise as possible to frighten away the rats. The glass was missing from the two windows, a blind was flapping in one but at least the room had no missing floorboards. Vallabh unpacked our bedrolls, mosquito nets, a pillow and a clean set of uniform. He made the beds, erected the mosquito nets and put an empty crate between the two beds with the lamp on it. Later he appeared with a tin bowl, a jug of warm water for washing, some glasses, and a bottle of boiled drinking water. Not trusting it, Angela quickly opened our iron rations – Scotch. We added it to the water and sat on the narrow beds surveying the scene. It was certainly airy – apart from the lack of windows I could see a large hole in the roof. Some of the other actors were in a room nearby and had located the thunder-box – in a dark cupboard.

We decided it was time to explore and taking the torches made a cautious descent to the ground floor. There we found two tables laid with NAAFI cutlery, and learnt the cooking was being done over a wood fire outside the building. The cuisine consisted of Spam and more Spam with tinned vegetables, mainly served cold as the monsoon rain frequently doused the cook's fire. We were not hungry. Don Wilson arrived with a jeep and suggested we might like to look over the Garrison Theatre – the Town Hall that Jack had acquired. There was a performance in progress.

The steamy humidity outside was nothing compared to the wave of heat that engulfed us as we made a discreet entry. The Town Hall was crammed. Men were standing everywhere, the heat and sweat for the moment unnoticed. We joined them. All eyes were focused on the stage: Beryl Templeman in a spotlight singing, 'Long Ago and Far Away – I dreamed a dream one day.' The punkahs were doing their whirling duty, with little effect, but no one cared, enraptured as they were by her sweet song – each lost in their own dreams. I looked at her. A transformation. In a beautifully designed black dress, low cut to show her figure, her hair fashionably swept up, I thought of the girl I first met in Jack's office in a cheap flowered dress, then one of the ENSA secretarial staff. Here she was commanding a hushed audience at the mercy of emotions they had kept buried for years. When she finished, the applause, shouts, whistles for encores and stamping feet were deafening. The band struck up again, and Beryl obliged with another number.

Don led us out of the hall saying there was only one place in Rangoon where they cooked an edible meal, a Chinese restaurant. We should hurry there before it was full. It was better not to question what was in the dishes – enough to say there was plenty – well covered in spices and sauces. We returned to the Silver Grill, ready for sleep in any kind of bed. It had been a long day.

The most curious noise awakened me. It was daylight and Angie woke at the same time. There seemed to be water all around us. With the break of dawn the monsoon also broke, the rain lashing down in torrents. Our roof, which was full of holes, couldn't withstand the onslaught and the room had filled with water. We were sleeping in our two cots like boats, while our shoes and boots and anything else we had left on the floor were floating. Fortunately, due to wartime training, everything of value was on the bed with us. There was only one thing to do – we both lay back in our beds laughing – somewhat hysterically.

As always, Vallabh came to the rescue. With an assistant carrying pails and brooms, they mopped away until it was possible to put our feet on the floor, once we had wrung the slippers out. Our complaints about the roof brought the Pioneers around to nail a few boards together and cover it with a tarpaulin in hope of making us more watertight.

Angela and I began to explore the nightclub in daylight. It was strange that there were so many small rooms. There were lots of mirrors, not all had been smashed and we carried away two good ones for our own use. All the doors had sliding peepholes. There was Japanese money left lying on the floors, as well as some provocative photographs of Japanese girls. It didn't require much imagination to guess that the Silver Grill had been a gambling club or more likely a brothel. As the last building to be evacuated it was less damaged than most. The wretched girls must have had to make a frantic dash for it.

Playing to packed and enthusiastic audiences every night, each performance brought friends to the dressing room afterwards. Rangoon was full of men we had met on our travels, but unlike us, they had endured a long and costly fight to get there.

Angela knew a contingent of Americans who were camped around Lake Victoria. Actually, they had commandeered several of the once beautiful but now vandalised villas that surrounded the lake. It was easy to visualise how lovely this sad city must have been before it suffered the dreadful battles fought over it. Angela and I were invited to a Sunday lunch of Southern fried chicken. The Yanks had a generator producing their electricity. The lunch was a treat and accompanied by music, all the latest tunes from the States.

Afterwards we rowed out onto the lake. It was hot and sticky, with heavy cloud, almost mist – real monsoon weather. I was hoping for a swim to cool off. I had optimistically donned my swimsuit – most had – it was cooler. Out on the lake, there was a slight movement of air. I decided to take the plunge and jumped overboard. Bliss – so cool. I began swimming away from the boat. I called out for Angela and some of the others to join me. 'It's so refreshing.' They began rowing towards me. 'Yeah,' said one of our Yankee pals. 'It should be fresh – that lake is full of dead Japs.' I have never swum faster in my life. I might have had a shark behind me. I reached the boat and they hauled me back into it.

When I regained my breath (they were laughing their heads off) I laid into them for not telling me, which caused more laughter. 'Here, take a swig,' said one, producing a bottle of Scotch from the bottom of the boat. 'It'll kill the germs.' More laughter. I had to join in. I never did know if they were telling the truth. It *could* have been a joke, but all those bodies had to go somewhere.

There was great excitement when Mountbatten, the Supremo as he was known to all, arrived in Rangoon. A guard of honour was laid on in a clearing near the airstrip, all of the Forces represented to welcome the popular leader. Five of us squashed into a jeep, wrapped up in our cloaks against the pouring rain. The canvas top over the jeep did little to keep us dry – we did not care – we were fired with patriotism. It was hot and humid, so we were damp not cold. We stayed in the shelter of the jeep until the stamping of feet and presenting of arms alerted us to the arrival. As Mountbatten's jeep drove up, he jumped out, followed by his aide. Magically, a crate of solid wood was produced, and the Supremo leapt onto it in order to address the assembled forces. He looked magnificent. Speaking in a loud clear voice (without a mike of course) he could be heard despite the monsoon, which suddenly began to rain with its full force. We left our shelter to listen to his words. I cannot recall them exactly, stirring as they were. He was full of pride for the tremendous advances, assuring us of more – we had the enemy on the run. Charisma he had by the bucketful. At that time anyone would have obeyed any command he gave, instead we cheered him until we were hoarse.

*   *   *   *   *

Within days of leaving Rangoon we were in the north of Ceylon. From there we moved down to Trincomalee – so changed since my last visit. There was no Eastern Fleet, it had moved on, and no WREN accommodation, instead we were in basha huts right down on the beach. The theatre was still there but the atmosphere was changed. The audiences were plentiful, warm and laughing, but the men themselves seemed downcast, as though they had been left behind. This was so in each camp we visited. Most of the hidden airfields I had stayed and played in before, were gone – the jungle would soon take over. It was impossible not to sense the air of dissatisfaction, who could blame them? Most had been away from home and their loved ones for years. Now that victory seemed imminent, how much longer was the unspoken question.

We ended up in Colombo, not at Mount Lavinia but at an ENSA hostel. By this time I was ill. I had finally fallen foul of the dreaded amoebic dysentery. The symptoms were plain: utter exhaustion, loss of weight, appetite, and complete debilitation. Lying under my mosquito net I felt homesick for the first time. I longed to be at home with my parents, an emotion new to me.

Hugh Latimer, who was in charge of us and knew Ceylon well, insisted I have a check up with a private doctor he knew, who confirmed that I had 'amoebic'. By the way, the doctor informed me, I had a grumbling appendix that should be removed before starting any treatment – it was probably riddled with the amoebic bugs.

Jack was advised by telex from Hugh, and I was given permission to have the operation in a nursing home in Colombo. Fortunately, we were at the end of the tour.

The sister there told me that I must have proper treatment as amoebic dysentery was serious and recurring. Antibiotics were almost unknown then, but she told me of a new medication called Entero-Vioform, which was effective but rarely obtainable. She added I should return to a temperate climate sooner rather than later.

Angie and Hugh came to visit when I was out of pain with the news that Jack would be arriving shortly. I asked Hugh to telex the name of this unobtainable medicine; Jack just might have a contact or know how to obtain some.

Two days later Vallabh rushed in with the news the Major Sahib was on his way. The cure was miraculous – not only his presence – but also he produced out of his pocket, like a magician, the

Entero-Vioform pills. He had obtained enough for immediate use from American friends in Bombay. He would stay at the hostel for a few days, officially to welcome Gracie Fields and make certain everything was ready for her one big performance, though unlike some other stars she was undemanding.

After pleading with the sister that I must be well enough by now – I had been in hospital for thirteen days – I was allowed to go back to the hostel when Gracie and her husband (Monty Banks, a pre-war movie star and now her manager) came to stay. Only Jack and myself were about when Gracie arrived. We just chatted, mostly about the north of England, which of course I knew.

Angela and Hugh had now also fallen foul of the amoebic bug and were in beds upstairs in the hostel dosing themselves on pills. Rangoon, without doubt, was the culprit.

Gracie was to perform for one night only, on the racecourse of all places, and troops were amassing from far and wide. Jack had arranged for a stage with special lighting effects, which he was overseeing for most of the day. In the evening he took me to the concert and we sat on the rear of a truck, parked on high ground to have a good view. She sang her heart out with that powerful voice and no microphone. 'Coom on lads – what do yer want next?' she would yell out in that Rochdale accent. She was tireless. That performance was one of the most moving I have seen in my life.

*   *   *   *   *

Jack had to leave, but I stayed on in Colombo until I was fit enough to get on a plane to Bombay. The plan was to perform *While the Sun Shines* one last time at the Excelsior in Bombay. Angela was returning to England, and a visit to the Tropical Diseases Hospital in London. Hugh was due for his discharge from the Forces, which his illness would expedite.

When I was notified I would be airlifted to Bombay the next day, a longing to return there was marred by a dread of the flight. At

4.00 a.m., feeling terrible, I joined a crowd of servicemen hoping to get a lift. When we climbed aboard the old Dakota I made for my favourite spot, the huge load of mailbags stacked at the front of the aisle, where I could flop out and sleep. The bucket seats were unbearably hard, but I must have slept at least for part of the nine hour journey.

On arriving in Bombay, I was glad to be met by Stafford and not Jack. I needed a bath, to wash my hair and to try and do something with myself. Jack was in Delhi for a few days; I should have revived by then. Soon Angela arrived, and then Hugh, giving us the complete cast, and after a dress rehearsal we opened *While the Sun Shines*, which ran for a week. We were now housed in the ENSA hostel near Green's and the Taj Mahal Hotel. Once the play was over Angela left on a troop ship for England. I would miss her.

It was now August and I knew I should make efforts to return home – necessary for my career and my health, also my work here was finished. Jack said the arrangements would be made in due course, but it was becoming increasingly difficult to get a passage. The truth was that the parting now facing us was dreaded by us both – we tried not to think about it. The magic Entero-Vioform had effected some sort of recovery but I still had little appetite or energy.

Jack made frequent flights to Delhi, and after one such trip I went in the staff car to meet him. After the plane had touched down he walked towards me across the grass – my God! he was covered in red and gold with extra pips and flashes on his shoulders. It could only mean he had been promoted to full colonel. He adjusted his cap as if to salute, but just looked embarrassed. I laughed and put my arms around him, I didn't care who the hell was watching. 'Congratulations, what brought about this sudden elevation?' He told me he had been allocated the unenviable task of arranging entertainment for the whole of South East Asia.

I was absorbing this when he gave me a small package in which there was a beautiful ring of small square-cut sapphires, diamonds and emeralds, set in three separate layers. It was exquisite. I wore it always.

I did have one last job before I went home, with the American equivalent of ENSA (USO) at the Garrison Theatre in Calcutta. Jack and Stafford persuaded me to help them out when one of their leading actresses became ill. My American accent was good, and Jack promised it was just for that one play.

Jack and I arrived at the airport just before dawn. As usual a crowd of officers was hanging around for planes, and a group of gold braid, top brass, also waiting. Jack climbed out of the car, telling me to wait until he had found my plane. His high rank should increase my chances of getting to Calcutta. He was Singapore bound. He joined a gathering of similar officers; they were all in earnest discussion.

The dawn streaks turned to daylight. This was becoming late for a take-off. Presently Jack returned. 'What's the delay?'

'Something serious. We're awaiting more information.'

He rejoined them.

I was bewildered. I watched the various groups, all talking amongst themselves. It seemed hours before Jack returned. Even Vallabh asked me if we were still going to fly to Calcutta. I told him that I didn't know. All the planes stood silent. As Jack came back to the car he told the driver to return to Bombay. I gazed at him amazed. He was silent. His face very set. I asked him why we weren't leaving today.

'No planes are taking off at all until we have more news.'

'What has happened? Something wrong?'

He turned and took my hand. 'As far as we know, something that's going to change everything has happened.'

I could see from his face that whatever it was he found unbelievable. 'A bomb – not the kind we know of, but an extraordinary new invention named the Atom Bomb has been dropped on Japan. It has caused unimagined chaos, death and havoc.'

'By us?'

'No, the Americans, but it is a combined operation.'

I was trying to absorb this extraordinary information. 'It might mean the end of the war,' I almost whispered.

'Yes,' was Jack's only reply.

We were still clutching each other's hands. I thought of all those wretched men trapped out there in the jungle, those still starved and tortured in the prison camps. Could it mean the end to all these dreadful years? I dare not believe such a thing could happen. The Japanese, who never surrendered, could they be forced to by this new bomb? I voiced my hopes to Jack. He agreed. Of course he longed to see the end of the war too. A sudden end, utterly unexpected, unthought of. And yet . . .

That evening we had a dinner together and decided to go to the ballroom at the Taj. Jack had been in the office dealing with queries from the artists and from the many companies out on tour. Lines were jammed.

It was dance night, and the band, Sonny Lobo, was playing lively tunes. No one was dancing. The tables were not as full as usual, and conversation muted. There was no air of celebration, only one of shock and bewilderment, provided by rumour rather than hard news. Jack said it was the city of Hiroshima that had been hit and completely devastated. 'They *must* surrender now – do you not think?' I queried.

'We can only wait. I'm trying to keep all the companies working as normal – as to our own departures – again it's a waiting game.'

After the second bomb was dropped on Nagasaki it was definite that the end was in sight – the Japanese Emperor had spoken. The appalling fighting and suffering of that long war was over. Bar the signing, it was finished.It had been ghastly with a ghastly end.

*　　*　　*　　*　　*

Work had to continue. Jack went to Singapore, I to Calcutta. For the nine-hour flight, I was lucky to find myself in a plane with proper seats. I was met at the airport by an officer I had known in Cairo. I asked him what the reaction had been to the cessation of hostilities at long last. He said it was so unbelievable it had to be properly absorbed, but that the longing to return home to England was going to turn into a frustrated stampede for troopships. He gloomily predicted that that although overdue to return to Britain, he would be here for many months. Entertainment was vital, but beginning to dry up. With the end of the war it would finish. I thought of Jack having to keep ENSA going all through Asia and the Far East.

The director of the American company and Dennis the young leading actor welcomed me with flowers, and we began rehearsing our scenes. Though Calcutta seemed empty without Jack and Stafford, the play was an easy frothy, light comedy with an evenly balanced cast of three men and three women.

Americans cannot resist seeing the local sights. As someone who had spent so much time in Calcutta they were amazed I'd seen so little of interest. But I was always working, or it had been too hot. Now it was cooler. Dennis and Brian (the director) were indefatigable, determined to see everything and have me accompany them. I was grateful for their tenacity.

One day they took me to the burning ghats. I was a little uncertain about this – our intrusion on what must be a private occasion, and my own reaction. As we walked towards the arched entrance, we were halted by a dreadful sight. Lying in a ditch beside the rough path was a boy, dead, between the shafts of an overturned rickshaw. He must have collapsed and died, either from exhaustion or disease. Now he was covered by a million flies, buzzing all over him. The sight was appalling, the stench sickening. I gazed at his corpse in utter horror until Dennis and Brian guided me away. There was nothing we could do. The memory has remained vivid all these years. Somehow, it was a part of India. The worst part.

No one prevented us from entering the ghats. The scent of flowers and burning incense was powerful. There was a temple at the far end of what appeared to be empty land. We moved on, so as not to be observed as there was a cortege approaching. This was a family of some consequence – although even the poor would give their all to honour their dead. A pyre had been built, of sandalwood impregnated with incense. The mourning relatives, all chanting and clad in white, were bearing the dead man. He was elderly with flowing white hair. His face resembled parchment. I had thought I might feel uncomfortable, but not at all. He was laid on the pyre, more flowers and incense were scattered. Then the fire was lit. It sprang into a blaze instantly and within a few minutes the corpse was engulfed with flames. We walked away towards the flowing River Ganges, where later the family would scatter the ashes and flowers. I could not help thinking what a wonderful end, not to be shut down in a wooden box.

* * * * *

After performing at the Garrison Theatre, and several camps around Calcutta, the Americans pressed me to join them in more productions, but I knew that I must return to England. Common sense told me that I must try to leave before the hot weather returned. The rush for passages home had doubled now that the peace had been signed. The talk now had shifted to political concerns, the promised Independence of India, the dismantling of the British Raj.

It was the usual dawn take-off from Dum Dum airport – I was back on the mailbags. Jack was at Bombay to meet me. Happiness again.

I had begun collecting clothes for my return. Shoes could be made in India; they were not only hideous but difficult to obtain in Britain. Fabrics of all kinds and clothes were on coupons. Requests from home were many. My trunks were becoming full to overflowing.

I was in Bombay with Jack and our friends for Christmas and we danced in the New Year at the Taj ballroom. I had been in India since 1944 and it was now 1946. The war was over and I had seen it through to the end as I had hoped – soon we had to part. How to face up to the parting, and how long would it be for, all that lay in the future.

As predicted the riots began. There were massed marches of Indians in the streets shouting 'Jai Hind – Jai Hind', shaking their fists, throwing bottles and smashing windows. We were confined to the hostel with the shutters closed.

In early March, after two false alarms, there was a space for me on a troopship. Jack said he had managed to arrange a tiny single cabin for me, for which I was thankful.

I had many goodbyes to say to friends, also people I had known and worked with in ENSA since the early days, including the wardrobe department and the workshops who had created all the sets and furniture.

The worst and most upsetting was the parting with Vallabh. He grasped my hand, which was most unlike him, pleading with me to take him. I longed to, but it was impossible. 'Could I not send for him later? Could not the Colonel Sahib arrange it?' I didn't know how to explain that it was difficult enough for me to get away.

Vallabh was crying. 'When you go, all of you, we have fighting. Indian will kill Indian.'

I didn't know how to console him. Write? – no, I couldn't write, he had no address, he was always with me, and anyway he couldn't read.

Luckily Jack came and finding us both in tears, took Vallabh away, comforting him and promising him other work. I was desolate. How many times have I since longed for him and worried about him.

When the awful day came for my departure I was in Jack's room wearing a splendidly tailored dark khaki winter uniform. It had been specially made in England for a concert pianist, Irene Kohler and she had left it behind. It was hardly worn so the wardrobe altered it to fit me. I had no warm clothes. All my winter wear had been eagerly shared among my relatives and friends on leaving England. The shortages had already begun to bite. My luggage went ahead into the ship's hold, leaving me with the small amount of hand baggage I needed on the voyage. Jack and I were alone – he held me close. 'It'll be all right, you must know that, everything between us will be as we want it, believe me.'

We walked down the wide staircase to the waiting car. 'I've spoken to the C.O. I hope it helps. Here's a bottle that will. All ships are dry now.' At the docks we climbed out of the car. 'I shan't come aboard.' We had already said our goodbyes. I turned and walked up the gangplank.

I felt like an automaton, numb in mind and body. I handed over my boarding pass and followed a steward down endless narrow passages until at the end of one he opened a door. 'There you are, miss.' I was in the smallest inside cabin ever – I think it was a converted broom cupboard. The steward put my two bags on the lower bunk and was gone. The cabin was tiny, but at least I was alone and could indulge in my misery without being observed. Jack had given me a bottle of Gordon's gin, then extremely rare. He must have gone to some trouble to find it.

I went through the motions of unpacking, out of habit placing my personal possessions on the top bunk. I climbed on to it and found it impossible to do more than raise my head; there was no way of sitting up. Never mind, I preferred to be on top. It was hot and stuffy in the cabin. I did not want to go up onto the deck for a final look at Bombay, but in the end I was drawn there as if by some magnet. The ship was packed with officers trying to push themselves and their gear into overcrowded cabins. It appeared to be worse than any troopship I had travelled on before. Almost next to me was a dormitory for mothers and children. I made for the fresh air, but it was just as crowded on deck. Gradually I managed to reach the rail. I was homeward bound on a Castle Liner. My first ship had been the *Athlone Castle*, and catching sight of a lifebelt I saw this was the *Durban Castle*. I began to feel a little more at home. It was already evening and the sunset, always brief, turned to dusk.

There was the Gateway of India where Jack had first held me so close and – no stop right there, said an inner voice – no memories. But there was the Taj Mahal Hotel with his room looking this way. Perhaps Jack and Stafford were watching from the window. No, of course not. Jack would still be working hard at the office. He would not be watching my departure. He was far too sensible. He was a man, for heaven's sake. Perhaps he had already forgotten. Now, you are being stupid – making it hard on yourself. Idiot, this inner voice told me.

Rapidly, Bombay retreated to a grey line on the horizon, so different from that magical gold rising from the sea that had begun a life of amazing happenings for me. Now it was over, only the deep ache of love remained. I left the deck and pushed through the crowds. A gong banged somewhere for the first dinner. I tried to find my way back to the cabin. No friends, no company of actors. I was all alone for the first time. Perhaps I will have a splash of the gin after all. Oh hell!

The door seemed to be wedged shut. I leaned my whole body against it and forced it wide enough to see what was blocking my entry: luggage, bags and suitcases – plus clouds of cigarette smoke billowing out into the corridor. A woman's voice in a thick accent was saying something about trying to let me in. Let me in! Was I in the right cabin? I glanced up at the number. On the lower bunk sat a woman with short hair puffing away at an evil smelling cigarette. She was wearing some kind of uniform, but not one I recognised, and spoke in an accent, either Middle European or Russian. She apologised for the mess.

I was bewildered and angry, suffocated by the smoke in that tiny space. Was this really happening? Apparently she was put onto the ship at the last moment, after arriving from Delhi, hence the loads of luggage now occupying the cabin. She was Russian and an interpreter. There was nothing we could do about the situation. It was going to be an uncomfortable voyage anyway, but in the company of a chain smoker worse. The moment had arrived to open the gin. Holding out her glass I was afraid that she going to kiss me, but once it was filled she took a huge swig. I cautioned her that this was my only bottle.

'No worry – we go to bar.'

I told her the bad news of a dry ship.

'What is that?'

She soon found out. My gin was demolished before we entered the Red Sea.

The food on the ship was terrible. Much of the overcooked grey meat and boiled puddings were left untouched, especially with no beer or wine to wash the stuff down. There was a group of POWs from the Japanese torture camps on board, though many were in the sick bay. They were given a special diet (ours would have finished them). Unused to proper food for so long, they needed all the nourishment that could be provided. Terribly emaciated and underweight, the doctors were making every effort to enable them to return to their families in reasonable condition.

Most of the men on board had been away for five or six years, and were nervous and preoccupied about being reunited with their wives and families. We were all concerned about the future. There were some regulars, but the majority were wartime conscripts or volunteers. They would sit in groups talking quietly about possible careers. The despondent mood was odd considering we had achieved peace and victory, and made a strange contrast to the singing of the 'Skye Boat Song' that I remembered on leaving.

We wondered what it would be like in England under the new Labour Government, which had been elected in the absence of millions stranded in various hotspots without a voice. In the Far East we had little knowledge of the momentous political events going on at home. I suppose it would have been impossible to organise. How could voting papers have reached us out there, when we seldom received any mail? Perhaps the change would be for the better – who knew – we would soon find out.

On a grim sunless day, with the sea an all too familiar grey, I recognised the Isle of Wight. We were going into my home port, Southampton. Soon I was pointing out familiar landmarks to those gathered around me. It was raining and cold as we entered Southampton Water. Dark when we docked. At last some news was given over the tannoy. No one to disembark at Southampton! The ship would proceed to Liverpool for disembarkation.

Knowing that the *Durban Castle* was docking, my family would have gathered to meet me. I asked to see the Commanding Officer.

I pleaded with him that this was my hometown, that after three years away my entire family would be on the dock, waving their bunting in eager anticipation of my arrival. I was a woman travelling alone; I was the last member of a company that had long since returned home. In going on to Liverpool I would have to journey down with all my stuff, unaided. I would be an inconvenience. I won my case.

As we drew along the familiar quayside, I saw my family group anxiously scanning the decks of khaki for one lone female. I tried to attract their attention, yelling and waving, but my mother continued hurrying up and down in a state of agitation. Finally, some chaps around me got together and almost hung me over the side, shouting 'Hey Mum, look, here she is!' Finally, the family saw and broke into excited waves.

Then, walking down the gangway, I waved goodbyes to the friends on board. In my pocket I had several telephone numbers of wives I had been asked to alert of their husband's impending arrival home. I imagine the wives would have been just as nervous as the men. How to rebuild a relationship after so long a period apart had turned husbands and wives into virtual strangers?

As I stepped ashore, I knew I was not the same person who had left, and was thankful for it.

I hurried on to embrace my family.

PART IV

ENGLAND

THIRTEEN

London, 1946

The train shrieked, belching out steam, and hissed, drawing slowly into Waterloo Station. I let down the window to lean out. I had last stood on this station in 1942, ankle deep in shattered glass after the chaos and damage of a night's bombing.

I returned to London wearing Irene Kohler's cast-off dark khaki. I was embarrassed when people stared at me but I didn't possess anything else that was warm. The clothes I had made in India were for spring at the earliest.

My loyal Aunt Irene met me, astonished to see me in uniform. In England the war was long past, though the roof of the station was still without any glass. As Irene and I were trotting behind the baggage trolley, I noticed a cluster of young women being marshalled onto a boat-train, most of them clutching babies. 'American G.I. brides,' my aunt explained. They were gradually being transported to the States to join their husbands, the fathers of children conceived during the war. The US Forces had now returned to their homeland, so some spaces on ships could be found. I thought they might have an uncomfortable voyage ahead, reflecting on my own recent one. I also knew a few dreams were likely to be shattered, as the wartime view of America was largely what Hollywood had shown us. Every American soldier was a Clark Gable or a Robert Taylor, living the good life in a magic country of plenty.

Being back in London was strange. I had left in the midst of blackout and bombing – gone and finished forever one hoped – but the sad remains of buildings looked grey and shabby. Lights were still dim, Piccadilly Circus was hardly lit at all. I can't think why I'd expected it to be sparkling again when I knew there were power shortages. I missed the eternal blue sky and warmth, but was delighted to see healthy well-fed children once more.

Atlee's Government did their best over the lack of food, money, homes for the returning forces and their bombed-out waiting wives. Prefabs shot up all over the place and were immediately occupied. Although tiny, rather fragile constructions, they were better than no roof at all. Only homeless families with children had priority to apply. The Government with its dour faces and outlook (or so they seemed to us), had inherited a country on its knees. Five years of war had taken its toll. Forces were returning home worn out by fighting, some with wounds which would never heal. Everyone was short of rations, and just about everything except hope. No one wore stylish well-designed clothes because there were few to buy and those were on coupons. Most men dressed in an assortment of leftover service uniforms. Naval surplus duffle coats replaced overcoats. Ex-officers of high rank wore their great coats. There was also another kind of uniform, de-mob issue: off-the-peg grey pin-stripe suit, with raincoat, shoes and a hat.

This was the mood of Britain in 1946. We had fought hard and it cost us everything, but in the end we had done it. So the Atlee Government inherited a country that was willing to strive for its peace, putting up with being pushed around and told what to do. We were used to that, so we just got on with it. It had to be better in the end.

I stayed with my ever-hospitable aunt in St. John's Wood and lost no time in turning in my uniform. Extraordinarily, ENSA was demanding its return – who would wear it? I certainly had no further use for it, though I had to explain that I had nothing else warm to wear. Drury Lane was being refurbished for the much longed for Broadway production of *Oklahoma*, so ENSA headquarters had been moved to an unpleasant office. It was staffed by a rather snooty lady who treated me as an out-of-date nuisance and who handed me a chit to take to another department to procure the necessary clothing coupons. There was also a note for me to attend the Tropical Diseases Hospital, which I ignored. I had neither the desire nor the time to be messed around there having tests.

The coupons were intended to be used for sensible garments such as vests, knickers and stockings, but instead I had an extravagant time in Bond Street. I used them for buying one chic outfit: my excuse being that I needed to go for interviews with theatrical agents in order to find the necessary work.

Through the theatrical grapevine I was told that an actor whom I had known in the Sheffield days was off to Germany on a C.S.E. tour. The Combined Services Entertainment had taken over when ENSA finished in Europe. He had a flat he wished to let and I managed to obtain his telephone number. Half London was still in ruins and was packed with ex-services of both sexes trying to find anything with a roof. Accommodation was virtually unobtainable.

I was lucky when my old chum answered my call, very surprised to hear my voice. I had been long gone and forgotten, but now I was making up for lost time. He explained that there were several people after his flat, and did I know that it was just an attic conversion in Bedford Street, Covent Garden. I said I didn't care if it was in a hut as long as it had a telephone and a bed. Yes indeed it had a double bed, plus sitting room, tiny kitchenette and a bathroom on the floor below. I knew that he was always short of cash and doubted the situation had changed. The lease was for three months, so I offered him cash for rental in advance. I was desperate to seal the deal before anyone else could. 'You'd better come and see the place.' I knew that meant bring the money, so I arranged to be there the next day. It was mine.

Before I left England I had arranged for Drury Lane to pay part of my small salary into Barclays Bank at Kingsway, a short distance from Bedford Street. I was several hundred pounds in credit, the most I had ever owned. Money went further then, there being so little on which to spend it. I was delighted that my frugal savings turned out to be so useful. I had received an increase in salary somewhere along the line and I had been away a long time. I noticed when I glanced through my statement that Patrick had stopped my meagre wife's allowance early in 1944 soon after he had received my farewell letter. I didn't care, I was glad not to be beholden to him in any way.

The attic, once I'd climbed several flights of rickety stairs, proved to be more than I had been led to expect. There was a telephone, a fair-sized living room with dining table, and two windows overlooking Bedford Street. On the landing was a small kitchenette with a tiny stove and a sink, a few crocks and utensils. No fridge of course, but they were scarce then and not expected. The bedroom had a small window, which looked down on the alleyway with the Adelphi Theatre on the other side. I was about level with the 'flies' in the roof. Money changed hands, and I was entirely happy. I had brought fabrics from India. I enjoyed, and was quite good at, decorating. My pal and his girlfriend didn't care what I did, anything for an improvement.

They told me the other occupants were a theatrical agent on the floor below, an office open only in the day and never at weekends, and a 'lady' who only had regular customers and was in fact quite proper. I rarely saw her gentlemen callers. On the ground floor was an Italian café, whose piles of rubbish and the stink of their cooking first thing in the morning lost me as a customer.

Money and explanations finished with, the three of us made our way across to the local pub and I was introduced to Queenie, the landlady, who was a gem and provided me with my one hot meal a day. For only two shillings and sixpence the pub served a two-course meal, always with treacle pudding or home made pies and tarts. At last I began to put on some of the weight I'd lost.

I was glad I had given the Tropical Diseases Hospital a miss in order to get on with my life. Sometimes the dreadful exhaustion that lingers on after amoebic dysentery would attack when I least expected it, but in time I overcame it, youth and an excellent constitution was on my side.

I moved into the attic immediately. Taxi drivers would then, for a tip, heave bags and belongings up three flights of stairs. There were no parking restrictions: in fact there were very few cars because petrol was still scarce. My mother sent my tin trunk and a wardrobe trunk up to London via Southern Railway. Standing it upright in the tiny bedroom it provided my only cupboard and drawers. I made curtains out of my fine white cotton Indian saris with edging. I spread my Naga cloth from Kohima on my trunk, and my exotic Ashanti tribal wrap from West Africa on the bed. I hung my pictures, made cushions for the chairs and painted the fireplace. From the electrical shop around the corner I hired a wireless, the only home entertainment then. It was the first place where I had any sort of home of my own and I was really happy there. I was alone and I had my own bath and lavatory – something I had craved for years.

I was especially in love with the area, much of which had been badly bombed. There was a dairy round the corner in Maiden Lane and the lady who worked there would come and clean for me once a week. There was lovely fresh bread and meat (my one chop), in New Row, loads of other shops, and of course, Covent Garden. I learnt all the songs from the show at the Adelphi Theatre, I think it was Cochrane's *London Town*. Recognising the finale, everyone singing with gusto, I knew when it was getting late.

Word soon got around as to my whereabouts. All my actor and actress friends sought me out. Mine was the place to drop in, it was in the midst of all the theatres and theatrical agents, so I heard all the gossip and news. The boys, now men, returning from the war, talked about the difficulties of re-establishing themselves. There were lengthy discussions on whether it was best to hang on trying for work in the profession, or to embark on another career.

I had letters from Jack – many – this kept me going. I missed him very much. Two were waiting for me on my arrival in England, which raised my mother's eyebrows, as did the ring on my finger. She said she had never seen anything so exquisite. There were no recriminations about Patrick, or, 'I told you so,' for which I was grateful. Only when I was settled into the attic did my mother urge me to take care and not let Patrick know of my whereabouts. She was worried that he might become violent. I did my best to reassure her and told her I would only deal with him through legal channels. My parents never asked why I had left Pat; I suppose they thought it was up to me to give an explanation. I never did, nor did I talk about my messed up marriage. It was a closed subject. It was as if it had never happened.

I had a long letter from Stafford Byrne full of news and complaining that he did not think they would ever get away from India, the boats were all full and the waiting lists endless. The political scene in India was becoming increasingly violent. When he and Jack had gone for a swim at Juhu beach one day they ran into a political gathering. The mood turned ugly. Their open car was surrounded, the crowd began rocking it and spitting at the two men. There was nothing they could do but remain seated, staring straight ahead. Thank goodness Jack was in civvies, as he managed to edge the car through the mob. They missed me, wrote Stafford. Jack was lost and lonely and my picture was everywhere. Jack was kept busy trying to organise entertainment without enough artists. The date of our reunion appeared remote. I cabled Jack telling him I was now installed in my own place and giving the address. I had a reply from him enquiring how large the flat was. 'Big enough,' I cabled back.

Now I was settled for three months, I concentrated on my highest priority – legal advice for a divorce. I had been appalled by the newspaper headlines quoting the figure of 65,000 couples lining up for the divorce court. The number was bound to increase as many were still overseas. The wreck of wartime marriages had forced special courts to open to deal with the pressure. It would be years before all these sad marriages would be terminated.

My old friend Hugh Latimer was now reunited with his wife Sheila and their little daughter Carol, whom he had never met. He was, as always, a help. He arranged an introduction through a friend for some radio work, but even more important, he knew the best divorce lawyers in London.

Highly nervous, garbed in my new suit, I found myself at their offices. The charm and experience of the young solicitor allotted to my case made me feel at ease. I told him the history of my unfortunate marriage and my reasons for seeking a divorce. I discovered the only grounds accepted was adultery: it was the sole quick end to a marriage that a court would accept. What was worse, the vital evidence of adultery had to have been committed here in England. I would have to contact Patrick, and persuade him to produce the irrefutable evidence. I was aghast. How long would this take, I asked, and was told that as this was a highly respected firm my application should come high on the list. Now it was up to me.

When I left the solicitors it was a beautiful late spring afternoon, warm and sunny. I walked through the side streets back home deep in thought, and by the time I had arrived at Bedford Street I knew what I had to do. I must talk to Patrick, if I could find him. I knew that Harry Hanson had retired but was rumoured to have kept his little theatre in Hastings, possibly from sentiment. He had retained a few of his loyal older employees, who might have had difficulty obtaining work. The theatrical rat race was worse now than ever. Repertory, as he managed it, was soon to become a thing of the past.

Intuition told me that Pat would most likely have returned to his roots. Harry Hanson would always employ him. Most of the Hanson-Black companies in the past had played twice nightly. I guessed that at the little theatre in Hastings, his first and last, the same tradition of hard work would apply. I judged the time in the evening likely to be the break between shows – took a deep breath, then dialled the number. My heart was thumping as I heard the phone ringing. The stage door keeper answered, I asked if I could speak to Patrick and gave my name. He told me to hold the line – he was there – I had been right. I waited, agonisingly, but not for long. His voice came on, breathless and eager. It was so strange to hear him again. I thought it best to come straight to the point and dash any false hopes my call might have aroused. I plunged in,

'About the divorce. Can we meet and talk?'

His voice became icy. 'I suppose you want me to come to London. Where are you living?'

Mindful of my mother's warning I replied, with some truth that I was mostly with my aunt in St John's Wood. I knew he didn't know where she lived. 'Yes,' I said, 'if it's possible can you come to London, then I'll fit in with you.'

Thursday was a free day for him and he could come to Victoria Station. 'When?'

'As soon as possible.'

'Next Thursday,' was the curt response, '12.15 at platform eight.'

'Thank you. I'll be there.'

We hung up. I was trembling, but I'd done it, made the fatal call and achieved the necessary result. I felt weak and drained and yet tears were pricking my eyes and slowly running down my cheeks. Was it relief? I don't know, but I don't usually cry about anything.

*　　*　　*　　*　　*

Thursday morning found me in a state of nerves after a bad night's sleep. I decided to dress my hair up, which I knew Patrick did not like, he preferred it long. I was calmer by the time I reached Victoria, though unfortunately late, because there had been some hold up on the underground. As I hurried across the station to meet him I could see him stamping about – furious. He greeted me by saying he only intended to give me another five minutes. This was not what I had planned. I apologised and made my excuses. He abruptly demanded, 'Well, what do you want me to do?'

Knowing the man, the obvious suggestion was to have a drink.

'Where? I don't have much time.'

I suggested the Café Royal, though why I can't imagine. I hadn't been there since the early days of the war. I hoped it was still standing. We took a taxi. I felt guilty for being late so I paid. I was sure he would be short of cash. Harry was not over generous with pay.

We were both silent for the entire journey. Eyeing him surreptitiously I thought he looked sadly out of place without a uniform. Thankfully we pulled up at the Café Royal. The doorman welcomed us into the plush warmth. Seated in a banquette, Patrick asked me what I wanted to drink. 'I'm having a large brandy and ginger ale.' The waiter took his order and looked at me. I nodded in agreement but asked for a single as there was no point in getting smashed, I had to remember all the briefing from my solicitor.

Pat was still staring straight ahead. When the drinks arrived he took a large gulp. 'So, you're with Jack Hawkins? Perhaps that's why you're wearing your hair in that style, to make yourself look older and more sophisticated. He's too old for you.'

This onslaught took me by surprise. 'Jack is in India, I have no idea of the date of his return to England.' This caused another heavy silence, so I pushed on. 'About the divorce, I do think it better for both of us if we can begin the proceedings as soon as possible.'

'So you're determined not to give our marriage a chance.'

'Oh Pat, we have been through all this by letter and I've nothing to add. We're now even further apart. I need my own life.'

'With Hawkins no doubt.'

'Jack has nothing to do with our marriage problems. I don't know what the future will bring.' I pressed on, there wasn't much time. 'I know about your affair in Cairo with a girl called Mary. I was hurt at the time, but that is not the reason for the break up. Unfortunately adultery is the only way we can obtain a divorce.'

'Who told you about her?'

'An officer friend of yours, but forget it, it's of no consequence now. That's the past and we have to think of the future.'

'You certainly don't care about mine.' His voice was bitter.

'Yes I do, very much, but I couldn't make you happy. You will find someone who will take the place I never really occupied.'

He ordered another drink and paused, taking a large swallow. 'I'll do the right thing of course – give you evidence.'

Surprised, I muttered, 'Thank you' in a low voice. My solicitor had told me that it was the way it should be. That is how it was at that time. I suddenly felt as though I was playing a scene from a farce. The man had to be found in bed with a woman when the hotel maid brought in the breakfast tray. There were ladies you could pay for this service and it didn't matter if you spent the night playing cards as long as you were found sitting in bed together, it was sufficient evidence. It was also an unwritten code that the man in the case provided the necessary scenario. I was hopeful, if doubtful, that Patrick would co-operate. Before any more could be said I produced a card.

'This is my firm of lawyers, I've written the name of my solicitor on the back. Please make all contacts with him.'

Pat looked at the card then put it in his breast pocket. 'So, we finish here. I gather I shall neither see nor speak to you again.'

I nodded. 'I know it's harsh, but if we do make contact it's referred to as collusion between couples – an arranged divorce. So from now on all correspondence has to be through solicitors. By the way, do you have your own?'

'Can't afford one and frankly I don't see why I should.' He gave a dry laugh, 'Incidentally, judging by this card these people are very expensive. I'm not paying, so who is?'

I knew he thought I was being helped by Jack, which was not true. I would never have allowed him to help me with something that was not his fault. In fact, through hard work I did manage to finance it myself, though I was grateful when my father gave me fifty pounds towards the court proceedings.

I stood up, telling Pat that I didn't expect any money from him for my legal costs. To my surprise he paid for the drinks. We left, walking into Regent Street to say our goodbye. It was a wretched grey day – matching our mood. He turned on his heel, with a military abruptness and made for Piccadilly Circus. I walked in the opposite direction. I was to meet my Aunt Irene in a small restaurant at the upper end of Regent Street near the BBC, where she had worked as telephone supervisor since early in the war. The last I saw of Patrick as I turned to watch him disappearing, he was entering the Criterion bar.

I fled, as fast as I could go with my thoughts in chaos. Seeing him again had given me more distress than I had envisaged, mainly I think because I felt absolutely no warmth towards him. I knew my decision, made in Cairo, had been the right one. I had endured years of agonising waiting. I prayed that it might not be too long now.

By the time I pushed open the door of the restaurant I was feeling almost elated. At last Patrick had agreed to give me my freedom. Irene was already at the table and she smiled. 'I can see by your face that the news is good. Sit down and tell me about it.'

＊　＊　＊　＊　＊

In my nightgown I hurried down the uneven staircase before the agency opened, and a queue of hopeful actors made the journey up to the first floor in search of an interview with Rene Noble for a job. There was silence. The Italian café had yet to open. But my early morning ritual was rewarded – I could see some mail lying on the worn mat. It was usually bills, unpaid by the owner of my attic abode, but not today. I could see an airmail letter with the familiar stamp –from India – it had to be Jack. I jumped the final stairs and rushed to pick it up. It was difficult to read in the poor light of the squalid entrance, so clutching it firmly I leapt up the stairs two at a time into the sanctuary of my own flat. Sitting on the bed I could hardly believe the first sentence – they had a boat at last – sailing between the 15 and 17 May. Stafford had been able to arrange a passage on the same ship. The rest of the letter was full of love, the excitement of our reunion, the many presents he was bringing, some of the clothes (mostly shoes) that were being made but were not finished when I left. He also wrote of the fabrics and rugs that he had bought for the home that one day we might have together. I was delirious with happiness.

Jack was more than overdue for his release, but had felt he must wait for a replacement. Now an officer who had served under Jack in Bombay was returning from leave to take over the command of what was left of ENSA.

The next four weeks were full of letters and cables, during which I tried to arrange my life to be free for Jack's return. He begged me not to get a job that would take me away, or involve me so deeply that we would have no time together. This was difficult, but I managed to eke out my living with radio, and luckily had two short film parts. I also performed for a week at the lovely old theatre on Richmond Green managed at that time by Laurence Naismith.

Having avoided work for the immediate future I had to do something to pass the time, so I invited my mother to stay, if she didn't mind sharing my bed. She needed no second invitation. She longed to see where I had taken root. She wasn't too enthusiastic over the carpet-less stairs, but once in the sitting room she appreciated my efforts at décor. I think she found the whole atmosphere rather Bohemian. However she was terrified of the various noises in the night, finally waking me to tell me in a frightened voice that someone was dragging something heavy across the roof above; she thought it was a body. I told her it was only the rats who played about at night. This shot her out of bed. Rats! I tried to explain to her that they were all over London – we were surrounded by bombed buildings. 'You mean you have them in the flat?' I had to admit they were around. She begged me to call in an official to do something about it, and caught an earlier train home.

Two days after she left I opened the door of the oven and a large rat jumped out and landed in my lap. I don't know which of us was the most scared or surprised. It was sufficient for me to dial the number of the Westminster City Council and was put through to the Sanitation Squad. They were hard pressed and overworked, but one afternoon a member of the Rodent Exterminators finally arrived. He was pale grey of complexion and reminded me of Peter Cushing as King Rat. He only lacked the whiskers. On looking round the sitting room he rubbed his hands gleefully.

'My heavens, miss, you've certainly got 'em here!' He explored the wainscoting with a digging implement. 'See these holes, they are all around.' He proceeded to make them larger, at the same time putting down piles of evil looking powder. He told me not to touch it; the rats would eat it and die.

'Not in here, I hope.' How would I get rid of the corpses? He told me not to worry – something about dying of dehydration which sounded very unpleasant.

'Where else?' he asked.

'Only my bedroom, they make a noise overhead at night.'

'They would, most likely it's where they nest. Oh miss, you don't sleep in that bed under the window?' He was really agitated. 'They can jump in windows you know. Those big 'uns come off the ships, they carry bubonic plague and they bite.' He was at his most sinister.

'Well I've been inoculated against bubonic plague, but I could close the window before I go to sleep.'

He gave me a very odd look. 'You can call me if you have any further trouble.'

*   *   *   *   *

I was so happy, I could hardly believe it was me. I loved my little garret, the shopping in New Row, the pub with good food. There were plenty of cafés and small restaurants in that area, a baker with home-made bread – the smell was so seductive – a grocer, and a greengrocer. Everything I needed was right on the doorstep. I used my old service knapsack as a shopping bag and this usually began conversations – but everyone talked to one-another then. I frequently met friends from my travels, theatre folk too. In that vicinity there were many.

A letter from Port Said – wonderful, he was on his way. Poor Jack – four pages full of the agonies of the voyage. Six colonels holed up in one cabin. I laughed at the thought of it. Stafford was in some dormitory, his sufferings had to be the greater. At least the colonels had brought aboard plenty of booze.

Another loving and funny missive from Gibralter with news that the ship would dock at Liverpool. If I had made arrangements to be out of London would I please cancel them and be there to meet him at the station. I had, of course, done nothing but wait and plan. Finally, a cable arrived to say they were landing on June 7th.

Feverish excitement – what to wear? I splashed out and bought myself a saucy little hat to add to my Bond Street suit, which had used most of my coupons. I must visit the butcher to try and wheedle another chop and anything else he might have to offer. I tempted the butcher with Jack's future ration book and the fact that he had been in the Far East for six years. I was promised two chops and perhaps a piece of ham or corned beef.

FOURTEEN

Jack Home

Even in the sea of khaki disgorging from the train at Euston Station, Jack's tall broad frame was instantly recognisable. Apart from all the red and gold trimmings, and there were several of those, he stood out from the crowd. He was searching for me and I was being swallowed up in the masses. Eventually I leapt onto an empty baggage truck waving my arms, and his face was suddenly lit by a smile. We managed to carve a path towards one another. Oh the heaven – he was here – his arms enfolding me. Then over his shoulder I saw Stafford, grinning broadly and standing back. I turned and we laughed and hugged. He told me he was thankful to hand Jack over to me, the journey had been hell. I could imagine what it had been like, patience was not one of Jack's virtues.

Porters existed in 1946, so arranging all the tin trunks and bags was easier than I had expected. Jack has armed himself with sterling. Before I knew it the whole load was on the very truck I had been standing on. More cash was produced as we were wheeled towards the taxi ranks and somehow everything was squeezed onto and into a taxi, with Jack and I squashed in as well. Stafford was staying with friends. Jack gave my address to the driver and we moved out of the crowds, holding hands so tightly, in case this was not really happening.

In his letter he had asked if he could join me – if I would have him – until he knew what his next role in life was to be. It was Whitsun, London was more or less empty, but accommodation was, as always, full. Jack had written suggesting we go away for two weeks holiday, but I had not thought too seriously of the idea.

I wondered what he would make of my 'eyrie'. When we arrived in Bedford Street, how in hell we were to get all those trunks and his gear up the small well-trodden stairs. However, he had a way of making things happen. Before I realised what was going on, I found myself surrounded in the flat by tin trunks and baggage. Jack paid off the taxi driver enlisted to help with the lifting and shoving and was washing his hands in the sink. He came back to me, laughing with happiness and grabbing hold of me we whirled around the room until we flopped onto one of the window seats.

'Darling, it's wonderful. You clever girl.'

'It's not very big,' I apologised.

'Don't worry. We'll sort it out. Wait until I show you some of the things I've brought.' The trunks were treasure chests. The wonderful rugs went on the floor instantly. There were saris for me, fabric for curtains when we had a home, and all my completed orders from various shops in Bombay. Jack also told me the Bombay workshops had carved and made a replica of a Regency sofa for us as a wedding present, which was being sent on another ship.

Having at last closed all the trunks and covered them with a colourful Indian rug, I produced the half bottle of Scotch I had been hoarding. We sat on the window seat, and drank to one another – together at last in England. Jack fished in his pocket and pulled out a small package. He took my left hand and placed a ring on my finger, it was the bluest sapphire from Ceylon, set in diamonds, a ring to wear forever. It was a moment of surprise and pure joy.

Whit Sunday brought absolute peace and silence. We were entirely undisturbed. There was no agency open on the floor below, and either the lady on the floor beneath was away with one of her gentlemen, or she was having a weekend of rest. There was no sound from the Covent Garden market – even the Italian café had closed. It was what we longed for and needed. We talked – some of it news and plans – many of them Jack's. He was to re-start his career immediately.

I should have guessed.

He telephoned his father. I imagine after six years the old man had been uncertain of ever seeing his youngest son again. I am sure it was an emotional call. He lived in his own house (Jack's really) with one of Jack's elder sisters. He told his son that all his suits – overcoats and everything – had been carefully tended during his long absence and were in perfect condition, as was Jack's car, a beautiful old pre-war Sunbeam "drop-head" which had been on blocks in the garage, drained of petrol and protected against rust. Jack assured him he would be out to Southgate to visit as soon as he could.

Around mid-morning I thought I should take him across the road to meet Queenie. She was overwhelmed to say the least as Jack was still in uniform, having no 'civvies'. It was drinks all round, then down Bedford Street and Garrick Street to the Arts Theatre Club, where Jack told me we were lunching with Alec Clunes. They were planning a production of *Othello*, Jack to play the title role and Alec opposite as Iago. Talk about jumping in at the deep end!

I had only known Jack surrounded by military and fully occupied with his job of organising ENSA, making a success of it all and cutting through red tape when he had to. Now I was about to see him as the career man, dedicated and ambitious. Enthusiasm he always had – when dealing with the many problems in India – now it was infectious and bursting out of him. This was the man who in India said that he did not think anyone would remember him. He was not even certain if he could still act!

*   *   *   *   *

Over lunch I listened. The conversation was so fast-flowing there was little need for me to do anything else, except (I hope) look decorative. Alec suddenly turned to me and asked my opinion on Jack opening with a starring role in a play at the Arts. I was enthusiastic. It was a splendid way for him to re-launch his career if a suitable play could be found. A selection of plays was then avidly discussed. Jack liked the idea of a revival apart from the classics.

I ventured to mention George Bernard Shaw, and that collection of clever young men all looked at me (I almost blushed, but I had cured myself of that embarrassing habit some time ago). 'Excellent idea,' someone remarked. Immediately all the Shaw plays with a male lead of importance were discussed. The favourite was *The Apple Cart*, and all were in favour of Jack playing King Magnus with rehearsals to commence as soon as possible. Alec would find a three-week slot for this comeback for Jack in the forthcoming schedule of plays for the Arts Theatre.

On our way back to Bedford Street, I queried the Arts Council tour of *Othello* that was also being planned. They were to play in any of the cities of Europe that had a theatre or suitable building still standing. Many had been enemy occupied during the war. Jack was to lead with *Othello* and *Candida*, Alec Clunes *Don Juan in Hell* and Fay Compton, a then famous theatre actress, was to be the female star; the remainder of the company was yet to be cast.

'It sounds exciting but hard work and uncomfortable at times. A grand ENSA! I don't understand why you want to go away again.' I added quietly as we climbed the rickety stairs to our sanctuary, knowing that it would involve yet another parting.

'No, you'll come with me. I'm certain that there will be a part for you. I'll make sure there is.' This was something I feared – being fitted into his production. I would never know whether I was earning the work on my own merit, or that Jack had arranged it.

'How long will you be away?'

Jack answered that they were still in the early stages of the project and he had to play King Magnus first. Of course he had no desire to go away again playing in semi-demolished cities but alas, finance and the Inland Revenue were the reason. In his final bundle of Forces mail there had been a demand from the taxman. After six years of service life, the welcome from his country was a demand for payment in full for his final year of work, *The Importance of Being Ernest* and Edmund in *King Lear*, both with John Gielgud. Two thousand pounds! I was aghast. It was a huge sum and there was no hope of paying it when just out of the army with very little money.

'So you see, my darling, I have to do this tour to pay the Inland-blasted-Revenue. Hopefully, we can then begin afresh. Anyway, I long to tackle *Othello*, it's a great challenge.' I looked at him, his eyes shining and sparkling at the prospect. He told me he had been studying the play on the voyage home – it helped to maintain his sanity.

I kissed him. 'You'll be fine, I can't wait to see you, but as you say, 'Magnus' looms ahead. What the hell are we going to eat tonight?'

'Those chops you cooked last night were delicious. By the way, I didn't know you could cook.'

'I can't,' I replied with truth. I'd left a comfortable home far too young and thereafter lived in digs or hotels. When I had occasionally shared a flat, it had been with an older actress, or Irene, and they had cooked the rare meal. Cafés were the main source of hurried eating during the war. 'Anyway, I'm afraid there is little else to cook. We've eaten the ration for the week!'

'How about an omelette?' he offered, 'that's one of my few culinary successes.'

I gazed at that face I loved, heaved a sigh, and told him the sad truth about dried eggs.

'We have some corned beef. I suppose I could try making a hash with some potatoes.'

Jack laughed. 'We'll wander through Soho – I know all the good restaurants there, one is certain to be open. If not, we could go across to the Savoy. They will be pleased to see me back and my credit's good.' I rushed to do my hair and pretty-up.

I was in a whole new world.

Bliss does not last, it cannot, but without a dose or two in life, one is missing out. Sure enough, with the weekend over the agency re-opened. The smells from the Italian trattoria were more pungent. The telephone jangled constantly. Friends called to know if Jack was safely returned. There was an offer of work for me, and a call for Jack to hurry to the Arts: they were already forging ahead with the production of *The Apple Cart*.

Rene Noble, the owner of the theatrical agency, had apoplexy when she saw Jack coming down the stairs and I was forced to introduce them. Thereafter she put it around that he was one of her clients!

I was alone, trying to concentrate on the tedious but necessary task of learning lines as I had another week at the Richmond Theatre ahead. The background music from outside the window indicated that the show at the Adelphi Theatre was approaching the interval. Suddenly a sharp piercing whistle from the street below sent me rushing to the window. I knew it had to be Jack because he was the only man I knew who had that trick of the Cockney whistle with two fingers in the mouth. Wonderful for hailing taxis! Looking down into an empty Bedford Street I could see Alec Clunes. Beside him was parked a large yellow Sunbeam – hood down – revealing a two-seater with lush leather upholstery, huge wheels and headlamps. Jack was leaning against this magnificent vehicle. He had told me that he had been a collector of unique motorcars and this was his last pre-war one. Gazing in admiration, I threw down the front door keys as bidden. In the evenings it was the simplest way of getting in because in the day the front door was always open. There was extraordinary trust and lack of fear at that time. When they arrived in the flat Alec remarked that it was an unusual way to greet visitors. I laughed.

Jack had been out to Southgate to visit his father. Alec had used up his precious ration of petrol to drive him there. Jack had been walking around wearing a combination of uniform and civilian clothes and so needed some of the suits and shirts so carefully tended by his father during his long absence. Of course, he wanted his car too. Amazingly, once filled, she had started at the first turn of the ignition key, but unfortunately you could not fill up her tank with the measly ration allowed. She also gobbled up petrol at an impractical rate. Although parking problems were unheard of, and vandalism yet to come, I did suggest that it might be better to find a garage. Alec miraculously achieved this in a few days.

The following day was Sunday. Determined to make use of this beautiful vehicle whilst we could, Jack drove me down to the river near Staines. He owned, he told me, with another actor friend, a half share in a bungalow-cum-cottage on the riverbank – they enjoyed a mutual passion for fishing. Bit by bit I was asembling the jigsaw puzzle of Jack's pre-war life.

We purred along in comfort on almost deserted roads. The interior of the car was luxurious: mahogany and soft grey leather. There were no motorways or Heathrow Airport; the air was fresh, and to be relished in an open car.

I enquired if Jack had alerted Arthur (Hamblin) and his wife of our impending arrival but was assured it was not necessary. His friend would either be fishing or in the nearby pub. In fact, it was almost as if we had been expected, for they rushed out to greet us as soon as we drove into the driveway.

Returning happy and contented after a truly enjoyable day, I asked Jack more about the couple and how often was he able to stay there? Apparently not as frequently as he wished, but he would occasionally drive down after the theatre.

'Did Jessica go with you?' I cannot think why I asked, I never spoke of his past marriage and he rarely mentioned it. Now that we were on home ground, I needed to know more of Jack's background.

His reply was abrupt, 'No, she didn't care for it.' The subject was not mentioned again.

The late evening sunshine was to be enjoyed. I put my head back against the soft seat and we both began to sing.

*   *   *   *   *

The handsome solicitor and I faced each other across the desk. He was beaming and I was laughing. The news was good: Patrick had provided the necessary evidence and it had all been recorded. He had spent the night with a lady in a hotel somewhere on the south coast. The woman owner of the hotel was more than willing to come to London (with good expenses) to provide the evidence in Court. It was better than I had hoped for or expected. I was laughing because the charming fellow on the other side of the desk had mentioned the name of Pat's partner in this charade.

'You know her?'

'Yes, indeed. She's an actress and an old friend of his. I expect they were working in the same company.' I was not prepared to elucidate, but I am sure they had fun and enjoyed their 'night of sin'. I was glad for him.

'When do you think we'll go to Court?' This was my main concern because my whole life and future revolved around this dreadful day.

'Too early to say. As you know the waiting list is interminable though now we have the evidence we can push ahead. But we're thinking about next year – March if we're lucky.'

I stopped laughing – it was a lifetime away. Next year – and it could be longer – I had to hang on until then. My solicitor looked at me sympathetically.

'There's something else.' I looked up enquiringly. 'At our first meeting you hinted that there was someone in your life, indeed I can't imagine there wouldn't be, but you told me he had nothing to do with your divorce. Knowing the full story, I believe you.'

I tightened up immediately. 'I don't wish him to be involved in any way.' I was nervous now – uncertain.

'No reason why he should be. Is he back from India?'

I paused, but was forced to answer. 'Yes he is, but only very recently. He is to go abroad on the Continent for three or four months.'

'Just as well,' he replied. Rustling some papers, he asked me if I had ever heard of the King's Proctor.

'Vaguely, who is he?'

'Well, hardly one person. It is the legal name for an official body of the law that supposedly pries into your private life during a divorce, to ascertain that there's not collusion between the parties. That the innocent party – you – isn't breaking the rules. It's unfair because the guilty party – in this case that husband of yours – is free to do as he wishes. You have to be careful.'

I took his point and stood up to leave, looking thoughtful. 'We're getting there,' he said reassuringly. 'It would be unbelievable if you didn't have a good man and a splendid future ahead. I know it seems a long wait, but you'll get through it. However, I'm glad you're not contemplating going on the Continent with him.'

Walking home deep in thought along Charles Street and the Haymarket, I knew that one decision had been made for me. There would be no question of my being 'fitted in' for the tour. Although I hated the thought of parting it appeared to be a dreadful blessing in disguise. I decided to ask Queenie if she knew of a room to let nearby, as Jack should be seen to have a separate address, although all his mail was delivered to the Savage or Arts Club.

I simply had to get on with my life until I was liberated, and work as much as possible. The divorce expenses were mounting and I had to pay for them. By the time Jack finished the tour the Court hearing could be imminent.

*　*　*　*　*

I was running down the alleyway between the Adelphi Theatre and my building, my coat collar turned up, and held tightly around me, for underneath was only my nightgown. It was Sunday morning and completely deserted. I reached my destination – the paper stall in The Strand – without encountering a soul. I flew back to Bedford Street, out of breath by now, and flung the newspapers on the floor. Jack made tea whilst I rapidly turned pages to the theatre columns. 'This is great – the Sunday Times'. It was only then that he joined me. Trying to look nonchalant, he took the paper out of my hands, putting the tea on to the table while I searched through the other papers. They were unanimous in their praise for Jack's performance and welcomed his return. A successful actor prominent on the London stage since first appearing as a boy in *St Joan* was now back to take his rightful place once more. He was smiling. 'They're good.

I'm delighted so many of the critics remember me.'

I was convinced of his success, but one can never be certain. The first night the tiny theatre had been packed, buzzing with anticipation and there had been tremendous applause. The reception was mainly for Jack's 'Magnus' – an exacting role and quite a load to carry for a first appearance in many years. I was sitting out in front suffering first night nerves, for once not for myself. I did not have Stafford with me as he was on stage playing one of the smaller roles. Alec was with me but he kept disappearing. I hadn't seen Jack all day, indeed I hadn't expected to. He was at the theatre and later, at the National Gallery. I learnt, over time, that looking at paintings was his way of coping with first night nerves.

Now we were both relaxed. Drinking tea, eating toast, talking about the first night and our small celebration afterwards. Not a party, we simply enjoyed eating at a table with a few close friends. Now was the moment of satisfaction – excellent reviews from the press.

Jack rented a room, rather a dreary one two doors away in Bedford Street, but it was cheap and clean. As he spent all his time there learning dialogue, I doubt he had even noticed his surroundings. I hoped it would pacify my solicitor, although I had heard nothing further. As we were both busy rehearsing, we did not see each other as frequently as before.

Later that Sunday, while a group of us were again at the Arts Club having lunch and discussing the notices, I noticed a young couple sitting on one of the window seats, who only had eyes for each other. They were enchanting – like a pair of cherubs. I asked Alec, who was next to me, who they were. 'Oh, that's Dickie Attenborough and Sheila Sim. They were recently married, I believe. Sheila's on tour with *Arsenic and Old Lace*. I expect he met her train – she's probably breaking her journey so they can lunch together.'

'They love each other very much,' I said quietly. Of course, I now recognised the couple. I had seen *Brighton Rock,* in which the very young Richard Attenborough gave a memorable performance as

Pinkie the boy-gangster. I had seen both of them in the occasional British film which made it to India. I turned my eyes away, hoping that one day we could be in that state of married bliss. In the unseen future Dickie and Sheila would become close friends of ours.

* * * * *

The unpleasant letter handed to me by my neighbour, the theatrical agent, bore the news that the telephone was about to be disconnected – the account was overdue. Rene insisted that it was nothing to do with her; she had paid her contribution. We did have a communal line but with separate numbers. Both should have been long since paid by my landlord, who owned her office and my attic – but was now out of reach in Germany. I was perfectly happy to pay my three-month share, but it was minimal in comparison. A total of £60 was overdue, then an enormous sum. Rene and I were in unison: our telephones were essential, for her business and for me to be contactable for work – apart from my private life. Had I the sixty pounds? Rene was pleading. Apparently she had not. The agency could not be very lucrative. How was I supposed to raise such a sum? I had no intention of asking Jack, who was so generous in every way. He was deeply into *Othello*, rehearsing every day, with the departure imminent – not the moment to talk of telephones. Did Rene know any means of contacting our landlord? She said she had the number of the C.S.E. headquarters, so I told her to trace our errant landlord whilst we still had a telephone. Somehow I would dig deep into the sock for the money.

Within a day I received a phone call from Germany with profuse apologies. It was extraordinary that in the rush to get away the telephone account had been mislaid! However – if I could pay the account, my tenancy would be extended for another three weeks at least. I accepted with relief. I was nearing the end of my stay in Bedford Street, and though I had not given it much thought I had nowhere else to go.

*   *   *   *   *

Stafford had whiled away some of his time waiting in India for a ship by writing a play, with myself in mind for the lead. Most flattering. I had read it, so had Jack, and he thought it a good role for me, and the play worth a 'try-out', if Stafford could find a suitable theatre. I introduced him to my old friend Peter Coleman, now an actor-manager again, who liked the play and said he would play the male lead opposite me, and Derek Francis the other. Peter was producing and directing in one of the Moss Empire Theatres around London, so the play was accepted.

It was to be my first job after Jack left, so I was thankful that I would be too occupied to be unhappy – for a while.

Jack wanted me to attend the final rehearsal of *Othello*. As anticipated, he gave a fine performance. I could imagine, with the make-up and costume, that he would be magnificent. He was leaving the next day.

It was deeply depressing watching him from the attic window as a bus with all the actors aboard collected him en route for a train to the Continent. He looked up and waved, blowing a final kiss. No longer in the army uniform but casual civilian clothes and hair longer for the two roles, he climbed aboard to join the company, who were all laughing and greeting him. Oh, I knew how it would be, excitement, discomforts, parties – all shared. When you're working so closely it's like a family – squabbles and all.

I turned away to the empty room where only his tin trunks remained. I must hurry. I was off to the first reading of Stafford's play. Within half an hour I was walking to the Prince of Wales Theatre where the actors were gathered in an upstairs room. It was a glorious autumn morning and my heart lifted. I was myself again with no distractions. When I was working that was how I needed to be – single-minded. Peter was introducing me to the members of the cast that I did not already know. Scripts in hand, we were off.

FIFTEEN

Moving On

Stafford was worried about my not having anywhere to live. My exit from Bedford Street might coincide with the dress rehearsal and opening night of his play and he was fussed that it would affect my performance. I hadn't given the situation much thought. Jack's leaving was sufficient upheaval and I was completely absorbed in work. It was a real 'clothes horse' of a role. I had managed an interview with one of Moss Empire's executives to plead for a financial allowance towards the hire of expensive clothes and he had acquiesced, so I was dashing about choosing elegant outfits and paying little attention to my domestic arrangements.

Stafford had many friends in the profession. One with a room available in Sloane Street was Joan Craft, who by coincidence was the Stage Director for C.B. Cochran and the show at the Adelphi, my next-door neighbours. Stafford urged me to take this opportunity and move before the final rehearsal and opening. So I gathered together my few possessions in preparation. After the day's rehearsal he was coming to take me for dinner.

I was in my tiny bedroom when suddenly there was a noise outside the window. Looking out, I saw a young man, wearing his old army jacket, on a ladder cleaning the windows below. He gave me a cheery wave, which I acknowledged before turning to pack more into the over-flowing wardrobe trunk. Suddenly there was a loud cry and a crash. I rushed to the window and could see the young fellow lying beside his ladder and pail, moaning most dreadfully with blood pouring out of his mouth. Distraught, I rushed to the telephone, dialling 999. I realised that apart from the Italians, I was possibly the only person in the building.

At that moment there was a shout from Stafford in the street below, so I flung down the keys, returning to the bedroom window again. The sight was awful – what could I do? I ran to the stairs, meeting Stafford and telling him what had happened. He came up into my room, looking out at the pitiful sight. 'We can't move him, that would be too dangerous, not knowing the extent of his injuries.'

We hurried down the stairs together, hoping the ambulance would arrive and found the Italians clustered in panic. His cries were heart-rending, and the injuries so serious because he had fallen on the wretched wheel they used for grinding their knives, but there was not a thing we could do to help.

'He was so young,' I said, 'and still wearing his army jacket.' I hung on to Stafford, glad to have him there for comfort. 'I can't wait to leave here now. I want to go as soon as possible, if Joan will have me.' Staff said we both needed a stiff drink, so we crossed over to Queenie's. The pub was fairly empty but bad news travels fast. Someone had known the window cleaner who was indeed recently de-mobbed. He had four young children and no job and was only cleaning windows to earn a few shillings, so of course had no insurance. He died later that night – the wretched knife grinder had pierced his lung. Queenie soon organised a collection for the young widow. How she would manage with four children was an appalling thought. I had just come through a time of many deaths, but the war was behind us. The tragedy was somehow made worse by knowing that the fellow had fought through the war and survived, only to lose his life falling off a ladder in a London street.

The next day, being Sunday, I was packed and ready to leave, Stafford had arranged some form of transport for me. I had no regrets leaving – that young man's dreadful accident haunted me.

*   *   *   *   *

Joan Craft looked in dismay at my tin trunks and bags. I don't blame her. I am sure at that moment she was regretting her decision to give me a roof over my head. Luckily it was much easier to manipulate them down her basement steps than the back-breaking task of heaving them up the unsound stairs to the attic had been. But Joan was not a first rate Stage Director for no reason and soon had all Jack's gear stored on and under the old staircase to the main house, which had been closed off when it was converted. Joan had her own room and we shared the bathroom. There was a pleasant sitting room with a real fire, leading on to a tiny garden. The fire was a godsend in the bitter months to come, because of course there was no central heating. There was a tiny kitchen in which I began to learn the rudiments of cooking, but unfortunately, little food. The rationing seemed even more stringent than it was in wartime. The lavatory was outside – only a few short steps across a tiny yard – but when the snows came! The rent was very low.

*   *   *   *   *

Then followed the worst winter of my entire life. I hasten to add that this had nothing to do with my flat-mate. Although we were complete opposites in every way, we became good friends. Joanie was small, tough and direct. She had to be, she held an important and demanding job and ruled all the staff under her. She had to deal with rough, and often surly, stage-hands, overseeing props, scenery and effects – all the hard work that goes on backstage, especially with a musical, and which never gets the applause. I hardly saw her. She was at the theatre every day, and of course, in the evenings. She was highly energetic, so when she had time, she would clean the flat. I really did not think about it much. I looked after my own room and cleaned the bath. She always made food ready for her after-theatre supper; if I had not eaten, and there was enough, I joined her. When I look back on it now I realise how selfish I must have appeared, or lazy, but it was simply lack of thought. It was not my flat and I had only briefly shared with a girl before. I was so wrapped up in the problems of my own life, and so heavily involved with work, I was hardly around.

Stafford's play occupied so much of my time because I wanted to do my best for him. He sat through most of the rehearsals, making any necessary changes. Each night, after the curtain came down, we would sit in my dressing room and have a post-morten discussion on the performances.

The showing of the play was successful in one way. The many theatrical agents and managements that Stafford had been able to persuade to come and watch it helped me considerably in the future. Offers were made of tours – and another showing with a star name, preferably a man. Dennis Price, who had worked with Stafford pre-war, was high on the list. Of course Dennis was now a major film star and not at all free to do an unknown play. I knew I did not wish to tour, I had done enough of that in my early days. I needed to stay in London for many reasons; the divorce; to hear from Jack; to wait for his return; my contacts were in London.

So I suddenly hit a black patch. I had been fortunate with work, but by the end of October there was nothing. I put it down to the change of address and telephone number. If you are not obtainable there is always someone else. All was silence on the divorce, just the endless waiting for a date. Silence from Jack, except a brief note from him after the opening of *Othello* in Prague, saying what a success it had been. He, personally, had received great acclaim for his Othello. He sent all his love but I was not to anticipate much in the way of communication. The acting was exhausting, also there were after-show parties given by the many occupying 'brass hats', local mayors, consuls, ambassadors et al which were not easy to cut. As he had to shower away all the black make-up before he could appear, he was not only tired but late. Then he was always travelling. Surely we had been through this before? Not hearing did not help my state of mind. Depression set in.

My various travelling companions had found me during my Bedford Street days, including Pamela and Robert, although as they had parted company she was alone. Bob Ayres and I would run across each other in the job hunt. His Canadian accent was an asset. He became quite successful playing Americans, making film appearances and later in television. Joanna was married and living in Chelsea, we would meet occasionally. Later she followed her actor husband up to Stratford-on-Avon and they had a son, Anthony, named after her brother who sadly died of wounds received on almost the last day of the war in Europe – a heartbreak for the brigadier and his family. On looking at her baby, I am certain the last thought that would have occurred to her was that she was nursing a future chef, whose amusing television appearances may be the result of the theatrical blood in his veins. Otherwise Anthony Worral Thompson had a military background going back generations. There is no question that he made a wise choice of career. Angela and I were in constant touch, but she preferred to live out of London, with her mother, now remarried.

It was Rosamund Merivale that I saw most, so it was a happy day when I could tell her that the large bed-sitter flat above me was becoming vacant. It was still impossible to find anywhere to live and Roz was desperate. Having Roz on the floor above was a lifesaver and we spent much time together. She knew a wide circle of actors, was always having groups around, and somehow we would find bits to eat though drink was a problem—but often helped by generous guests. She was waiting for James – the Canadian Major she had fallen for in Cairo – to marry her, and had put her career on hold. It was taking too long of course as he was heavily involved in Canadian politics. She was in the same unhappy state as I – we were consolation for one another.

*   *   *   *   *

When you are in a dark pit, there is only one way to go – up and out. Not easy I found. November had come with a bitter cold that I had not experienced for many years and my thinned blood, watered down by the tropics, was not equal to the English winter, nor was I equipped for it. Before Jack had left he had bought me a chic and attractive overcoat, the colour was a warm, golden yellow, and I blessed him every time I wore it. Being loose, I could wear it over a mass of sweaters and it still looked becoming – especially over black. I piled on all the clothing that I possessed without looking too lumpy.

I was not the only one suffering. The streets were full of hurrying, huddled figures with fading tans, looking pinched and grey. This was their first winter home and it went from bad to awful with snow, sleet and icy winds, not helped by the daytime electricity cuts.

Roy, Joanie's friend, moved into the basement for a short stay. Either he gave me 'flu or it was the other way round, we were certainly never in close contact as he was at the other end of the flat, however, we were both ill. Joan was working all hours and desperately endeavouring to be Florence Nightingale in her limited spare time. I had never had influenza before, so it was quite a shock to feel immobilised with aches and pains, the chest wheezing and the temperature steadily rising. Roz ventured down the basement steps, took one look at me and sent for the only doctor she had known.

I am afraid this elegant man, dressed for Harley Street, was rather surprised by my basement surroundings, the bars on the windows and the rumpled bed. But he was sufficiently concerned to ask if I had contracted malaria and suffered any recurrences. I was able to reassure him about that, much to his relief I am sure. He left me some pills with strict instructions to stay in bed and above all to keep warm, remarking that it was far too cold in this room. I agreed and thanked him for calling. He never sent a bill – perhaps he thought I could not pay it.

How can you keep a basement warm, or free of draughts? It was cold and damp and the sunshine never penetrated. I looked out from my bed at the small patch of grey sky, heavy with the threat of snow and thought of the eternal blue skies, the palm trees and the blessed sun. How I longed for them. But I was in London, this was my life and I must get on with it.

Work was the only way out. No money – or very little – is a great impetus. Roy, was out of his sick bed and rehearsing a play, another try-out of a new author. He returned from his labours blue with cold, except for his red nose. I had forced myself as far as the living room, lit the fire and was heating some soup that Joan had thoughtfully left for the invalids.

'Do you want to take on a role in this play? It would suit you very well. It's a good part for a glamorous girl. I told them I knew you and they were delighted. The producer asked me to give you the script to read. The money is rubbish of course, but that's normal.'

I laughed for the first time in many days. 'Glamorous. You have a vivid imagination!' There I stood draped in a blanket from Burma, my hair hanging down, absolutely no make-up, a graveyard cough and sore nose.

I was at rehearsal the next day.

Christmas was fast approaching. I knew I would have to spend it with my parents. It would be my first in England for many years. My brother was still in India so I'd asked Stafford if he would like to join me as he was alone. I thought it might make, what was of necessity going to be a rather frugal affair, more enjoyable for all of us. My father had decided to take us for Christmas dinner to the local hotel, which was old and welcoming, near the River Avon in Christchurch. Joan once asked me why I did not visit them more often and it was difficult to explain the reasons to her. Possibly because I knew they were worried about my lack of money and my future. I felt uncomfortable about that. Also they had their own circle of friends, I was part of a different world.

My life began again. I had a telephone call from Jack. Would I make my way to Brussels as soon as possible? He was arriving there with the company this coming weekend and they were having a few days break in the city. He longed for me to join him. How? It was all arranged. Take a train to Harwich, then boat to Ostend – catch another train to Brussels then a taxi to the hotel. I would arrive late at night, but there was a room and bath booked for me. He would arrive by train the following morning. *Please* would I meet him at the station. There would be no problems, the bookings had been made through our old friend Bunny, who had worked with the welfare team in India and was now with a travel agency. I just had to collect the tickets, plus the small amount of foreign currency that we were allowed. Once we were together I would have no worries.

I was ecstatic – no word for weeks and now this! Typical of Jack – and our life. What an idiot putting myself through all that mental torture! I should know the man by now. I scurried around to find one of the many suitcases. I wondered what on earth to put in it.

The North Sea crossing to Belgium was on a small troopship, loaded with soldiers either in uniform or civvies. I found myself a sheltered corner on deck with a group endeavouring to keep warm in a biting wind. One of the men produced a bottle of Scotch. Another went off in search of cups, paper or otherwise. The company was entertaining, all rejoining occupying forces after home-leave, and all bound for various destinations. The journey passed easily, though I was disappointed that none would accompany me on the train to Brussels as Army transport awaited them. I did not relish the thought of travelling through Belgium alone. Although I had been around so much of the world, this was my first step on European soil. I spoke little French then – anyway the Belgians spoke with a strong Flemish accent.

I passed the lengthy ride in silence on an ill-lit train, the other occupants staring straight ahead. The lighting was due to economy I presumed, the same as at home. It was only when they realised I was English that interest and kindness were shown. Not knowing how long the journey might be, or how many stations I should count, I was becoming rather agitated. All was darkness outside – including the many halts. At Ghent the carriage all but emptied. Finally we slowly entered into what had to be the outskirts of a city. The couple opposite me rose, smiled and nodded, adding 'arrivés'. I thanked them, collecting my case from the rack above.

From then onwards it was easy. A taxi, the name of the hotel, and in minutes I was there in front of a brightly illuminated entrance. The porter opened the taxi door, collecting my case, then ushered me into the foyer.

I could not believe it – lights and warmth – there was actually central heating! Up in a lift to my room, which was welcoming, warm and luxurious: the bathroom even had towels on hot rails. The boy who had brought my case and laid it on the rack was waiting. Oh Lord, a tip! I had little currency left from the £10 we were allowed to take out of the country – and that I was saving for a taxi to the station in the morning. I dived into my bag, finding some packets of cigarettes that I had bought on the boat for this purpose. He accepted them, smiling politely. I explained in my halting French that I was hungry. He replied in good English that he would ask the waiter to bring a menu. Despite the lateness of the hour an excellent sandwich with a glass of wine were brought to my room. I was to discover that this was a land of plenty compared to Stafford Cripp's austerity Britain – including unlimited cigarettes!

Next morning found me running down the platform, keeping abreast of Jack's compartment. He was leaning out of the window with a broad grin of delight. As soon as the train came to a halt, he opened the door and jumped out to fling his arms around me, giving me a great bear-hug. There was so much to say we did not know how to begin, so I said my hellos to the members of the company that I knew, including Terence Plunkett-Greene, late of the Southern India Area, now, thanks to Jack, busy organising the travels and many needs of this tour. Jack said that they could not have done without his expertise and good humour. It had been no joyride – I could believe that – apart from the success of the plays and the huge welcome they received from audiences in what remained of once lovely cities.

Terry eased Jack and myself into a taxi. We shot off ahead of the others, holding hands tightly, exchanging all our news. Jack had the most exciting, fascinating stories to tell, some of them riotously funny. I was just happy to be with him, enjoying the sheer pleasure of being together.

The luxuries in the shops amazed me – nylon and silk stockings, not seen since the war, beautiful cashmere sweaters, chocolates, candied fruits, rich pastries. All of which were on ration or unobtainable at home. One could hardly believe the war and all it's horrors had been here, but it most certainly had. We had been so far away and were totally deprived of European news.

Jack was buying anything I admired so I held my breath. Chocolates and sweets for me to take home and Christmas gifts of scent: I was given my first bottle of Caron 'Bellogia'. Jack thought it the right perfume for me. I still have a bottle on my dressing table half a century later.

The food was a treat and there was no shortage of wine. Spirits were not available but we made do with champagne instead, the very best and plenty of it. Aside from weddings, champagne had not entered my life until now, but Jack was an expert at making champagne cocktails and we extracted every moment of pleasure from our brief reunion.

I was desolate about having to return for Christmas, because Jack hoped I could stay on and see him perform *Othello*. I longed to do so, but had promised my family. I knew they were looking forward to having me at home. Jack comforted me, and himself, with the hope that it would be our last Christmas apart.

The bitterness of departure was eased by an airlift home in a light aircraft with ten passengers. We landed at Croydon, which then had a small airport. But it would be March before I was to see Jack in London.

*   *   *   *   *

1947 entered with heavy snowfalls and driving winds, which continued for weeks. Electricity cuts were frequent. The streets were dim – Piccadilly almost unlit although there had been sparse return of the pre-war illuminations to provide some cheer over the holiday. The best sight was the giant Christmas tree in Trafalgar Square, a gift from Norway and sent in gratitude for our help during the war. Once lit and reaching to the sky, this seasonal remembrance cheered us all.

But 1947 was to become my year, in every way.

Returning to the basement flat after Christmas the telephone was jangling urgently. I ran along the passage to the living room and picked it up. It was Roz, who had seen my arrival so would I hurry up to her flat as soon as I could. Emerging like a mole from down below into the street, I rang her bell. Rosamund was down and opened the door in a flash. She looked different, flushed and obviously bursting to tell me something. I followed her up to her comfortable room with the pleasant view of the gardens opposite, now glistening with snow. There was a fire crackling in the grate and she produced a bottle and two glasses. What heaven, I could warm my hands and frozen feet. In answer to my enquiring look she told me that James had finally made it over from Canada and they had been together whilst I had been in Brussels and during my Christmas visit to my parents. I looked at the very single divan bed and she laughed, guessing my thoughts. 'Yes, it was a tight squeeze. We didn't get very much sleep.' I sat by the fire with my drink, waiting. She dived into her handbag for something, then put a wedding ring on her finger. I jumped up to take her hand and gaze at the gold band with surprise and delight.

'Yes, we were married, in the church just across Sloane Street. James managed to arrange the ceremony very quickly with the vicar, because he only had a few days here. He bought a special licence.'

I was so happy for her – she had waited all those years since Cairo. I kissed her, drinking to their future happiness. Apparently it was not only a hurried wedding but also a secret one. Why? Roz said she found it difficult to understand the reason but James had asked her not to tell anyone for a few weeks, something to do with his political career – there was an election for which he had to return. I was as mystified as Roz, but what did it matter. His

reasons had to be sound and it was only a temporary situation.
'Who went to the church with you?'

'Not a soul. If you'd been here you would have accompanied us.
As it was, we just collected – or rather the vicar did for us – some
helpers in the church.'

So I was the only person to know this momentous piece of news.
Roz was so thankful I was back, she just had to tell me. She kept
gazing at her ring, happy to have it on her finger. As secrecy was
necessary, for whatever reason, I suggested she hung it on a ribbon
or chain around her neck. We sat happily by the fire talking of her
future in Canada. I told her of my wonderful few days with Jack
in Brussels. Roz was planning to go to California quite soon to
stay with her stepmother, Gladys Cooper. Sadly, her father, Philip
Merivale, had died late in the war, before Roz had been able to go
to America to be reunited with him. Her brother John Merivale,
an actor, was with Gladys and working in Hollywood. When Roz
went to stay with them in Beverly Hills, James would visit from
Canada, and that's when the family would be told the news. When
she returned to England she would make plans to move to Canada
to begin a proper married life. Well, at least one of us had achieved
happiness with a long awaited marriage.

The next morning I received a letter from my solicitor to say the
date of the Court hearing had been set for the third week in March
and it was imperative that I attend. At last, a move in the right
direction.

The weeks passed and the snow and cold continued. Work, which
had dried up on me before Christmas, was suddenly coming from
all directions, which was a great blessing, for the costs of the legal
drama ahead were mounting. My solicitor was insisting that I had
the best representation and had arranged for a barrister – a top
one, as I discovered when I paid the account! It seems ridiculous
that divorce was so long drawn out, expensive and emotionally
wearing in comparison with today's 'quickies'. The mere thought
of having to appear in Court I found daunting.

Getting around London was increasingly difficult in thick snow.

Everyone had ceased to care about their appearance and wore trousers, boots (if you could get them), otherwise thick socks – sometimes tied over trousers around the ankles, layers of clothing, scarves, hoods and gloves.

I was rehearsing a play from America, *Cry Havoc*. It had an all woman cast and was about nurses caught up in the war, on one of the islands in the Philippines, a dramatic play with a sad, violent end. I knew the director, George More O'Farrel, and most of the actresses in the cast. Mary Kerridge was leading us. She was a fine actress and a good friend, the wife of John Counsel. They ran the Theatre Royal, Windsor, where I had occasionally worked.

We rehearsed in a building in Marylebone High Street, owned by the BBC. The play was also being televised. The façade was standing but once you entered it was virtually a shell. There were two makeshift offices, with a staircase that appeared to lead to the sky. Having climbed to the top, there was a platform with unsteady planks to edge your way across while beneath was just rubble and a long drop. The planks safely negotiated, you leapt into another part of the building that boasted a roof, and in which someone had placed a couple of oil stoves. We rehearsed there until a theatre became available.

*　　*　　*　　*　　*

Whilst I was playing in *Cry Havoc*, Jack returned to England. He wanted me to meet him with a hired car as he had collected so many things on his tour. Roz had left for America and we had made an arrangement for Jack to rent her flat in her absence, so I was thankful I did not have to ask Joan for yet more luggage space.

He was amazed at the sight of thick snow, which was now packed solid, and would take a long time to disappear in the still zero climate. His last date had been in Nice, in glorious South of France sunshine. He had certainly been enjoying high living, lunching with Somerset Maugham in his villa on Cap Ferrat.

He was not pleased that I had to rush off to work in the evening, but I showed him the flat and assured him that I would hurry back as soon as the curtain was down. I added that I'd prepared a stew (I was learning), told him it was in the oven, and asked him to please light the gas at a certain time.

Cry Havoc by now was in its final throes. I suspected that it was not the moment for a depressing all-women wartime play. On the bright side, as far as I and other members of the cast were concerned, it had been seen by most agents and many managements, which might prove beneficial for future work. I was about to make my dash for home and Jack, hardly bothering to remove all my make-up, when an agent I knew came backstage. As he had come chiefly to see my performance, I simply had to agree to a drink with him in the nearby pub.

Eventually I made it back to Sloane Street and Jack's warm embrace. The fire was lit, the table laid and he had opened a bottle of champagne brought back from France. I went to the oven to produce the stew. He had forgotten to light it!

*   *   *   *   *

We were back at the Arts Threatre Club, where *Othello* was the chief topic of discussion. H.M. Tennant was the important management then with 'Binkie' Beaumont ruling over all from his office at the Globe Theatre. He had decided to place *Othello* and possibly *Candida* for a short season of three months in a West End theatre. I was delighted and Jack secretly pleased. He deserved his *Othello* to be shown to a London audience as he had received great acclaim on the tour.

It had, however, been very exhausting. He needed a rest, but Binkie wanted to go ahead soon. Another difficulty was Alec Clunes, who firmly refused to continue playing Iago. Whatever the reason, it involved recasting and at short notice.

A notable contribution that Alec Clunes made in post-war London theatre was to employ as many actors and writers as he could, especially those who had returned from the war with no work and had to face up to starting again from scratch. Thanks to Alec, many long-absent talents appeared in revivals of some of the finest plays, as well as premieres of new ones. Laurence Olivier and others in management adopted this same worthy approach to casting. It was much appreciated by the actors who had been serving in the forces or incarcerated in POW camps.

I was suddenly called by the Rank Organisation: would I go for an interview with Antony Bushell in connection with Laurence Olivier's keenly anticipated film of *Hamlet*? He was to direct and play *Hamlet*, as he had with his film of *Henry V*. When in my teens working in northern rep, I managed to see many films, sneaking in during the afternoons. I recalled Antony Bushell as being one of the best looking of young British actors, tall and blond haired, with striking eyes. I mentioned to Jack that I was off to meet him; naturally Jack knew him. They had last met during the early part of the war when they were first in uniform. 'Give Tony my best' was his parting request. This I did not do, I did not want to create any special interest. Indeed I was curious about the whole summons from the casting director.

Anthony Bushell lived up to past memories. Not only was he tall and good-looking with blue eyes that crinkled when he smiled, he was full of natural charm. He took my coat (my Burma Green blanket from my bed-roll made into a wonderfully warm and smart coat by Roz's dressmaker). He knew that I had been the Far East for some time and asked me about my war. We spoke of that for a moment over a cup of tea. Then he said 'You see Laurence (he never called him Larry, not on set anyway) is most anxious to employ actors who have returned from service in the war.' I agreed that this was a laudable policy and to be welcomed.

Soon the reason for my interview was explained. 'As you know, there are few women in *Hamlet*. I nodded, I had heard that the teenage Jean Simmons was playing Ophelia and Eileen Herlie the Queen. He went on to tell me there were to be ten actors playing ladies and gentleman of the Court, in attendance, and on set most of the time. So it was vital that experienced actors were cast. There would be a great deal of ensemble acting and occasional close-ups. Every day on set – that would mean for the entire film. At last, some months of regular money, I thought. It would pay for the divorce. 'You're used to working in period costume of course.'

'Oh yes,' I answered quickly, 'both in drama and comedy. Restoration, Victorian . . .' He stopped me, laughing, saying that he knew a certain amount about my work or would not have asked me to join them. My heart leapt. So I was in! The money was good, it would keep me until the Decree Absolute was through and I was free.

He said I was to go the costumiers for measurements and fitting. Later, I would receive a call to go to Denham Studios for hair, false pieces and styling. We would commence shooting in April. 'See you on the set' was his farewell. I left, brimming with excitement and happiness at my sudden turn of fate. I would be working with interesting and top actors and my financial worries were resolved. My Court appearance would be over by the time filming started. I would also be free to be with Jack, to attend his first night of *Othello*. I fled as on wings to meet him, to tell him my news.

*　　*　　*　　*　　*

Almost alone, I sat in the darkened stalls of the Piccadilly Theatre where a dress rehearsal was in progress. The majority of the company was at ease in their performances; they had been playing *Othello* for six months. Some changes may have occurred in minor roles, but the important replacement was Iago, where Anthony Quayle had stepped in at remarkably short notice. I felt he had been given rather a raw deal. Most of the ten days of his rehearsal had been with the director or stage manager, or Jack's understudy. It was no fault of Jack's if he appeared to be unhelpful; he was exhausted and badly needed rest. With the sudden change of climate he had developed a cold, causing the usual panic about his voice, his most precious instrument, which had to be guarded for the first night. Jack was unhappy about the theatre too. He did not like the Piccadilly. It was considered by many actors to be a white elephant, tucked away behind the Regent Palace Hotel. He summed it up by saying it had 'no passing trade'. I could see what he meant: hardly mainstream Shaftesbury Avenue, with posters, names above the entrance and photographs going unnoticed.

I was watching Tony closely. He was giving what I thought was a remarkably new interpretation of the role of Iago, original and well thought-out. I had not seen Alec Clunes' performance, though I am sure, fine actor as he was, he would have been playing the role in a more traditional style. Jack had only managed two rehearsals with Tony, and in those I suspect he was 'walking through' them, guarding his vocal chords. I wondered if he appreciated how different Tony's performance would be to Alec's. When Jack made his entrance I was electrified. He looked magnificent in the dark make-up, his eyes flashing in the lights, and in the colourful robes his whole presence was commanding and charismatic. Now he was the best, holding the stage, his voice was unique. How I loved to watch him act. No wonder he found Othello exhausting, with a gamut of emotions through the play, culminating in the final agonising scene with Desdemona, when he strangles her. Then the terrible cry of remorse, and his tragic death. No wonder all the actors I have known who braved *Othello* found it not only physically and mentally draining, but also depressing. There is little room for anything else in their day, which is spent conserving their strength for the performance.

Backstage I found Tony Quayle and Jack flopped out in chairs, both clutching a glass of Scotch. I quickly kissed Jack. 'Alright?' he asked.

'Much more than alright – I'll tell you later.' I turned to Tony, who was looking thoroughly disheartened. 'I think your interpretation of Iago is brilliant.'

He brightened a little. 'I felt I must try for something new and different. I want to make him more of a rough solider – a sergeant major type. I'm not sure that I'm getting it over in the way that I'd hoped.'

'Oh yes you are. You had no audience out front tonight to enable you to judge reactions.'

He gave me a wry smile. 'That's true. It's also my first real rehearsal with the full company.'

'I know you haven't had much of a chance, but I promise you that tomorrow night it'll be different. Everyone will love it. Critics as well as the audience.'

'I hope you're right. You've encouraged me. Anyway it's too late to change my performance. I wish I had more time.'

I could sympathise. When you step into another actor's shoes, in a company already well worn-in, you are the odd one out. Tony had been left pretty much to his own devices.

We neither of us mentioned our meetings in Cairo. That was in the past; we were concentrated on now, and the future. We all were.

I was consumed with anxiety on the first night. Stafford was sitting with me in the stalls, amid the buzz of excitement and greetings. We waited quietly for the curtain to rise. We were both in evening dress, which was mandatory in those days. I had visited a second-hand dress shop in Knightsbridge, managing to buy (without coupons) a black chiffon dress with jet trimming which suited my figure and colouring. Being so small a size I could easily slip into it. It was an important investment as I was to accompany Jack to the party the famous 'Binkie' was giving at his lovely old house in Lord North Street. I was a little scared of facing a gathering of so many West End stars that seemed like a club of which I was not a member. I felt I would be regarded with suspicion, possibly be compared to Jessica Tandy, though we were not remotely alike. This would be Jack's first party with old friends since he left the London stage for the war.

I was right about Anthony Quayle, whose confident performance and fresh interpretation of Iago made the audience sit up. Jack received a wonderful ovation of welcome on his first entrance. Once on stage, I only had eyes for him. He was magnetic and powerful. However, though no one would have noticed as I did, he was being slightly thrown off-balance by Tony.

During the interval, whilst Stafford and I were having a drink, we laughed at the contrast of the colonel in India and now Othello! Then he spoke of Quayle's Iago. 'What courage to tackle such a well-known classical role in an entirely different way.' Courage was one of Tony's undoubted qualities. I was glad my intuition that Jack had been slightly thrown went unnoticed by Stafford.

Jack's dressing room was the usual crush of backstage visitors after a first night. The theatre manger had escorted Stafford and me through the 'pass-door', which leads directly on to the stage, so we were first in the dressing room to give our congratulations. I hugged him with joy. Then Stafford and I went to work pouring out whatever drinks we were able to provide for the invasion, which was considerable. Jack was able to plead the excuse that he was expected at 'Binkie's' and had to remove all the body make-up, so disappeared into the shower with his dresser. When Stafford bade his farewell we were alone.

'Well?' he shouted, above the running water.

I shouted back that I could only add to the praises of before, that he was giving an electrifying and moving performance, looking so great in the robes and make-up of the tortured Moor.

'That's not what I mean and you know it. I blame myself.'

I said nothing.

'I should have attended more rehearsals with Tony. He was so different to Alec – even more so tonight. It threw me at first.' He emerged draped in a towel.

'Darling, you couldn't rehearse with that cold and you had to guard your voice. I never did see Alec's performance but it was obvious that Tony would try for something different. They're not remotely alike as actors.'

Jack was rapidly climbing into evening dress. 'Entirely my fault for not paying more attention.'

I changed the subject, saying how much I was dreading meeting, and being inspected by, all his old chums.

'Oh rubbish, you look so great you'll be the most lovely there.'

That's part of the trouble, I thought. 'You're biased. They will resent me, the women, in the way that Fay Compton has done since I met her.'

Jack laughed. 'Oh Faydie, she resents all women, especially if they are young. You mustn't think she has anything personal against you.'

This proved to be true. We became friends, then good friends. Eventually, as she grew old, very loving ones.

We entered the gracious old house. At a glance I could see the well-chosen pictures and antiques, the drawing room with its beautifully lit panelling. Tonight it was filled with twenty or so top stars of the theatre drinking champagne. They effusively applauded Jack's arrival and he was immediately swept into their midst and ardently embraced by all the ladies. I stood aside. Binkie politely decided that he had to do something about me. He smiled his rather wicked, cherubic smile and began to perform some introductions. He remembered my name, which was amazing. I interrupted him, putting him at his ease, telling him I knew several of the guests (untrue) and that I could make my own way around. He left me with obvious relief.

'Diana darling, your glass is empty!' Diana Wynyard's glass was refilled. She was one of the brightest stars in the Tennant galaxy at that time, as were most of the others clustered around Jack. Well – it was Jack's night. I did know Rachel Kempson, who came over to talk to me – a lovely actress and person, married to Michael Redgrave, the mother of his talented children.

Champagne was handed to me but my confidence, so carefully built up over the years, had deserted me. I clung on to the balustrade of the ornamental staircase that descended into the room, still endeavouring to look svelte and sophisticated and, I hoped, succeeding. I looked around wildly for John Gielgud, whom I'd met in Bombay and was a good friend of Jack's: alas, although I knew he had a house nearby, he was not there. Tony Quayle had possibly declined in favour of a quiet dinner with Dot, his great love, the actress Dorothy Hyson. How I envied them.

Presently John Perry was at my side, refilling my glass. I did know John, who was Binkie's partner. I had once attended an interview with him at the Globe Theatre, the offices of Tennants, braving the coffin-like lift up to the office. I am sure the lift was devised to make actors about to be grilled for a job even more nervous than they already would be.

John was now charm itself. I knew him later to be extremely kind. He tried to put me at my ease and force me away from the banister rail where I appeared to have taken root. 'Come and join the others, do have some food.' I did not want to do either, although the spread of delicacies on the table would normally have tempted me. When Jack looked over occasionally to be certain that I was all right, I would raise my glass to him brightly, to show enjoyment. He saw John Perry with me and was satisfied. It was his night. They were all delighted to have him back where he belonged – in the London theatre. It was not that there was any hostility towards me; indeed little, if any thought was given to my presence. I was just not part of *them* – the chatter was all theatre gossip.

As finally we left, I knew that Jack was happy. He had been the object of much admiration – well, why not – he had given a great performance after being away for years. But he was coming home with me, to be together. This was the moment when we were both relieved and relaxed, thankful the long night was over. After any performance an actor's adrenalin is high. A first night such as this, with a role so demanding – well, we were up for most of what was left of it.

SIXTEEN

Divorce & Work

I was sitting on the top deck of a London bus, crawling even more than usual. Unbelievably we had suffered another snowstorm the previous night. It was still snowing and the streets were packed hard with it. I was becoming agitated about the time. I did not need this, my stomach was already churning with nervous anticipation. I was hoping to reach the Law Courts by 9.00 a.m. and had allowed ample time, but today, any amount of time would not have been enough. It was 8.45 and we were in the Strand in an unmoving traffic jam. I would have jumped out and run, but I had no boots and the snow was ankle deep. There had been no sign of a taxi in Sloane Street, or I would have been in it. Impatiently, I went downstairs and onto the bus platform. If we moved a little further I would try to make a dash for it. Hanging on to the rail, I was about to jump and to hell with the snow when, to my relief, I spotted a taxi immediately behind. I leapt off the bus, the snow softening my landing. I tore at the door of the cab. 'Please!' The driver looked at my desperate face in surprise. 'Somehow can you get through this traffic to the Law Courts by 9 o'clock. I have to appear to plead my divorce.'

'Get in love, I'll do what I can.' I have always had a great regard for London taxi drivers. When you are in a tough spot and short of time it is amazing what they can achieve with their skill and incredible wheel lock. He did it. Weaving in and out, avoiding the deep ruts when he could, he deposited me at the gates of the Courts with five minutes to go. As it was a short but difficult journey I wildly over tipped him, he deserved it. 'Good luck, hope you win.'

He gave me the thumbs up sign.

My solicitor was waiting. 'We're in hut number seven.' I looked at him with surprise. I had visualised a mahogany courtroom, such as I had seen in films and when I played in court scenes on stage, but it seemed this great drama in my life was to be enacted in a Nissen hut. There was a whole line of them, temporarily erected to cope with the overflow of divorce cases. We found our way, arriving at the exact moment of nine o'clock.

'I've been fortunate in getting our case heard early in the day. In fact I think the deadline is either lunchtime or early afternoon. Our barrister should be here.' We sat close together, for warmth as much as anything, it was freezing. We were to be second on the list. There was no sign of the barrister.

I had bought a hat especially, as it was essential to wear one in Court. I felt it should not be too smart or becoming, so I had bought one made of felt, which needed no coupons. Anyway I was sure I would never wear it again. I asked Raymond – we were on first name terms after all this time – if I were suitably clad.

'You look splendid, as always. I'm sure the judge will treat you kindly. We're fortunate, I've checked on it, we have a pleasant one. Some can be a bit surly.'

'This weather doesn't help anyone,' I added, 'I don't know about you but my feet are frozen.'

My solicitor was on his feet. The first case was already in the adjoining courtroom and he was obviously becoming alarmed at the absence of our expensive, renowned barrister. Cut off by a thin partition, one could hear the murmur of voices. It was nearing the conclusion, we were informed by a clerk of the court, and we were next.

'It must be the snow that's holding him up, probably been in the country for the weekend.' It was a Monday, so a possible explanation, but that did not help me. I was getting into a panic. If we missed our place would we ever get another? I could not go through it all again.

The clerk arranged for another case to go in ahead of us, there were plenty waiting and I am sure delighted to be ahead in the queue. Just on eleven o'clock, when yet another case went in to be heard, a court official delivered a note. Raymond read it, his face impassive, but I could sense it was bad news. He looked at me.

'A telephone call to say he can't travel up here today. He is snow-bound in the country.'

I was aghast, but also determined. 'I can't wait around any longer. We have to get through this case today. If I have to do it myself, so be it.' I could face anything but the torture of waiting for another date.

Raymond nodded. 'We have the witness here too. I don't know when we can arrange for her to come back to London.'

'Please, please ask the clerk to get us in there as soon as he can, because if we have to wait until after lunch it may not happen. The judge may call it a day, and with this weather he has a reason. Then what?'

There was a quiet conversation between the two men. I watched. I did not care if I had to stand in the box without the damned barrister – it could not be worse than the waiting.

It happened, we were given the final hearing before lunch. Either the judge would be in a tetchy mood, having to endure all these cases with much the same sad tales to tell, or he would be longing for his lunch. Probably he might make a quick decision, hopefully in my favour. Suddenly, we were called. A lady joined us, I do not know where she had been, I hadn't noticed, but I presumed she was our witness – the seaside landlady. I smiled at her and she grabbed my arm, wishing me luck. We went into the Court. I was ushered into the dock. I felt as if I were facing a major trial – which it was to me. Our witness accompanied my solicitor into the centre of the court, sitting on benches.

I took the Bible in my hand, reading the oath held in front of me by the clerk, in a clear voice. The judge adjusted his glasses and looked at me. From that moment onwards I was fighting for my future.

His initial questioning astonished me. This 'Mary' the ATS girl, was she the only reason for my application?

'Oh no, my lord (I knew to bring in respect without overdoing it), I forgave my husband for that indiscretion.'

'Ah, you took him back and yet he was again unfaithful.'

'Yes my lord.' No point in explanations. I had been instructed only to answer the question.

'You were apart a long while. You think there was more adultery?'

'Most likely. I have no proof of that.'

The judge looked at the papers in front of him. 'Except here in England. I have in my possession positive evidence of adultery, also a witness. Will Mrs (I cannot remember her name) please stand. I have a bill for a night spent in your hotel for a couple occupying a double room with a double bed. The man, we know, is this lady's husband. I believe you took breakfast into their room?'

The witness had been sworn in. 'Yes my lord, I did.'

The judge continued. 'This lady you see standing here, was she the other occupant of the double bed you saw that morning?'

I held my breath – then, bless her, loud and clear 'Oh, no, my lord, nothing like, obviously not.' Inwardly I heaved a relieved sigh.

'Thank you. You may be seated. I find it difficult to understand why your husband should behave in this manner.' He was looking at me closely, taking in my whole appearance.

Oh God, how do I respond? I was in a corner. Did he want more background? Would he tell me to try again with Patrick? Act? – no, it came from the heart. 'My lord,' my eyes were pleading, 'it would be impossible for me to take my husband back again.' I lowered my head, adding softly 'there has been too much unhappiness.'

There was a deathly pause, I looked up again and met his eyes.

Suddenly he said 'Decree Nisi granted. Application to be made for Decree Absolute. Costs awarded to the plaintiff. Court adjourn for lunch.'

Everyone stood until the judge had swept out.

Raymond rushed over to me, helping me out of the box. I was glad because my knees were wobbly. 'I was about to disobey the rules and stand up myself to help you, but you were wonderful.'

The lady from the hotel joined us, saying we all needed a drink and she was going to buy it. 'Especially you, poor girl. What a time you've had.'

Realisation was dawning on me. 'I've got my freedom!' I felt as if my world had tilted on its axis. 'Yes, where's the nearest pub where I can treat us all to a reviver. I certainly need one.' 'No, I'll be the host,' said Raymond. We were still arguing and laughing when he steered us into one of those splendid hostelries near the Law Courts. The three of us flopped into the leather chairs. With drinks on the table, we thanked the landlady witness, who was much enjoying her day out to London. We began to thaw out and to celebrate my victory.

More than anything I wanted to see Jack. To tell him. I had been in despair and overwrought. Now I was feeling on top of the world. Our friendly landlady wanted to continue with lunch – inviting us to the Piccadilly Hotel where she was staying. (I would not have minded if it had been the Ritz. The costs meant little at that moment of relief.) I thanked her, but declined. I knew Jack would be anxiously waiting. My solicitor said he would be delighted to continue the celebrations but he had appointments at his office. We dropped our witness off at the hotel. My solicitor, to whom I shall be eternally grateful, leapt out of the taxi. It was to be the last time we met, although there was future correspondence. The judge had awarded me costs, proving that there were no doubts about my rights in law. Although I knew I would never receive a penny from Patrick. I didn't care. I was free. The cab drove on to Sloane Street.

I possessed my own front door key. Jack had given me the spare whilst he was occupying Roz's flat. I ran up the stairs, longing to tell him my news and found him in his dressing gown, nursing a cup of tea. So unlike him – always up as soon as he awoke – he said it was army training. I realised that possibly he had not slept until the small hours. I hadn't met him after the theatre the previous night as my own day had begun early. Now it was over.

I felt euphoric. He read my face. 'It went well, thank heaven, was it too awful?' I began to tell him the tale of my courtroom drama. How the famous barrister had not shown up, so was not there to represent me. Then I realised Jack was only half listening, so I stopped.

An anticlimax.

A moment we had talked of, and longed for, over the years, was nothing in comparison to his evening ahead, *Othello*.

'Can I get you something to eat?' No point in a celebration drink – impossible until after the theatre. I was glad that I had spent that short time recovering, calming down, with the other participants of my experience. Jack said he had eaten some toast, he was going to have a bath then make for the theatre, he had some scenes he was intending to run through with Tony Quayle. His dresser would bring him some light food from a nearby restaurant. Then, of course, he had to begin with the body-makeup. This was his life for awhile. He held me close. 'Darling, I'm sorry. We should be having a wonderful dinner together tonight.'

I kissed him. 'It can wait. We have to hang on until the Decree Absolute. Then we can have a real celebration.' I decided to leave him to relax and concentrate on his role.

The basement flat was empty, unwelcoming. I realised I was hungry. Suddenly the telephone rang. I was surprised by the foreign accent of the man on the other end of the line, an old friend from Egypt. He was staying at the Savoy with others whom I'd known in Cairo. Could I possibly join the party and dine with them that night? They were going on to Paris the next day. I was delighted to hear from someone I hadn't seen for several years. He and his brother had been the most generous hosts on many occasions. Yes, I would be happy to see them again. It would be a great pleasure to be at the Savoy for dinner. I hung up. Now full of energy and anticipation, I rushed for the iron and board, trying to decide, what of my limited wardrobe would fit the occasion.

It was an evening of luxury and pleasure. After dinner, the ballroom and dancing – then the cabaret. I glanced at my watch at about the time that Jack would be in his dressing room taking off his make-up. The cabaret was due to start at any moment. I decided I couldn't leave so abruptly. Anyway, it was a show much praised in London with a star I wanted to see – when did I ever have nights such as this? I chose to stay and enjoy myself. We went on to a nightclub after the Savoy. I told myself that Jack always had visitors after the performance. He would be drinking with some old friends. Perhaps he would not even miss me.

It must have been about three o'clock when I was finally dropped at Sloane Street. I descended the basement steps carefully. I had had more to drink that day than ever before. I was not drunk (fortunately I have an extraordinarily good head for drink, which goes with my sense of balance). No, the descent I was making was from my high excitement and strain of the day, followed by an unexpectedly glamorous evening. I undressed, flopping into bed; my mind, over-active, was reliving the whole day. Suddenly tears came – then in a flood. I was shaking with sobs. For what? I had what I wanted – my release, freedom. I suppose I was crying for a marriage that should never have happened. A foolish young girl rushing into what was intended to be a lifetime commitment, but which instead ended in the divorce courts. I fell asleep with Pat's name on my lips.

* * * * *

There was a constant banging noise. I thought for a moment that it was my head, which certainly did not feel like my own. Lifting it off the pillow with difficulty, I looked at the window. Jack was peering through the bars, looking exasperated. I hurriedly put on a dressing gown, signalling to him that I was going to open the door I ran my hands through my hair thinking I must look dreadful.

'Where were you last night?' he asked. 'I thought you'd come to the dressing room.'

'I'm sorry darling, but I had an unexpected invitation to dine with friends at the Savoy. I stayed on to watch the cabaret.'

'It seems you made a night of it. I'm off to the theatre for the matinee.'

'Oh Lord, is it that late? I have to be at Motleys for a costume fitting at 2.30.'

'You'd better get yourself together. You rotten old stop-out, leaving me wondering where you were.'

'I'm sorry I couldn't reach you to explain. Quite honestly you have so many visitors I thought you wouldn't miss me.'

He ruffled my hair and kissed me. 'Who was the lucky fellow?'

'Not one, a whole crowd of Egyptians I knew when in Cairo.'

'I forgive you. I'll see you tonight. We'll have some supper together. I must rush or I'll be late for this cursed matinee.' He ran up the steps.

*   *   *   *   *

I was in the tube train making the long journey to Uxbridge and the studios. I had been called for make-up and more important, hairstyling. The hairdressers at Denham were experimenting with braids and false hair of my own colour. I was to keep the length, even allow it to grow longer. The final choice was two plaits in long loops on each side of my head with a tiny silver crown perched on top. Prop jewellery had been selected to enhance my heavy satin gown, the sleeves and train were lined with purple velvet.

I had come to terms with the tough schedule that lay ahead. We had to be at Denham Sudios for make-up and hair by 7.00 a.m. The corseting, the petticoats, the dressing must be finished before the arrival of the stars at 8.00; after which all the attention focused on them. I would be forced to catch the workman's train at 5.30 a.m. from Knightsbridge to arrive on time. I didn't look forward to that early start for months ahead, without a break. I took some comfort from the thought of being able to pay the heavy legal costs of the divorce, but knew I would have precious little time to spend with Jack.

His film contract with Sir Alexander Korda had been signed.

His first film, *Bonnie Prince Charlie* with David Niven, was to be made at Shepperton Studios. He would begin shooting almost immediately the run of *Othello* and *Candida* finished.

I found the hours at Denham longer, and certainly more tedious, than twice-nightly Rep. Indeed more uncomfortable. Tightly corseted from early morning, hair pulled tight with the false plaits and crown, it was almost impossible to sit in such a voluminous gown, even if there was a seat to be found. A film set only provides stars and directors with the prized canvas chair. At that time the days were supposed to finish at 6.00 p.m., but there was usually an extension until 7.00 o'clock. Inevitably the union shop steward in charge of the crew would agree to the extra hour (extra pay) needed to keep the film up to schedule. The actors were not consulted.

Technicians unions ran studios in 1947.

Usually at 9.00 o'clock when I reached Sloane Street I was too tired to eat more than a quick snack of whatever was available. We also worked Saturdays until lunch time, so there was no time for shopping and I relied on Joan for any food.

Our small group of courtiers spent most of our days draping ourselves around the sets in background shots. Occasionally we were seated in ornate chairs, a piece of good fortune that fell to the ladies. We were not allowed to leave the set in case we were needed and with so many hours spent in each other's company we soon began to form friendships. All five men had been in the war, two incarcerated in PoW camps since Dunkirk. Patrick McNee, later better known for *The Avengers*, had been in the Navy and also happened to live near me. We became good friends. Hours were whittled away in conversation. Waiting is always the worst side of filming and the most longed for moment was the appearance of the tea ladies wheeling their trolleys with urns of rather foul tea, but there were cheese rolls and biscuits. No one had time for breakfast before the morning dash from home, so our stomachs were rattling with hunger – anything would have been welcome. The next break was for lunch. We longed to loosen our corsets, but it was imperative to rush to the canteen to find a seat. We soon became more organised, sending the men ahead to grab a table, or at least places to sit. These were few. The stars using the canteen had tables reserved, or food sent to their dressing rooms. The menu was dull, but for us anything was acceptable, especially when eaten seated.

Over one such lunch the conversation centred on divorce. Most of the men, like myself, were in the throes of it, or awaiting the Decree Absolute. The exception was Desmond Llewelyn. He too had been 'in the bag' in Germany, but was rightly proud of the way his wife had stood by him through the years of absence. Dan Cunningham was bitter about his wife, who had left him for a director. He sourly pointed out that Desmond's wife had been an officer in the ATS, so would have had scant time for temptations, and the thick khaki stockings and bloomers would also have been a disadvantage. John Roberts was also divorcing his wife, regretfully, as they had a young son. As we sat in silence musing over our misfortunes, I gloomily remarked that 1940 had not been a very good year.

While hanging around on set, Desmond and I passed hours talking of our mutual fondness for classical music, and we would hum passages to see if the other would recognise them. He became well known in later years as 'Q' in the Bond films, demonstrating all his amazing inventions to 007, 'Oh, do pay attention, Bond!' He filled that eccentric role to perfection.

Great news! A knighthood for our star and director, now Sir Laurence Olivier. Applause greeted him when he next appeared on set with Anthony Bushell at his elbow. All the acclaim was received with genuine pleasure. He was popular with everyone, actors, crew, up in the gantries, on the floor, waving to them all with a modesty that was part of his charm. Watching him directing was an education.

We were kept occupied as much as possible. When not performing background reactions and sweeping curtsies, we were given individual tasks such as running down castle corridors in fright – or what ever facial expressions were needed. I would look forward to seeing Jack on Saturdays after the theatre and part of Sunday too, depending how tired we were. The early mornings and long days were taking their toll on me, and Jack was nearing the end of the Piccadilly run, which had been a strain on him.

* * * * *

Jack's brief days of freedom came and went without much time spent together. He was off on location to Scotland. He had a short break, filled with fittings for costumes and wigs, before going away.

We were adjusting as best we could to life at Denham. Dan and Desmond both owned small cars. Petrol allowing, a morning roster for the pickup was arranged. Jenny Grey, Patrick McNee and myself fortunately lived in the vicinity of the two drivers. They would take turns, while we would all try to provide black market coupons for petrol. This gave us an extra hour in the morning. I bought a collapsible campstool, putting it underneath my skirt and train and multitude of petticoats and finally placing my bottom on the canvas seat.

Relief to the boredom came in a different form. I was approached to play the lead in *The Dominant Sex* at the Theatre Royal, Windsor. Despite the complications of rehearsing and performing a play while under contract at Denham, John Counsel at Windsor was adamant about wanting me for the two-hander, and getting round the difficulties. Though I could not guarantee attending much in the way of rehearsals, the performances of the play coincided with a week that the courtiers had off, when the scenes with Ophelia were to be shot. As a kindness to the relatively inexperienced Jean Simmons (she was seventeen), an effectively 'closed set' would apply for the directing of her key scenes. So provided the problem of the rehearsals could be got around I should be available.

When Tony Bushell stopped in his tracks to enquire what on earth I was perched on, I demonstrated to him my seating arrangement, and seized the opportunity of asking him about Windsor and John Counsel. Tony raised his eyebrows and reminded me that *Hamlet* had first call, and I was taking a big risk. He thought having a rest would be preferable, but wished me luck.

I learned the lines during the interminable waits on set; Edward Sinclair, who was cast opposite me and lived in Datchett, collected me from the studios in his car. We rehearsed after filming finished for the day at his house, then he dropped me back to Sloane Street. Luckily, the film schedule didn't change and I got there for each performance of the one-week run at Windsor. It was a frantic time and the last night brought a specially happy conclusion – there in the prompt corner was that wonderfully familiar figure waiting to embrace me – Jack. He had been on location with David Niven in Scotland.

In August we were to have two weeks holiday – a decision made by the unions. Strikes were often threatened, so our hard-pressed star-director was frequently attending meetings. However, no one was arguing about the holiday. The studio closed for two weeks – with pay! An unusual bonus.

To get away from London was my priority. I needed fresh air after being cooped up in musty studios for days with my body tortured by corset bones. I needed sun, swimming, sea air – so I headed for my parents. I slept for hours undisturbed in my own bed and room. I insisted on repaying some of the money I had borrowed for the Court hearing, though my father would only take a small amount. I think he was relieved that I appeared to be financially afloat.

On my return to Sloane Street there was a pile of mail waiting. Straight away I could see the important envelope from my solicitors. There it was, my Decree Absolute, at last. No tears this time, just laughter and relief. After all these years I had my freedom. I looked at the empty flat – there was no one to tell. Then the phone rang. It was Jack. 'I hoped you'd be back tonight. I'm finished for the weekend and thought I would drive down so we can be together. I'll be with you in half an hour.'

Somehow I didn't tell him, it was too important to say over the telephone. I rushed to my cupboard and found one of the silk dresses made for me in India. Pale blue and becoming to my tanned bare legs and arms, my hair bleached by the sun – I felt wonderful. I dug out my white high heels, not worn since India and splashed myself with the remains of Caron's Bellogia. Then he was there.

I flung open the door as he rushed down the basement steps and jumped into his arms. After a moment he held me away from him. 'Let me look at you – my heaven, you are marvellous. Your lovely hair and eyes all a-sparkle. You've been sunning yourself down there.'

We moved into the flat, then I told him my news.

'This has to be one of the best evenings, we must celebrate.' There was never anything in the flat, especially as I had been away, so we wandered round to the local pub, which had become a popular meeting place for nearby residents, including several actors who lived locally. Through Cadogan Square we walked arm in arm, all the trees were flowering, so beautiful in the evening sunlight. A tennis match was being played in the gardens. As we reached the pub, Jack said we would go on to his favourite restaurant in Soho for dinner. He flung open the door to shouts of greeting. We had been out of London for a while. Somehow we did not mention the great news, it had nothing to do with others and neither of us spoke of our private lives. It was our affair.

To them we were just a couple in love, who would marry one day.

On my return to filming on Monday, I found I was not the only one with a tan unsuited to the gloom of Elsinore. I ran into Tony Bushell in the corridor. 'My God, is that what two weeks holiday does for you?'

I laughed. 'I'm on my way to make-up to tone it down.'

'It's not just your colour. You've obviously relaxed and rested.'

'And I've had some good news,' I added. 'My divorce was finalised.'

He laughed out loud, throwing his head back. 'Mine too.' We

exchanged a few words about our unfortunate and mistaken marriages.

'So how does it feel to be free?' Tony asked me.

'Great,' I answered with feeling.

He looked quizzical. 'I mean do you think one ought to do it again? Personally I feel nervous.'

'Oh, I think it's like falling off a horse, an air crash, or a car accident. A quick return to it is essential. The longer left, the more difficult.'

'Wise words. I think you've someone in mind.'

I smiled enigmatically and went on my way to powder down my suntan.

When our group met up in full regalia there was more laughter. The entire 1940 vintage had received their decrees. A massive clearout must have been going on at the divorce courts to shift the backlog.

* * * * *

We, the courtiers spent the following weeks seated in a semicircle around a stage, which had been built on the set, where the play-within-a-play would be enacted, and later the duel. We watched all the action unfold before us, reacting as directed when we were in shot. The action before us was absorbing – and we were *seated*. So the last few weeks of *Hamlet* passed quickly, culminating in the great fight to the death between Hamlet and Laertes. The fight was fast and furious – it was Sir Laurence doing his stuff – breathtaking in its ferocity and heart stopping in its speed. Terence Morgan, who was playing Laertes was at the mercy of an opponent who was not playing by the rules. The moves, so carefully choreographed and rehearsed were forgotten. Terry felt he was really fighting for his life.

Suddenly like a gust of wind a familiar figure in a different guise made an entrance on to the set, followed by a dresser and make up. It was Peter Cushing in the flamboyant wig and costume for Osric (in which he gave an excellent performance). I rushed towards him and we embraced. I knew he was now married. He had met his wife in an ENSA tour in the latter half of the war, her name was Helen.

So, the last days of *Hamlet*. What lay ahead? During the waits the gossip was of the forthcoming tour of Australia that the Oliviers were to embark upon. Some of our group were eager to be part of the company and there were to be auditions for the hopeful ones. I asked Tony Bushell about the tour – should I go for it? He shook his head, This tour isn't for you. The plays are obviously chosen for the Oliviers. There would be nothing worthwhile for you, and you would be away for nine months, though we would be delighted to have you along.'

To go away again for that length of time. What about Jack? It was not to be considered. I put it out of my mind.

So for me the end of *Hamlet*. It had hardly been a star performance. Although I had been there throughout the film, no one would ever notice my flitting around. But it had paid for my divorce, which was the real object. I had made new friends and even had money left in the bank. My solicitor wrote to tell me that Patrick had refused to pay any costs that I had been legally awarded. He thought it un-gentlemanly and unfair that I should be forced to pay them on top of all the other legal accounts – including the absentee barrister.

I wasn't surprised by his reaction, so accepted the inevitable.

We said our farewells at Denham Studios to Make-up, Hair and Wardrobe. The beautiful satin and silk gowns, once so exquisite, hanging there, worn and tired. Last of all I pushed my head round Maud Spector's office door. She was the casting director for Rank Films. When she saw my face, she told me – no goodbyes, she had a film part for me and would telephone.

Work was suddenly materialising, appearing from unpredicted sources – even Tennants approached me. This was what I had been struggling for all my life in the theatre. I knew that if I pushed and fully concentrated on my career, then all the years of hard work since I was a child could bring a reward.

But, and a big one, there was something else. The theatre had always been my greatest love. I was never happy when out of it and more at home on a stage than anywhere. But another love had now taken over, begun long ago in Bombay when Jack walked into my life. Grown stronger over the years, we had survived the testing time of the return to England and our lives here. Now was the moment of decision. With us both being totally occupied with work, we had not given our future the serious thought it needed. Jack had been thrown by the possibility of the Australian tour. That passed. Now I received a tempting offer to go to Canada with a company, in which I was to play the female leads. Major Barbara was one – I had already played that twice – and another was a part I longed to tackle, Candida. The director's only concern when we finally came face to face was that I was too young. I quickly reassured him that I was experienced in playing older women.

'You convince me. That's great. Shall we agree? We'll be away about six weeks. Three weeks rehearsal here in London.'

I hesitated. He pressed on, 'I know the money isn't terrific, but you'll have the best we can arrange with accommodation, all expenses paid.'

Something was preventing me – damn it. Finally, I spoke. 'It's not that,' I reassured him. 'I'm waiting to be married,' I blurted out.

He was completely fazed. 'Couldn't you put it off until after the tour? Of course the management will then wish for a showing here, to which you'll have to agree.'

I paused, 'I'm sorry, can I let you know tomorrow?'

'I have to know.' He thought I was procrastinating. 'I have to find another actress and quickly.'

'When's the deadline?'

'As soon as possible. At the latest, tomorrow morning.'

What a dilemma! I nodded my head. 'I wouldn't dream of letting you down. He'll be back from filming tonight. Ring me in the morning. I'll give you an answer.'

We stood up.

May I ask who the lucky man is?'

'His name is Jack Hawkins.'

'Ah,' was the reply.

SEVENTEEN

Marriage, 1947

The rain was streaming down the bars outside the window, sploshing onto the sill, drumming on the dustbin lids. Inside the three of us were clustered around the two-bar electric fire. The room was dark. Being in a basement it was always so, even on a bright day. No lights were on as we needed the warmth from the fire, and electricity was in short supply. We were urged to conserve it; sudden cuts occurred without warning. The previous winter we had no electricity at all during daylight hours. It was my first winter back in England and the coldest I can remember, with thick snow for weeks after Christmas.

Jack was uncorking a bottle of champagne. I cannot imagine how he had come by it or what it must have cost. I was endeavouring in the half-light to arrange my new hat, using the mirror over the mantle. Stafford had the glasses ready. We happily drank to each other – the future – anything. Peering into the mirror I was satisfied with the reflection; the hat was really becoming. Bonnet-shaped and blue, with black underneath and black feathers draped around the brim: it sounds hideous now but it was the height of fashion then. The dress was a beautifully draped crêpe from Paris, which I had bought ridiculously cheaply from Roz, who had acquired it from her stepmother Gladys Cooper. It was too tight on Roz but fitted me perfectly. My shoes, the best suede court shoes, were sold to me by another friend; they were pre-war and unworn, but too small for her. I suffered.

Jack kissed me. 'You look so lovely I think I might marry you.'

Stafford said the car was outside so we had better finish the champagne and be off to the Registry Office. It was still pouring with rain when we emerged from the basement. Jack was desperately trying to hold an umbrella over my new hat, but thankfully he had had the foresight to order a car from the mews at the back. He did not want the hassle of searching for a scarce taxi on our wedding day. We fell into the dry interior with gratitude.

Stafford was our witness. It was right that he should be with us on this day. We swept through the bleak wet streets into the King's Road and halted at the local Registry Office. It was not the elegantly decorated office in the Town Hall of today, but a shabby building opposite – at least it was still standing. There was no church wedding for us: divorce prevented that in those past unforgiving days of Christianity. But nothing, not even the weather, could spoil this day for us. We were at last about to achieve the ending we had been hoping for since the magical day when our stars collided in Bombay on 2 January 1944. Fate had brought us together at a time when we were both in need of some happiness – now at last we were reaching the longed-for conclusion.

Jack and I had wished for a quiet ceremony, mainly because we were both working so it had been difficult for us to arrange a day. We did not wish to involve our families, once we started on that kind of wedding there would be no end to the complications. Anyway it was a second marriage for us both, and too soon after the war to spread out with a great celebration. We decided early in the week that Friday was the day – Jack bought a Special Licence, so here we were happily sealing our future together.

Jack helped me out of the car, opening the umbrella again. We ran up the stairs ignoring the bare boards and cracked tiles on the walls. When we entered the Registry Office it was warm, even with flowers on the desk. To me, it was all beautiful. When Jack took my hand as we began the ceremony, the insecurities, the battles I had fought with life, faded into insignificance. The unhappy world of doubts and long partings, all uncertainty, receded. The years of waiting were past, divorces now completed. Any feelings of guilt I might have suffered over my sad marriage, those seven wasted years locked up in the past of wartime darkness, had been banished by the surprising news that Patrick was already remarried.

Jack had suffered from his wife's unfaithfulness in America, followed by the Reno divorce and her hasty remarriage. Further bitterness was caused by the realisation that his daughter would be brought up by another man. All that was now left behind in India, where my arrival at the beginning of 1944 may have helped to ease his pain.

Down the stairs, out into the rain again, we hurried to the car where one lone photographer waited, but thinking of the feathers on my new hat, we didn't stop for a picture. Something we regretted in later years. There was no record of our special day to amuse our children and grandchildren.

A few years ahead we would have had a phalanx of photographers surrounding us, and would have been unable to get away without giving them something for the press. But that day we were away in our dreams of a fresh beginning – a new life.

In the car we made the short journey to our local pub with its warm mahogany interior. This had become the favourite meeting place for nearby residents, including some of our theatrical friends. Gatherings at home were uncommon still. There was a virtual absence of any drinkable alcohol (except on the black market) and all food was on coupons and scarce – this combined with the lack of light and warmth, made home entertaining a rarity.

Our plan was to meet a select few for some champagne. Floyd, 'mine host' at the pub, on hearing our news from Jack, had managed through contacts somewhere in the City to obtain a case! I was overwhelmed. Only the previous day we had invited Alec Clunes, who was surprised at the suddenness of the event, but delighted. At that time Jack was preparing to direct Alec in the leading role of Christopher Fry's new play, *The Lady's not for Burning*. This became a prestigious success for all concerned, the play being bought for John Gielgud, who later performed the lead to great acclaim.

When we arrived at the pub – hurrying in out of the still pouring rain – a huge welcome awaited us. Floyd's wife, Doll, rushed to be the first to kiss us, opened the counter door of the bar, and ushered us upstairs to their private room. On opening the door, there were shouts of congratulations from our friends. We had no idea how the news had spread of our finally tying the knot, but it was a happy surprise. The room was decorated with flowers, Doll had supplied some delicious canapés; champagne flowed. The bride in black could not have been happier, and the bridegroom looked splendid in a well-cut dark suit he had had worn in a pre-war play.

Alec was complaining to me that we really should have told him earlier, he would have arranged a reception for us at the Arts Theatre Club. I explained that it was a last minute event. We both had a free day on Friday, so we decided to get married, with the least possible inconvenience to anyone.

The champagne consumed, Alec insisted that Jack and I with a few close friends continue our celebrations at the Arts. It seemed right that we were there sitting at a table enjoying lunch, for the Club in those days was a great meeting place for actors. It had become a second home to us when Jack returned at last from India and I was nearby in Bedford Street. In those long-gone days of 1946-47, the Club was a nest of young talent. Peter Ustinov, Peter Brook, Christopher Fry, and many others would gather to share their hopes and plans for the future, their talk always inspiring and uplifting. I was fortunate to be there with Jack, listening.

In our country struggling to recover from the devastation of war, we all shared the same hopes of a better, brighter future. It just *had* to be. That was the mood of 1947. We always were a land of optimists unable to admit defeat, even when it stared us in the face.

Afterword

The pretty girl on the television was ecstatic. She had capped her run of luck by answering the final question correctly and won thirty thousand pounds in a Saturday night quiz show. Jumping off her chair and gleefully hugging everyone nearby, she was asked by the presenter on what she intended to spend this windfall. On her wedding dress was the reply. She was going to sweep down the aisle in her dream dress, a huge bouffant skirt with flowing train – the works! 'Competing with the footballers' wives?' the presenter quipped. 'And how much will that cost?' 'Ooh thousands,' the happy lady airily replied, bounding off-screen to be embraced by her proud fiancé.

As one of those remnants of the long past Second World War generation, I winced at the thought of all that material going into one dress. Frugality was hammered into my brain and bones during all those years of shortage. I keep everything from bits of string to face cream pots, so I am one of those old bores left over from the Forties, uncomfortable about throwing things away in these days of 'chucking out'.

Extravagant weddings are on the increase, and fashionable. But when the great day and the party are over and that dress hangs in the cupboard taking up too much space – was it worth it? Does it make for a better and happier marriage? All you need is to be so in love with the fellow there waiting for you that you float down the aisle transformed – the watching guests swept along with you in a glow that has made you beautiful. Miles of satin and cascades of tulle cannot do it – only that secret ingredient can make this transformation.

In 2007 the country celebrated the Diamond Wedding of the Queen and Prince Philip. The nostalgic photos of the truly happy royal couple from that day brought into vivid recollection my own state of bliss, for Jack and I were married only a few days before the Royal Wedding – our day being 31st October 1947. The then Princess Elizabeth and I were enjoying the special time of being newly married. It was all about discovery, learning to live a life for two instead of the lonely one. The security of being part of a loving relationship stayed with me until the day that Jack was snatched away – like a physical blow, which made me realize that I was alone. Over all the intervening years since I have never recovered from this loss.

The 31st October 2007 was a beautiful day, warm with autumn sunshine. The garden squares around my home were still dressed in their brilliant colours, the leaves on the trees not yet blown away. Looking down from my rooftop I could see the lunchtime throng. The warmth had caused a rush for an outside seat at the pubs and restaurants nearby – anywhere to enjoy the sun whilst it still shone. Our city is so alive these days when the weather is fine. I went down from my eyrie to join in, walking slowly – drat it – enjoying the day. I walked around the square towards Sloane Street where our day began in 1947.

So my Diamond Anniversary was without the bridegroom. Sixty years of marriage to the same man and over half of that time alone. Not what was predicted for me after Jack's death in 1973 when I was still in my early fifties. But after heavy heart-searching I did what I thought would be the best, for me, and my dearly loved family, who were of an age when they sadly lacked the help and guidance of their father. I'm afraid, try as I did, that I was no substitute for Jack.

Life after Jack has been full and occupied, though fraught at times. Adventure and challenge have been there for me, so the time has gone swiftly. Suddenly I am faced with the sixty years that have been swallowed up, and I am old. Our many friends have been solid for me throughout, so it has been with deep sadness that

I have had to lose them one by one, feeling more bereft with each loss.

The twenty-six years of marriage to Jack taught me that I was a woman equipped to deal with most of what life could throw at me. His legacy was not of wealth but of something more valuable. Being with him in the exciting, wondrously good years, was followed by the grim and terrible years. His courage when he lost his voice – his golden asset – he managed to treat with black humour. His immense bravery in becoming a guinea pig for a new device in America that was promised would restore his speech, instead cost him his life. How could any man fill that empty space in my heart? So I raised my glass to 'our' day and thought of Jack, as I do frequently, with great love.